CHANGING REGIMES AND EDUCATIONAL DEVELOPMENT IN CAMEROON

Changing Regimes and Educational Development in Cameroon

MATHEW B. GWANFOGBE
Bamenda University of Science and Technology

SPEARS
MEDIA PRESS

DENVER

SPEARS MEDIA PRESS LLC
DENVER
7830 W. Alameda Ave, Suite 103-247 Denver, CO 80226
United States of America

First Published in 2018 by Spears Media Press
www.spearsmedia.com
info@spearsmedia.com
Information on this title: www.spearsmedia.com/product/changing-regimes

ISBN: 978-1-942876-23-6 (Paperback)
Also published in Kindle (ebook)

Spears Media Press has no responsibility for the persistence or accuracy of urls for
external or third-party internet websites referred to in this publication, and does
not guarantee that any content on such websites is, or will remain, accurate or
appropriate.

To all Teachers past, present and future

CONTENTS

Illustrations

Maps

Figures

Tables

FOREWORD

Mathew Basung Gwanfogbe's *Changing Regimes and the development of Education in Cameroon* presents a valuable and stimulating contribution to the fields of history and history of education. For the first time, a Cameroonian has provided an incisive and an inclusive outlook on the historical development of educational traditions currently in place in Africa in general and in Cameroon in particular.

In Africa today both traditional African and imported education co-exist and are useful to the vast majority of Africans. However, they sometimes clash or, cause divergence, contradiction or confusion rather than harmony and regularity or uniformity. That is, the roots of the bulk of Africa's education sector problems are, in dualism of the continent's educational inheritance, which Mazrui (1986) called a "triple heritage". It is a tripartite bequest of educational thought and practices from Arabo-Islamic influences; Western-Christian legacies and deep-seated African traditions that now together live in most communities, and countries of Africa. Cameroon's education problem is exacerbated by its chequered history with German, French and English imperialist education experiments, as they are witting or unwittingly vying for primacy or meaningfulness in the struggle by Cameroonians for survival, and subsistence. All education systems must prepare citizens to cope with and adjust to local and external change. Accordingly, educational reform is an on-going process without an end (Cockson, Sedovnik and Semel, 1992). According to Nsamenang (2005a; p.325) "Africa has made attempts to reform the systems of education it inherited from European colonizers. Unfortunately, the reforms have tended to be incomplete so that some inconsistency with African cultures and economic and ecological realities prevails" (p.328).

In reality, "For Africa, institutional education is an intervention, par excellence, because Africa's indigenous educational, traditions predate the advent of institutional education" (Nsamenang, p. 277). A Cameroonian scholar, Dr. Mathew B. Gwanfogbe, has taken up the challenge in Fafunwa's (1974) insightful clarification that we cannot understand the history of education in Africa without analysing how the imported systems mesh or mismatch with the indigenous educational system that existed long before the arrival of Islamic and Christian education.

From a historical perspective, Dr. Gwanfogbe's book, *Changing Regimes and the Development of Education in Cameroon*, richly analyses the educational problems of post-colonial Cameroon, as they derive from indigenous perceptions and attitudes of the pre-colonial traditional education, which are seldom in concurrence with those bequeathed by the imperialistic regimes of Germany, France and England.

Dr. Gwanfogbe's adroit and creatively innovative elocution of the complex history of Cameroon education edifyingly offers unparalleled insight into the commonplace bewilderment with why the nation's education systems and government's spirited efforts to evolve a relevant education system to bring development to Cameroon have literally failed or at best met with disappointment and incomprehensible difficulty.

Much has been observed and exposed about the history of education in Africa in general and Cameroon in particular. Now, for the first time, a Cameroonian has provided a comprehensive, systematic account of the history of education, which is consistent with and sensitive to the 'triple' inheritance of educational traditions in Cameroon and sub-Saharan Africa. Until Dr. Gwanfogbe's challenging book, very few people were aware that the impediments to the development and implementation of appropriate education policies attentive to Cameroon's development needs are derived from the influences of pre-colonial traditions and education history. In other words, many scholars and / or historians have tended to blame the colonial regimes only; failing to realize the inevitable impact of powerful contemporary educational values and practices.

Gwanfogbe brings to his forcefully argued and eloquent book, unsurpassed professionalism and career feats in learning pedagogy, educational administration, perceptive educational research, pioneering scholarship and a rich profile of seminal publications in education and history. He brings together telling primary sources, impressive statistical data and historical archival pictures. The result is a richly argued and well-documented treatise in which historiography is well alive in scholarly and polemical arguments synthesizing a broad; novel perspective on the history of education in colonized societies, with Cameroon as a case study. All readers will enjoy the engaging and lucidly simple style, which Dr. Gwanfogbe has brought to his topic.

This is a book that will be read widely for information, fulfilment, and edification.

Prof Daniel Abwa

PREFACE

Education in contemporary Cameroon like in most African countries is marked by confusion and a wide range of problems and difficulties inherent in the chequered history of Cameroon and in the pattern of the educational development in the country. Cameroon education consists of two, distinct systems inherited from colonial regimes which in their unreformed state are indisputably unsuitable for modern Cameroon. These two systems are juxtaposed with the pre-colonial African education system and the Islamic education system that existed before the introduction of Western education. Western Education was introduced in 1844 by the British Baptist Missionary Society and encouraged by successive colonial regimes (the German regime from 1884 to 1916, the British and French regimes from 1916 to 1961). Since independence and reunification in 1961, the failure to restructure education to reflect common national values and respond to the development needs of the nation has been identified by analysts with its colonial origins yet the different systems (Missionary, traditional, Islamic and colonial) had varying impacts and the inter-relationships between each system and Cameroonians differed. This book examines the impact of the respective education systems and changing regimes on developments in education. The role and motives of colonial regimes, Missions and Cameroonians are examined to assess the impact of the different motives and interrelationships on post-colonial attitudes to education. It is hoped that policy makers and educational administrators will realize that Cameroon educational problems have come a long way and cannot be solved superficially but through in-depth considerations of the past and present political economic and social conditions.

The central argument is that reform impasse in Cameroon education like in most African countries cannot be explained by a single factor without taking into consideration the past. It is for that reason that an overview of the pre-colonial traditional education system and the Islamic educational system that was introduced in parts of the country long before Western education has been taken into consideration. The respective colonial and Mission education systems which outcomes dominate current educational practices and the reactions of Cameroonians are examined chronologically from a historical perspective using mostly primary sources.

It was found that the Germans and the British colonial regimes were liberal to Missions as against a stronger French colonial control. The Germans' desire for a Protestant

Mission and the British indirect rule that left education to Christian missions and Native Authorities added to British tolerance to foreign Missionary societies, to establish a distinct system from that of the French. Besides, Cameroonians' interest in and attitudes towards western education also influenced the pattern of educational development. Finally, the constraints of global economic and political forces in the postcolonial era have reinforced the deadlock on institutional reforms. In summary therefore, the impact of the respective educational legacies and the perceptions and reactions of Cameroonians at different stages of educational growth are found to have combined with the socio-economic and political developments since independence to explain the stalemate in rendering education responsive to the needs of Cameroon.

To attain educational change, this book recommends the importance of creating awareness among teachers and parents and the wider public on the need for reform. It also suggests that further research be conducted on precolonial attitudes to education and on Cameroon cultures to identify indigenous educational ideas with relevance to modem education as well as those traditional values that can enrich the educational system and eventually generate common national and international interests.

ACKNOWLEDGEMENT

This book has been achieved with contributions, collaboration and encouragement from many people to whom I am deeply thankful. Unfortunately, I cannot name all of them here. I am particularly grateful to my colleagues and students of Ecole Normale Superieure annex Bambili, University of Yaounde I. For over ten years, students especially in Ecole Normale Superieure persistently encouraged me to publish this book which is partially a result of my lectures on the subject. I am grateful to them.

Professors Richard Aldrich and Martin McLean of the University of London were very helpful to me during my initial research. Their constructive criticisms inspired me to forge ahead. E.M. Chilver of Oxford was generous with her documents, ideas and German sources on Cameroon which helped enormously in reshaping historical facts. Shirley Ardener introduced me to the collection of the reminiscences of the colonial administrators at the Rhodes House Library in Oxford and to the "Exeter" association of the retired colonial administrators from whom I gained a deeper insight of the colonial situation. I want to thank Dr. Felicity Breet very specially for proofreading.

I want to very specially thank the Basel Mission authorities for permitting me to use some of their archival pictures.

I am grateful to Professor Daniel Abwa, Dean of the Faculty of Arts, Letters and Human Sciences, who wrote the preface for the book. I am also indebted to Professor Jerry K. Domatob, Professor Bame Nsamenang, Dr. John Babila Njingum and Dr. E.M. Nwana, who assisted at various moments.

My wife Helen Timia Na'sona has been a source of great inspiration. I will ever remain indebted to my uncle Ephraim Yangni who has ceaselessly motivated me since childhood. Finally, Na Mary and late Ba Njimontam Gwanfogbe remain rare as parents of their generation for the vision and determination they had for the education of their children.

ABBREVIATIONS

ACEC	Advisory Committee for Education in the Colonies
AEF	Afrique Equatoriale Française
AOF	Afrique Occidentale Française
BEAC	Banque Centrale des Etats de l'Afrique Centrale
BEPC	Brevet d'Etudes du Premier Cycle
BM	Basel Mission
BMS	Baptist Missionary Society
CAIP	Certificat d'Aptitude aux fonctions d'Inspecteur de l'enseignement Première.
CAP	Certificat d'Aptitude Professionnelle
CEMAC	Communauté Economique et Monétaire de l'Afrique Centrale
CBMS	Conference of British Missionary Societies
CCAST	Cameroon College of Arts, Science and Technology
CDC	Cameroon Development Corporation
CDCWU	Cameroon Development Corporation Workers Union
CEPE	Certificat d'Etudes Premières Elémentaires
CGCE	Cameroon General Certificate of Education
CNF	Cameroon National Federation
CPC	Cameroon Protestant College
CWU	Cameroon Welfare Union
CYL	Cameroon Youth League
GCE	General Certificate of Education
GCSE	General Certificate of Secondary Education
GTC	Government Trade Centre
G TTC	Government Teachers Training Centre
IMC	International Missionary Council
IMF	International Monetary Fund
IPAR	Institut de Pédagogie Appliquée a Vocation Rurale
KENU	Kamerun Ex-servicemen National Union
KUNC	Kamerun United National Congress
NA	Native Authority /Administration
NCNC	National Council of Nigeria and Cameroon
OCAM	Organisation of Central African and Malagasy States

PCA	Presbyterian Church Archive.
PCC	Presbyterian Church in Cameroon
PPA	Provincial Pedagogic Adviser
PSS	Presbyterian Secondary School
PWD	Public Works Department
RCM	Roman Catholic Mission
RTC	Rural Training Centre
SEP	Société Evangélique Protestant
SJC	Saint Joseph's College
SJC	Sacerdotes Cordis Jesu
SPEP	Support to Primary Education Project
TTC	Teachers Training Centre /College
UAC	United African Company
UDEAC	Union Economique et Douanière de l'Afrique Centrale
UNESCO	United Nations Educational Scientific and Cultural Organisation
UNO	United Nations Organisation
UPC	Union des Populations du Cameroun
WAEC	West African Examination Council
WTTC	Women Teachers Training Centre

MAP OF GERMAN CAMEROON

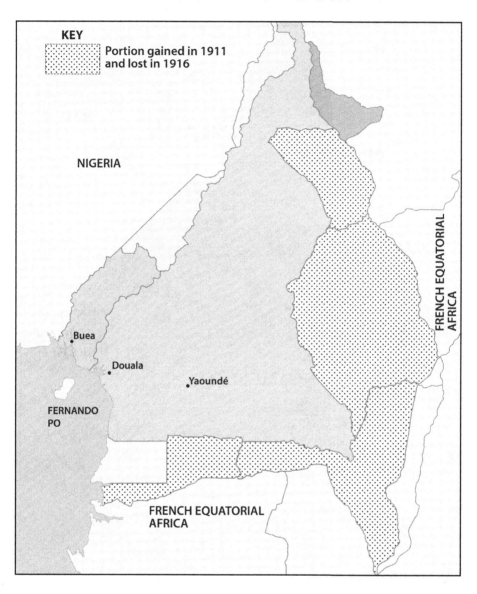

MAP OF CAMEROON AFTER FIRST WORLD WAR

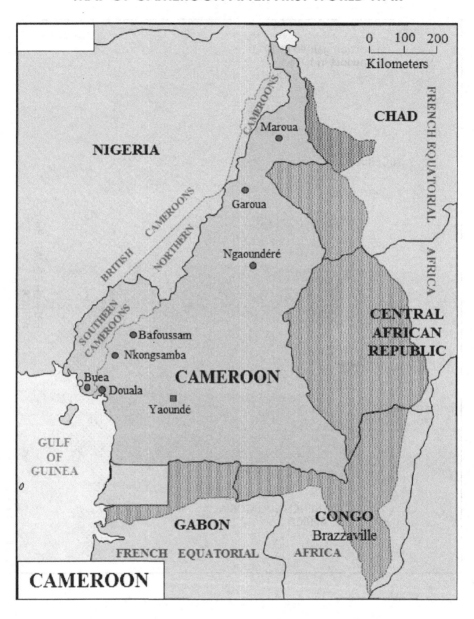

CURRENT ADMINISTRATIVE MAP OF CAMEROON

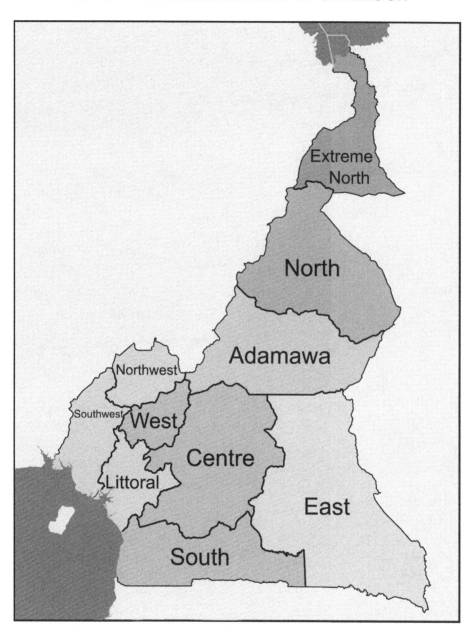

INTRODUCTION

Cameroon is located at the meeting point of West and Central African sub-regions and has consequently been variously described as a West African or Central African state. Since independence following the French and British colonial rule, postcolonial Cameroon has maintained very close economic and cultural ties with the other French speaking states of Central Africa sub region (formerly referred to as French Equatorial African states to which the south-eastern part of Cameroon belonged until its surrender to Germany as part of the accord of 1911). Thus together they belong to the CEMAC (Communauté Economique et Monétaire de l'Afrique Centrale) and earlier belonged to the Organisation of Central African and Malagasy states (OCAM), the Economic and Customs Union of Central African States (UDEAC) and jointly share the same Central Bank for Central African States (BEAC) which has its headquarters in Cameroon).[1] Cameroon's involvement in these financial, economic and cultural unions rather than West African associations justify its being considered a Central rather than West African state and gives an insight to why it is more involved with the *Francophonie* countries.

The immediate neighbours on the eastern border are the Republics of Chad, Central Africa and Congo. Within the southern region, the neighbours are the Republics of Gabon and Equatorial Guinea. Meanwhile on the western border stretching from the Gulf of Guinea precisely from the western end of Rio del Rey northwards to Lake Chad, Cameroon shares a common frontier with the Republic of Nigeria. Cameroon occupies a total land surface of 475,442 square kilometres; and a boundary length of 4,500 kilometres with only 500 kilometres of coastline on the Gulf of Guinea.[2] By size it is the 23rd largest of the 55 African states with a modest population of about 24, 000 000 people.

Since its first contact with the rest of the world, Cameroon has recorded a

---

1   These acronyms are in French; see list of abbreviation on page 16.

2   Gwanfogbe M.B. and Melingui A., Geography of Cameroon, Basingstoke, Macmillan, 1983

wide variety of political and cultural foreign influences.[3] In 1472,[4] the Portuguese led by Fernao do Pao arrived at the island of Biyoko which became known as Fernando Po until independence. On sailing to the main land, they noticed numerous prawns in the estuary of River Wouri which they immediately named *Rio dos Camaroes* (River of Prawns) from which the country derived its name. The Spanish traders on taking over Portuguese activities, called the River and land, *Camerones* and when the English arrived they called the area *Cameroons* while the Germans called it *Kamerun* and the French wrote it as *Cameroun*. Presently, it is known as *Cameroon* by those who use English as their first official language and *Cameroun* by those who are French speaking.

From the 15th century, Cameroon's contact with the outside world was centred on active commercial activities along the coast. By 1530, there was a shift from ivory and other agricultural products to the lucrative but inhuman trade in slaves. By 1560, the Portuguese dominance declined in favour of the Dutch, English, French, and German traders, particularly Germans from Brandenburg, then the Danes and Swedes increased the number of Europeans on Cameroon coast. By the 18th century the English activities surpassed those of all other Europeans on the coast. When Britain decided to stop the slave trade, they negotiated with the Spanish rulers who then had possession of the island of Fernando Po, to establish a squadron on the island to check on slave trading along the Gulf of Guinea. As an alternative to slave trade, the British took this opportunity to encourage several Bristol and Liverpool traders to set up floating hulks as trading posts on the Cameroon River.

The British influence on the coast expanded extensively because of commercial activities and naval surveillance of slave dealers and the growing activities of Missionary societies both on the mainland and island. To these activities was added an important diplomatic dimension, the creation of a British consulate. There was the frequent presence of the British consul for Fernando Po and the Oil Rivers of the Niger. By 1842, the British consul signed a treaty with Cameroon chiefs in Douala for trade in palm oil and ivory on condition that they stopped slave trading in their chiefdoms.

The predominance of British influence had a political, economic and cultural impact. Administrative systems of British pattern and commercial activities were

---

3   Kwast L., The Discipling of West Cameroon; study of Baptist Growth, Michigan, Berdmas Publishing Company., 1971. Also see Lekunze E.F., "Chieftaincy and Christianity in Cameroon, 1886-1926", Ph.D. Chicago, 1987."

4   Ardener E.W., "Documentary and the linguistic Sources for the rise of the trading polities between Rio del Rey and Cameroon, 1500-1650" in I. M. Lewis., (ed) History and Anthropology, London, Tavistock Publication., 1963

accompanied by an expanding British educational system established in 1844 by the British Baptist Missionary society and the education of some Cameroonians in Britain. King Bell, the ruler of the Douala people who was one of the principal authors of the letters appealing for British rule, was educated in Bristol. Other forms of cultural influences were manifested by the adoption of English names especially by the ruling class[5] such as "Prince" Manga William, "King" Bell, King Akwa etc. British trade and cultural activities especially through education and the active participation of Jamaicans working under the British Baptist Missionary Society introduced Pidgin English[6] which has become the lingua-franca in towns within Cameroon.

But despite the favourable circumstances and the voluntary decision of Cameroonians to associate with the British, the latter procrastinated for too long and were overtaken by the Germans. Influenced by Hamburg business people on the coast and because Britain delayed, the Germans succeeded in bribing and enticing some Cameroon coastal leaders to pass over their allegiance to German imperial rule.[7]

German rule lasted from 14th July 1884 to March 1916 when they were expelled as a result of their defeat in Cameroon during the First World War. During the three decades attempts were made, especially from 1910, to educate and extend the German culture through schooling and the establishment of German political, economic and social institutions.

On taking over Cameroon from the Germans, the British and the French partitioned the territory.[8] Britain took one fifth located on two contiguous narrow strips on the border with Nigeria starting from the Atlantic Ocean in the south to Lake Chad in the north. The two strips comprising British Southern Cameroon, from the Atlantic Ocean to the Mambila highlands, and British Northern Cameroon, from Yola to Lake Chad, were administered separately but as integral parts of the southern and northern regions of Nigeria respectively until 1961 when through a U.N. Organised plebiscite, the southern part chose to gain independence by reuniting with the French Cameroon (as before under German rule) to form the Federal Republic of Cameroon, while the northern portion decided to

---

5   The Cameroonian rulers were so interested in the British culture, that they gave themselves the titles of King, Prince etc.

6   For more on Pidgin English, see Todd, L, *Pidgin and Creoles*, London, Routledge and Kegan Paul 1974.

7   Dike K.O., *Trade and Politics in the Niger Delta , 1830-1885;* Oxford, Clarendon Press, 1956 pp. 216-217

8   Elango L, The Anglo-French Condominium in Cameroon, 1914-1916: The Myth and Reality" in *International Journal of African Studies*, 1987, p.82

integrate with Nigeria.[9]

Pre-colonial and German Mission education had been limited to the south for practical reasons and also for the protection of Muslim influence in the north. Consequently, Basel Mission education was limited to the south and never extended to the portion that became part of Nigeria in 1961. The French, on taking over their own portion in 1916, compensated the Basel Mission and replaced them by the Paris Protestant Evangelical Mission (Société Evangélique de Paris) while the British, after failing to replace the Basel Mission in their zone, allowed their activities to resume in 1925.

An important dimension of international influence that ultimately shaped the course of events affecting education in Cameroon today may be traced from British administrative strategy which remained peripheral throughout the colonial period. From 1916 to 1946, British Southern Cameroon was administered as a province under the southern region of Nigeria: From 1946 to 1954 the territory was administered as two provinces (Cameroon and Bamenda provinces) under the Eastern Region of Nigeria and from 1954 to 1958, it was administered as a *quasi-autonomous* region of Nigeria. Thus unlike other colonies, this portion of Cameroon never received much direct attention from London. Rather, everything had to pass through Lagos (capital of Nigeria and administrative headquarters of the British colonial regime) and for some time, through Lagos and then through Enugu (capital of Eastern Nigeria) before trickling down to Cameroon.

9   Ardener E.W., "The Kamerun Idea", in *West Africa.*, No. 2147 of 1958.

CHAPTER ONE

PRE-WESTERN EDUCATION SITUATION IN CAMEROON

African historiography on pre-European education has hardly considered the importance of traditional African education system. Those that attempt to discuss pre-colonial education tend to limit themselves to the era of Hamitic or Arabic predominance. This neglect has been attributed to the dearth of written sources covering the period before both Arabic and European invasions of the continent. Unquestionably, the influences of these two alien cultures have had significant impacts on African cultures and history. Yet there is no doubt that in spite of the impact of these foreign influences, the traditional African cultures, vestiges or legacies of pre-European and pre-Arabian times still survive.

Evidently, the survival of the pre- Arabic and pre- European African civilizations is a result of the fact that their practices had been so ingrained in its people that foreign influences, despite their intensity and sophistication, could not be totally erased. These indigenous practices had profound effects on everyday life and world view of the people, and could not therefore be easily suppressed by foreign systems of education. Apparently, the traditional institutions must have been so entrenched that replacing them have been difficult. Hence notwithstanding the repeated conquests and domination of the African people by Arabic and European regimes, contemporary Africa still exhibit surviving aspects of African educational systems albeit fragmented. The question is therefore to know if there were any educational practices in Africa before the external invasions or the continent was dominated essentially by primitive heathens who had no cultures that could be self-sustaining. This chapter seeks to find out whether aspects of pre-colonial traditional education exist and how they survived alien domination. This question arises because some Eurocentric have held the view that Africa before foreign domination was not capable of having a worthy education system.

In the 18th and 19th centuries, when historiography was revolutionized in Europe, some eminent historians stated that Africa had no history. By implication, they held that Africa had no culture and therefore no education. The German idealist philosopher, Hegel (1770-1831) stated explicitly that Africa "is not a historical continent, it shows neither change nor development" (Fage

J.D. 1981). He argued that since Africans were neither capable of Education nor development, they have never known any change. His line of argument was supported by Ranke who believed that objective history can only come from written documents and since Africa was generally an illiterate society, (in the Western sense of the term) there could be no history of Africa. The Hegelian view was reinforced by the application of Darwinian principle. This theory was used by the anthropologists in investigating and evaluating, in a non-historical approach, the cultures and societies of *uncivilized* peoples who had no history worth studying and were inferior to Europeans. The issue was put even more succinctly by A.P. Newton in 1923 when he stated that Africa had no history before the coming of the Europeans because history only begins when man takes to writing. He argued that African history could only be constructed from the evidence of material remains and of language and primitive customs which were not the concerns of historians but that of archaeologists, linguists and anthropologists. But today, the inter-relatedness of these social science disciplines for the study of history can no longer be disputed. They have become indispensable sources of history in nonliterate societies, and formidable supporting tools for investigating oral history.

Even as late as the beginning of independence in African countries, Coupland R., author of standard works on East Africa, stated that African history began only at the middle of the 19th century and that until then Africa was nothing but savagery. According to him, "Africa had stayed for untold centuries, sunk in barbarism...stagnant, neither going forward nor backward" (Coupland R, p. 3). Thus Coupland identifies African history (education inclusive) with the conquest and colonisation of Africa by the Europeans. It is equally important to remark that Trevor-Roper was even more vicious in re-stating this view. According to him it was worthless studying African history because African civilisation was "unrewarding gyrations of barbarous tribes in picturesque but irrelevant corners of the globe".

Meanwhile, another provoking attack on African history and education before foreign invasion by alien races was based on the Hamitic hypothesis. Prominent among the exponents of this concept was Seligman who in his publication, *Races of Africa* (1936), stated that the civilisation of Africa was the civilisation of Hamites and that African history was "the record of Hamites and their interactions with the other African stocks-the Negro and the Bushman" (Fage J. D. 1981). Undoubtedly, Seligman's myth served to consolidate the superiority of light skinned people over dark skinned people which characterised a part of European prejudice of the period. To re-enforce this prejudice, the fourth edition of *Races of Africa* in 1966 added a significant phrase that does not occur in the original text of 1930. In that edition, the Hamites are defined as Europeans belonging to "the great branch of mankind as the whites" Fage J.D. 1981). Thus

African education according to Western sources did not exist.

These attacks on the African past did not go unchallenged. Many refutations were made by African authors. Africans and non-African black people who became fascinated by their ancestral continent and felt obliged to rescue it from infamy and oblivion, wrote relentlessly to prove that Africa had a past and that African history is an integral part of the study of mankind. However, from the educational point of view not enough has been written about the past.

If William Boyd and Edmund King's argument (1977) that the training and instruction of the young for the business of life is one of the most ancient concerns of mankind is accepted, and Africans are accepted to be part of the human society, then Africans like all other human beings developed their own educational systems. After all Africans consciously instructed and trained their children to face life. These authors argue that any society, whether simple or complex had a system for training and educating its youths.

Undeniably, the goal of education and the method of approach differed from one society to another. In some societies education aimed at giving the individual a physical and skilful training with emphasis on character formation. In other societies, education catered for the whole being and his or her usefulness to society.

A. B. Fafunwa has argued that African indigenous education was clearly functional because the curriculum was developed to respond to the need of the society (A. B. Fafunwa, 1974). African education provided a means for survival. It prepared the youth for adulthood and integration in the society. The occupation of the individual, the social responsibilities, the political role as well as the moral and spiritual values were targeted in all educational considerations. Apprenticeship was highly encouraged through ceremonies, rituals, recitations and demonstrations. Youths were introduced to the art of farming, cooking, weaving, knitting, fishing, hunting, carving, building construction, wine production etc. by specialists who possessed great experiences.

Purely intellectual activities involved the study of legends, tribal or ethnic history, nature study and or environmental study (studying plants, animals, birds, the weather, seasons, soils etc.). Literature in the form of storytelling, poetry and praise songs was commonly practiced. The study of proverbs and riddles took the form of logic and stimulated creativity in reasoning.

African education therefore took an integrated approach wherein physical training combined with character building and manual activity with intellectual training. There was assessment at the end of each stage to evaluate the pupil's level of achievement. The final evaluation ended with a graduation ceremony and served as initiation into adulthood. Further education was acquired generally in secret cults where the secret of power was taught. Such secrecy could be real or imaginary. It was here that the peoples' understanding of the world and the entire universe was discussed; their philosophy, science and religion were taught. Generally, their world view shaped their philosophy of education.

African education was therefore functional. Unemployment of the type known today was unknown. Rather, unemployed people were referred to as lazy people because everybody could find some gainful activity to engage with. The aim and content of education were inseparable. Great importance was associated with the collective and social nature of the education system. The social importance had both material and spiritual significance. Education was acquired through gradual and progressive methods in conformity with the successive stages of physical, emotional and mental development of the pupil.

Since this type of education is referred to by Eurocentric scholars as schools without walls and classes and subjects without grades, and has remained largely unwritten, it has been condemned as primitive and uncivilized. This gives the impression that informal education as a whole has no inherent value. Yet it is evident that in spite of more than a century's introduction of literary European education in Cameroon, traditional African education practices still survive. Obviously, any meaningful education should be the aggregate of all the processes by which the individual learner develops the abilities, attitudes and other forms of behaviour which are of positive value to the society. Education can only be useful to a society if it is a process of transmitting culture in terms of continuity and growth. It should disseminate knowledge either to ensure social control or to guarantee rational direction of the society or both. Thus the usefulness of any educational system can only be determined by the extent to which it satisfies the needs of the society. But contemporary education (essentially western in content) in Africa fails to satisfy African needs even though it is considered modern.

Generally, western education was formerly introduced in Africa in the 19th century. The establishment of European trade to replace the slave trade necessitated the training of some Africans to produce those things that the Europeans would like to exploit. The introduction of Christian religion from European background also warranted the establishment of Christian missionary schools so that the converts could eventually be able to read the Bible and sing hymns. Subsequently, the establishment of European colonial rule in Africa forced the colonial masters to formerly train some Africans who would assist them in the task of administration. It must not also be forgotten that there were also Africans who were curious to know European education. These factors led to the implantation of Western education in Africa. But the new education was not widespread and did not effectively replace all traditional education

The number of educated Africans required by the imperialist administrators, European traders, farmers and Missionaries was often very small when compared with the population. Hence school facilities were made available only for the few people they required. This is why until independence; education remained the privilege of only a few Africans. The bulk of Africans who could not find themselves in the Western schools had to continue with the African education system. As such African education system continued to flourish alongside European education during the colonial period. The survival of this education system meant the continued growth of African culture and traditional African education.

Since the generation at the eve of independence still dominate the national scene in the respective countries, it is certain that people imbued with both western education and African education systems still influence national issues. But in most cases when issues such as the reforms of education are involved, those with western education want to dominate and very often dismiss the opinions on African education. Thus the probable reason for the repeated failure of attempts to reform education in African countries since independence can be explained by the fact that traditional African education systems are totally ignored in favour of alien systems which are usually incompatible with African cultures.

Indigenous Cameroon Education

The geographical location of Cameroon in Africa which stretches from the Guinea coast and equatorial forest through several climatic and vegetation belts to the Sahelian vegetation around Lake Chad in the heart of Africa, with people of diverse ethnic origins (over 220 languages or ethnic groups) makes one to see Cameroon as an amalgamation of African cultures. The diversity in climate, vegetation, ethnicity, language and culture has caused many to view Cameroon generally as Africa in miniature. Cameroon has pygmies, who are historically considered the earliest inhabitants of the forest; Bantus who are linguistically and culturally akin to the other Bantus of Central and South Africa. There are also people of the Sudanic origin who are linguistically and culturally related to the people of the upper Nile and the Western Sudan. There are Hamitic people of Fulani or Fulbe and Arab origins who are religiously and culturally related to the people of West and North Africa. These linguistic and cultural inter related-ness show that Cameroon has a representation of most of the ethnic groups in Africa. Cameroon may therefore be rightly referred to as Africa in miniature.

Since these diverse groups are largely related by language, and since language is said to be the vehicle of culture and education, it can be argued that the inherited indigenous or traditional education systems in Cameroon represent all forms of African systems. Cameroon systems of education were therefore similar with those found in most African societies. Generally, the educational systems had common aims and objectives although they differed in methods from place to place because of the socio-political, geographical and particularly economic imperatives in the respective areas.

Education in Cameroon started at early childhood. The birth of a child was considered a great blessing from God which deserved serious celebration. The celebrations varied at different ages of the child's growth and integration into the society. At all levels education either to the parents or the child was involved. Such education at the early stage was to remind the parents of their responsibilities towards educating the child to fit in the society.

In some societies the naming ceremony carried the first celebration. The extended family was involved. The fanfare and merriments were intermingled with significant educational values. The child's names were given with special significance to the day of the week, the month or season of the year. The coincidence of the birth to an important event in the family, the community or the village could also determine the name given to the child. All names had meanings and significance. For example, because of the strong belief in the concept of life after death, a child born shortly after the death of a closely related elderly person of the same sex in the family was believed to be the resurrected person and as such, the baby had to take the name of that deceased person.

Young parents having their first birth were particularly educated in child care. They were taught post-natal care for the woman so that her health might not be affected and in order to prepare her for subsequent births. Post-natal care for the baby included all health measures and rituals to ensure good health. Special foods and drinks were prescribed to the baby's mother so that her breast milk may flow without problems and contamination may be avoided. Elderly women including the mother of the nursing woman were her teachers at this-stage. They offered her close attention until the woman became pregnant for the second child. The attention given to the second child was less and much more that of supervision, since it was assumed that the parents had gained experience from the first child. Thus the art of motherhood and parental responsibilities were taught alongside that of communal solidarity. No fees were charged for this education except the fact that the young parents were expected to appreciate the assistance given by the community by reciprocating to the needs of others.

From infancy, the child was taught to socialize as a member of the community. He/she became the child of the community and not just that of a particular family. His eating, playing and all other social habits had to conform to that practiced in the entire village. The child's mother, however, remained the actual and steady teacher during this early period of growth. She taught the child everything required at this initial stage, including language and simple operations. The father was supposed to be too busy with the rest of the family responsibilities to pay adequate attention. More so, in polygamous situations, it was not possible for the father to give equal attention to all the children.

At the age of about three years, when the birth of the next child was expected, the extended family became more involved in the child's education. The grandparents in particular became more directly involved. In some cases, the child moved to stay and grow with the grandparents. Here the child was taught respect, obedience and good behaviour. All elderly men and women were to be regarded as mother or father of the child. In Cameroon there were no equivalent words for uncles, aunts, cousins because these people were seen to be fathers, mothers (junior or senior), and brothers and sisters respectively. Through small errands, the child was taught how to become useful to the society. The history of the family was also gradually introduced to the child.

From about six years of age, the child was introduced into the age-group or age-grade. In most societies, this association was particularly very important for educational purposes. Age-grade intervals varied from place to place. In some places the interval was two years while in others it was up to four years. Age-grade system was used for education, citizenship training, and communal labour, social and political participation. The age-grade practice was in all Cameroonian societies and could be compared with the classmate system in western education. Each age-group had a specific curriculum to cover. At the end of the course, there was an evaluation and those who passed had a graduation ceremony usually in the form of initiation into a new stage of life in the community. Exceptional graduates were earmarked for greater heights.

Objectives of Indigenous Education

The aim of indigenous African education was manifold but major focus was on producing an honest, respectable, skilled and co-operative individual who will fit into the social life of the society and enhance its growth. Like all other educational systems, indigenous African education system also encouraged physical training. But unlike European education where conscious training is programmed for all aspects of physical education, the African indigenous system profited from inherited skills derived from social and leisure life-style. This was particularly found in music and dance which were frequent and involved a lot of body movements. However, many competitive games such as wrestling, swimming, canoe races, running and hunting were organised.

African education emphasized character training. The parents, members of the extended family and the rest of the community participated actively in the education of the child. The philosophy behind this collective education was derived from the belief that the child belongs to a particular family only until birth and becomes that of the entire community from birth and especially when the child develops communicative abilities. The entire community would want to inculcate humble, courageous, honest, sociable and persevering attitudes in the child. This was generally so because the individual's behaviour was supposed to reflect that of the entire community. The teaching was direct from the seniors. Another method was through encouragement by members of the community. Children were also encouraged to learn through observation and imitation.

All parents, (especially mothers) were responsible for the education of their children at the initial stage. They started with language training and followed with sanitary and aesthetic education. All children were taught the importance of cleanliness. They had to wash their faces and clean their mouths before eating in the morning. They were taught to wash their hands before eating at all times. Taking a good bath at least once a day was said to be a means of giving the body renewed strength.

The development of character and communal spirit took various forms in different communities. Some used the wrestling exercises to instil the spirit of reconciliation and solidarity. Such healthy competitive spirits were also taught to peer groups right from the early age when in some communities mock wars were organized. Usually in all societies, both winners and losers were congratulated because the essence of each competition was to inculcate the spirit of tolerance and solidarity.

Further aspect of communal solidarity was taught by the establishment of laws (usually referred to by Eurocentric views as taboos) against killing, witchcraft, stealing, adultery, incest, disloyalty, infidelity, perfidy, corruption, etc. The divulging of the secrets of the society was tantamount to committing treasonable felony against the community and very often attracted ostracism. These measures were taken to ensure the imbuement of the spirit of honesty, kindness, uprightness, decency and cooperation. It was commonly accepted to remain childless than to have an uncouth child who will bring dishonour to the family and the society. Such education required all forms of evaluations.

There were both continuous and terminal evaluations. Continuous evaluation was particularly applied to disciplines relating to character development. To assess a child's level of understanding and ability to practice some basic concepts of ethics, some parents or teachers set up deliberate and even improvised tests for evaluation. This was particularly the case with attempts to test for the spirit of honesty, kindness, endurance, cooperation, concern or love for others, for animals and for what belong to the society. Through conversations, some children were also evaluated to gauge their levels of development in psychology, philosophy, sociology, literature and all such subjects that pertain to thinking and oratory. During moments of various forms of work (professional and non-professional), children's abilities and talents were also evaluated from their performance and demonstration of interest. The responses and reactions of the children were then carefully analysed over time to determine the character and ability of the individual in the society. The result was also used to help oriented the children in career development.

Terminal evaluation was largely deliberate. It was planned and had to involve a particular age group. In most societies, the elders had to set up a particular programme outlining the activities involved and the duration. The teachers concerned were professionals usually with recognized experiences or assumed inherited family expertise. There was first of all an intensive training covering all the required disciplines as well as what were considered to have been known and what was assumed yet unknown but appropriate at that age. Thereafter, a series of tests were organized to evaluate both theoretical and practical performances. The degree of success served as a means of orienting the children. There were hardly repeaters. But the best students in theoretical output were often directed towards priesthood and family leadership. Those excellent in practical work were encouraged to further develop their skills in the specific trades or professions. Where the test came before adulthood, there was likelihood for the individual to go through another test before graduation. Final graduation was generally initiation into manhood or womanhood. The graduation ceremony in some societies involved circumcision for boys only and in others for both boys and girls. This was usually at the end of adolescence. But it does not mean that circumcision was limited to this age group. It must be noted that circumcision at birth was commonly practiced in many areas.

Those challenging the pre-western African education focus their arguments on the absence of intellectual training. Yet a close study of the remains of the educational system reveals active encouragement of intellectual development. If reasoning abstractly can be accepted as an intellectual exercise, then much of Cameroon education before outside influence encouraged intellectual training. Some of the commonly used method of learning included observation, imitation and participation which are abstract processes. Besides, the child was taught the characteristics of seasons and how to determine the beginning of each season by observing atmospheric changes, the appearance or disappearance of certain fauna and flora. The effects of the changing seasons on the environment including the vegetation, the water level, and communication systems were taught to show how these changes could affect farmers, traders, builders, hunters, fishermen and all other forms of activities. Hence a child could identify activities that were appropriate for the respective seasons. These learning could be classified under Geography, Environmental studies, Nature studies, Rural Science, Weather Observation, Bio-geography etc., following Western classifications. They were therefore academic.

Local history was taught, first at family level, then at village or clan level and latter at tribal or ethnic level. Heroes were identified and songs of praises composed and showered on them which everybody including youths had eventually to learn. The learning of the history and the songs were undeniably, intellectual activities of no mean calibre. The study and identification of plants by names and utility to human beings as food, medicine, flowers, fuel, etc. constituted the study of Botany as the Western world came to call it. Similarly, the Cameroonian or African made good value of the age-old relation with animals. They were able to teach the youths how to identify and treat domestic and wild animals. They were taught animal husbandry including feeding and cures to various types of animal diseases and epidemics. Such studies amply covered aspects of modern veterinary sciences.

In almost all Cameroonian societies, proverbs, riddles, recitations, incantations and songs of praise constituted formidable bases for intellectual drill. They were taught not only for developing intellectual capacity but also for improving on the learners' reasoning. Arguments and conversations were considered to be more logical and stimulating with the application of proverbs. There is no doubt that to attain higher levels of reasoning, there was a lot of theoretical input on the part of the learners and teachers.

As earlier stated, more scholarship was attained by those who proved intellectually more competent at the level of the cults. In most African societies, there were and there are still many secret cults which have various functions. People, who considered themselves able, could join. And those who were seen by older cult members as being competent were invited to the cult. The cults generally had serious educational programmes requiring intellectual maturity before any-body was initiated. It was not uncommon to have such philosophical issues as ontological, epistemological, axiological, metaphysical, cosmological questions being debated. As for logic, semantics and ethics, cult members were expected to at least grasp the basics before initiation. The teachers were themselves experts and usually specialized as priests, diviners, herbalists, etc.

The songs and praises at this level had clear poetic and prophetic attributes. Songs praising the ruler were generally poetic and implied salutations. They were offered from memory and very often in chanting style. The themes of songs varied with the occasions and the person or people concerned; e.g. births and in some societies, the births of twins were given even more attention, deaths which in most societies had to distinguish between male or female, the age and the status. Songs at festivals (religious or others) also had specific themes. These were also done through incantations and recitations which could go on for a long time without repetition except when they were interruptions through choruses. Priests, diviners and healers were adepts of this form of oratory.

Mathematics was well developed. The children were introduced very early in life to the notion of counting and calculating. Through games, folklore and rhymes, these notions were further impressed. In all Cameroon languages, the concept of addition, subtraction, multiplication and division exist. This shows that pre-western education practiced Mathematics. They were also quite versed with quantities, although they might not have been as precise as the West who used percentages and fractions. Their competence in geometrical and trigonometric practices were more evident in construction. Most constructions, especially of houses were done separately on the ground before bringing the different parts together to assemble. That these pieces fitted together when assembled, were proof that the architectural level was well developed and the mathematical involvement was highly sophisticated.

Figure 1: Pictures of a traditional house under construction by Wilhem Zurcher in 1938; Constructing the foundation after the construction of the walls

Pre-colonial traditional education was therefore well developed in Cameroon like in all other parts of Africa before the introduction of Western Education. It is therefore false to claim that no education existed before the introduction of Western Education. Rather, it is certain that traditional education was highly ingrained in the society. This is true because even after a century's practice and dominance of Western education, the traditional education system remains very significant. The question is how this system of education has survived side by side with western education? The question is even more pertinent when we consider the fact that this system of education is not written. How did it prepare the people to receive western education? Was there integration or disagreement between the two systems? How has that affected the educational development? To better answer the question, it will be necessary to first of all trace and discuss the introduction of Islamic/Arabic education during the pre-colonial period.

*Figure 2: The process of constructing a house; top left, **setting up the first two walls;** bottom left, **preparing to fit in the last wall;** top right, **thatching after roofing;** bottom right, **a completed house.***

Islamic Education

Islamic education and the influence of Muslim culture have lasted for long in Cameroon. It was first introduced to the old Kanuri Empire before the turn of the first millennium. John Lavers states that the first Kanuri kingdom was in full contact with Dar al-Islam or abode of Islam and that the Kanuri king was converted to Islam in about 1880.[10] It is important to note that before the king became a convert, Islam had existed for a long time in the kingdom. S. A Balogun intimates that some of the people even read the Koran.[11] It is also said that after the conversion of the first Kanuri king, successive rulers became famous scholars and pilgrims. Kanem-Borno Empire, which evolved from the Kanuri kingdom,

10   J. E. Lavers; "Kanem-Borno to 1808 in *Groundwork of Nigerian History*, ed by O.Ikime, pp. 188-191

11   S. A. Balogun; -History of Islam up to 1800 in *Groundwork of Nigerian History*, ed. by O. lkime, p. 212

produced students who studied abroad in North Africa. Balogun goes further to argue that Islamic tradition became manifest in the growth of Borno and the neighbouring communities and that the principles of the religion served as the basis for governance. It should be remembered that the Kanuri kingdom later became an important emirate, the Dikwa emirate, which at one point was part of German Kamerun and became British Northern Cameroon until 1961 when it was ceded to Nigeria. From there, the Islamic education spread first to many parts of northern Cameroon and subsequently to other parts of the country.

Nature Of Islamic Education

Muslim or Islamic education has a religious emphasis. The single fundamental fact that determined and dictated the content as well as the evolution of Muslim education is the belief that God's final judgement to mankind was revealed in its entirety through Muhammad and is enshrined in the Koran.[12] The divine revelation embraces not only the dogmas of faith and the religious and moral duties of the believer but also guidance on the political, social and economic organization of the community. As such the basis of Muslim education unlike that of the indigenous had a well-defined policy. Its content was of divine origin. It aimed at directing the conduct of the individual and the community according to God's command. Since these bases are written, literary education becomes very important for any Muslim faithful so as to directly gain from what was revealed to the prophet by Allah.

Islam therefore requires education and the pride in acquiring the knowledge has always been a crucial factor. This is why it attaches great importance to the study of the Koran. Mohammed himself underscored the importance of education when he stated that, "...the ink of the scholar is holier than the blood of the martyr"[13] It is also held by Muslim theologians that "the learned are the successors of prophets".[14] Before receiving instructions in religious knowledge, the prospective scholar was taught the elements of reading and writing often with the Koran as the textbook. It is therefore clear to note that Islamic education possibly spread alongside the propagation of the religion.

The impact of Islamic education on the socio-political setting of those areas of Cameroon where the religion was introduced is said to have been far reaching.

12   A.L. Tibawi; "Arabic and Islamic themes", in *Historical. Educational and Literary Studies*. London, 1976.

13   GN. Brown et at (eds) "Government and Islamic education in Northern Nigeria 1900-1960" in *Conflict and Harmony in Education in Tropical Africa*, London, 1975.

14   A.L. Tibawi, *Op. Cit.* p. 190.

Islam introduced literacy to many of those who accepted the religion. Above all, the rulers who accepted Islam began to rely more on the advice of Muslim scholars. For instance, Mai Bukar Haji (1715-1737) of Wandala in the Mandara region replaced his advisers with Muslim scholars.[15] Towns like Maroua, Bogo, Mindif, Be, Ngaoundere, Tibati and Banyo received many Islamic scholars who established schools for the believers.

The spread of Muslim education was accelerated in the 19th century through the jihad. It started in Sokoto in North-western Nigeria and then spread from there eastwards into the northern Cameroon area. The leader was the Pulo Muslim reformer, Uthman dan Fodio and his representative in Northern Cameroon was Moddibo Adama. M. Z. Njeuma intimates that by 1850, the Muslim Fulbe in northern Cameroon succeeded in setting up over 40 administrative units in many parts of the region.[16] The headquarter or emirate was at Yola where the *Lamido* or the Emir exercised paramountcy over the administration of the sub-emirates and in turn represented them at the Caliphal government at Sokoto. Each of the administrative unit was a sub-emirate headed by a *lamido*. The Fulbe and other Muslim leaders principally from Hausa land became the rulers of these administrative areas.

It is important to note that Islam became the platform on which thought and aspiration revolved and anybody aspiring to power had to improve his knowledge of Islam by developing more interest in Islamic studies. Thus many schools were established following the jihads since knowledge in Islam became essential not only for worship but also for becoming good rulers because Islam formed the moral and legal foundations of documented governance.

The new converts to Islam endeavoured to study the Koran in order to know more about their rights and obligations in the new politico-religious setting. Social pressures became strong to convert or to conform to the dominant culture for reasons of self-preservation. Some people adopted Muslim names, modes of dress and mannerisms and learnt Fulfulde.

In the court of each *Lamido*, there were found many educated people whose task was to write, transcribe and recite religious and profanic texts. They were known as *modibbe* (plural of *modibbo*). They wrote many praise poems. For instance, Modibbo Bakari wrote elaborately and some of his historical writings and praise poems of the Sultan of Maroua have been translated into French by

---

15 J. Mouchet ; Notes sur la conversion a Islamisme en 1715 de la tribue Wandala in *Etude Camerounaise*, No. 15-16, 1946 ; pp. 105-107.

16 M. Z. Njeuma ; "Islam, Colonial rule and the early Christian Missions in Northern Cameroon." in *Cameroon Tribune*, No. 584 of 28th August, 1985.

J. C. Zeltner.[17] It helps to shed light on the history of Maroua and the advent of the Fulbe.

It is however important to note that although a lot of force was applied in propagating Islam, there is no doubt that Islamic education was not wide spread. This can be explained firstly because learning the Islamic scriptures was not a condition for conversion. Secondly, this was because the Fulbe used Islamic education to serve their political aspirations and to exploit the non-Fulbe population. Finally, because the Fulbe made constant raids for slaves from the population of the non-Fulbe population the later were often against Islam because they considered Islam and Islamic culture to be the religion of the Fulbe people. As a result, the Muslims remained limited in number in spite of the use of force and all other means to convert the population. All the same, Islamic cultures in some aspects such as marriage and mystical perceptions seem to agree with African world view and therefore attract even the non-faithful.

It is however important to point out a significant impact of Muslim education on the Cameroonian society. It stimulated the creative invention of Njoya, the Bamum king who in 1896 introduced a form of writing for his kingdom known as shûmom.[18] Bamum was a large and well-organized kingdom in the Western highland of Cameroon with the capital at Fumban before the arrival of Europeans in this region.

It is important to note that although Njoya claimed that he had no external influence in the invention of shûmom, there are reasons to believe that his inclination and eventual conversion to Islam suggest that he had a predilection for Islamic culture.

However, by 1916, there were more than 20 shûmom schools in Bamum land, which enrolled more than 600 pupils. Even during the exile of Njoya during the French colonial rule, shûmom continued to prosper and by 1933 when he died, there were more than 1000 literate people who graduated through Njoya's educational system. The Bamum history of 547 pages was written in shûmom and preserved in the palace at Fumban. The death of Njoya and the determination of the colonial government to undo all African structures that threatened the colonial administration ended the growth of that educational system. Nevertheless, before the establishment of colonial regimes, Western education was already introduced especially in the coastal regions where Europeans were doing business. What was the nature of this pre-colonial education and how was it going

---

17   E Mohammadou;"Introduction à la littérature Peule du Nord Cameroun in *ABBIA Cameroon Cultural Review*, No. 6 of 1963 p. 68.

18   N A. Njasse et al; *De Njoya a Njimuluh, cent ans d'histoire Bamoun;* Foumban, 1984 pp 30-35

to affect post-colonial education?

Pre-colonial Western Education

Pre-colonial Western education in Cameroon like in most African countries was predominated by Christian Missionary societies. Europeans of that age and even long after had regarded Africans as *uncivilized and barbarous*. This explains why the declared objective of the Missionary education was to bring enlightenment and to save African souls from damnation. At the same time, the growth of Missionary activities reflected the expansion of European trade and political influence in the world. Similar motives and values justified commercial, political and evangelical expansionism. The technical, industrial and military superiority of the West came to be taken as signs of corresponding moral and spiritual superiority. Many missionaries were no doubt motivated by spiritual goals and were among the few people who protested against the evils and excesses of colonialism, but this does not mean that they were not prone to think in racialist terms or, indeed, to practice some exploitation of their own. It is therefore no accident that the early missionaries did not consider African culture or environment in planning educational curricula. Subsequently, colonial administrators and postcolonial regimes continued the same practice by neglecting traditional education system. This reflects the European's opinion that Africa had little of value to offer.

Missionary education sought to make the Cameroonian just literate enough to read the scriptures either in his own language or in a European language. This explains why mission education was similar to that of working-class children in Europe in the 19th century. For example, 19th century working-class children were taught by monitors in schools owned by churches or voluntary bodies. The adaptation of that type of education was because to the European, the prevailing image of the African was, "a lazy scoundrel wallowing in heathen superstition."[19] They therefore considered it appropriate to establish the educational system then in vogue in England for working class people because the African was considered to be afflicted by similar weaknesses as their less privileged compatriots. It may be right also to explain further that the class prejudice in Britain influenced the curriculum of schools in Cameroon.

It may equally be argued that Missionary education also emphasized the spiritual value of hard work and the tenets of Christianity. But it did not take the missionaries long to realize that they could only gain African adherents by catering for material as well as spiritual needs. After all, "without food and clothing and several branches of secular knowledge, the Bible and the Gospel cannot exist

19   Baarman (ed) *African Reaction to Missionary Education*, New York, 1975.

in any country."[20] This realization had an important influence on the designing of school curriculum and it encouraged school attendance.

These were the basis for establishing Missionary education policies in Cameroon. Reverend Joseph Merrick (a freed slave from Jamaica), Reverend Alexander fuller (of slave parents) and Reverend Alfred Saker (and Englishman) were all sent by the London Baptist Missionary society to evangelise the Africans of this area. They came along with 42 Christian volunteers from Jamaica in 1844 and settled first at Fernando Po (Bioko) and later on at Douala and Victoria (Limbe).[21] From 1958, they left Fernando Po and settled on the Cameroonian coast. They founded the town of Victoria, which is today known as Limbe. Henceforth, Victoria and Douala became the focal points from where education radiated in Cameroon.

The first school was opened by Joseph Merrick in Bimbia in 1844. The second was started in Douala by Alfred Saker in 1845. Many other schools were later on opened along the coast. From 1844 to 1884 when Germany annexed Cameroon there were 18 established schools in Cameroon.[22] The Missionaries reduced the Douala and Isuwu languages to writing. The Bible and prayer books were produced in these languages. The Missionaries also set up a printing press in Victoria to help in the production of necessary documents for educational and religious matters.[23]

Vocational education was also encouraged to meet up with the material demands of the Missionaries. A kiln for producing bricks was built at Bimbia. This enabled the Missionaries to embark upon building their stations. The teaching of such trades as carpentry, bricklaying and sewing were also taught. In 1850, the Bethel chapel was completed in bricks through the joint efforts of the Missionary technician and their Cameroonian apprentices.

Another important area emphasized by Mission education was agriculture. In this domain, the Missionaries introduced new food crops and fruits such as potatoes, mango and avocado pear etc. They held that if the people could occupy themselves with useful agriculture, they could abandon slave trade and slavery and become more independent. But apparently, the new crops and fruits were intended to serve European demands.

---

20   A. Ayandele. The coming of Western Education to West Africa in West African *Journal of Education* Vol. xv, No. 1, pp. 22-23

21   Fernando Po and Victoria are now known respectively as Bioko and Limbe but we shall maintain the old names for convenience.

22   Victoria Centenary Committee, *Southern Cameroons.* London, 1958 pp. 41-54

23   W. Keller., *The History of the Presbyterian Church in West Cameroon*, Victoria, 1969, p. 4.

However, the Jamaican role in introducing Western education in Cameroon was very significant. It should be noted that it was really the freed slaves in Jamaica that initiated the birth and fostering of what crystallized and eventually went down in history as the first Christian mission to bring the gospel and education to Cameroon. While this may be accepted, it must not be forgotten that many missionary societies from Europe and America were at work in Africa even before the Jamaican freed slaves made their request to the London Baptist Missionary Society. Their desire alone was not enough. They lacked the material and financial means which the London Missionary Society had to supply. Besides, even if they did not come, it was possible that the elaborate missionary activities on the Niger Delta, Calabar and the Congo could have spread to Cameroon.

As earlier stated missionary education emphasized religious studies. The schools were generally, a little more than Sunday schools. Not much was done to adapt the Western Education to the realities of the pupils. The people's music, dance, habits and the entire culture were considered evil. Thus to be educated in the European school meant to be alienated from one's own culture and people.

Since the scope of education taught was very inadequate, it also became difficult for education to transform the society. Cameroonians were not involved in the formulation of the educational policy-a situation, which subsequently persisted during the entire colonial period.

Until the annexation of Cameroon there was only the London Baptist Missionary Society in Cameroon. They operated only on the coast with Victoria and Douala as their base. This was the situation of education before the establishment of colonial rule.

CHAPTER TWO

CAMEROON EDUCATION UNDER THE GERMAN COLONIAL REGIME (1886-1916)

Education under German colonial rule was motivated by imperial and Missionary interests as well as a Cameroonian desire to acquire western knowledge. But the preoccupation of the imperial Government with the pacification and economic survey of the territory initially limited Government direct control and favoured the predominance of Missionary societies in the provision of education. As a result, the pattern of education responded more to the needs of the Missionaries and the interests of some Cameroonians until 1910 when Government control was established. This chapter examines the implications of the varying interests of the colonial regime, Missionary societies and Cameroonians on the development of education. It assesses the impact of Missionary and colonial interest on the development of Cameroonian attitudes to education and the extent to which education under German rule confirms or refutes the interpretations of the colonial situation on education.

The first part of the chapter discusses the role of the colonial administration in the development and control of education with specific attention to policy on curriculum development. The second part examines the development of Mission education and relations with the Government requirements on the one hand and those of the Cameroonian population on the other.

The colonial administration and educational development

One year after the appointment of Freiherr Julius Von Soden as the first colonial Governor of Cameroon (1885-1891), he wrote to the Chancellor insisting on the urgent need for the establishment of a Government school if German Missionaries were not ready to take over education from the British Baptist Missionary Society. The Governor considered the continued expansion of the British Baptist Mission in Cameroon to be "injurious to the German rule".[24] He

---

24   Madiba E op. cit

reminded the Government of the commitment in the treaty of annexation in which the Government agreed to provide education and further stated that there were Cameroonians waiting anxiously to be introduced to western education and even ready to pay school fees.[25]

Besides the Governor's appeal, the German business people in Cameroon were instrumental in bringing colonial education to enhance their activities. The most prominent of these tycoons was Adolf Woermann, the Hamburg business magnate who master-minded German annexation of Cameroon in 1884. He was one of the greatest beneficiaries of the German annexation of Cameroon because of his extensive business activities in the territory. As a member of the Hamburg Chamber of Commerce, a member of the liberal party in the Reichstag and president of the *Kolonialverein*, Woermann evidently wielded tremendous political and economic influence. He was also president of the West African syndicate, which was founded through Bismarck's initiative in 1884 and comprised all important German business people on the West African coast. Thus Woermann had unquestioned authority on colonial issues in German West Africa. It was therefore not surprising that the German Chancellor asked Governor Soden to refer his report, including plans for educational development to Woermann.

After studying the Governor's report, Woermann submitted his recommendations to Bismarck in 1886. He strongly suggested the establishment of elementary schools with a curriculum comprising the 3Rs, religious knowledge, agriculture and the introduction of vocational education. As a business man who relied on plantation exploitation, commercial and shipping activities, his proposal was ultimately directed towards the training of a local labour force. Initially, German business people had to import literate workmen from Liberia and other African countries which was more expensive than employing local people. Thus by offering basic education and the elements of vocational skills, they could raise local labour. The religious knowledge content was aimed at inculcating Christian principles and the ethics of work.

Following Woerman's report and the pressure from the colonial administration in Cameroon, the first German teacher, Theodor Christaller, was appointed on the recommendation of the Basel Mission. After visiting schools in other colonies in West Africa, Christaller arrived in Cameroon and opened the first Government school in February 1887 in Douala. He had a financial grant of 2,500 marks from King Wilhelm II of Germany. The amount was increased to 5,000 marks in the following year. Christaller spent his first year studying the Douala language with the assistance of Bell's family. By 1888, he had produced a story book from which he could teach reading and writing in Douala. He worked in

---

25   Rudin H. op. cit

collaboration with two other Germans, Betz and Kobele, to produce a common curriculum for Cameroon and Togoland.

Figure 3: Theodore Christaller, first Western education teacher and his pupils in front of school house in October 1887

The curriculum involved a five-year course. Special attention was directed to the teaching, of German but this was only applied to Government schools. Mission schools continued to develop independent curricula. However, Christaller agreed with the Basel Mission on the use of the Douala language as a medium of instruction, and on a uniform orthography for the Douala language. Unable to achieve a full primary school course, Christaller requested the Government to establish a library in Douala to enable school leavers to continue reading. Unfortunately, his sudden death in 1896 left his plans unfulfilled.

It is difficult to speculate upon the course of German education in Cameroon if Christaller had survived until the education conference of 1907. As a person, he was very sympathetic to Cameroonians and much-more amenable to Mission educational strategies than all other Government officials. His attitude may be explained by the fact that he was the son of an old Basel Mission worker who had served in the Gold Coast (Ghana). However, it is doubtful whether he could have been able to oppose the hard-fisted imperialist rule of Governor Jesco Von Puttkamer whose governorship was marked by scandals and brutalities and exemplified the supremacist fantasies of the period.

The arrival of Governor Puttkamer (1895-1906) ushered in what Helmuth Stoecker has described as a period of "colonialist rule by terror and extensive child labour exploitation".[26] Puttkamer's twelve years of brutal and morally degenerate rule in Cameroon eventually provoked his dishonourable recall. Neither his predecessor nor his successor displayed such attitudes or perpetrated such abuses which terrified and seemingly kept away many Cameroonians from European institutions, including schools. As an individual, Puttkamer was openly opposed to educating Africans. He associated the Douala uprisings against the Germans in 1904 and 1905, with the education they had received and discouraged its expansion. To some extent this suspicion had the support of some Germans. Even the Council of Protestant Missionary Societies of Germany had warned in 1897 of the danger that loomed because of the spread of European languages in Africa and the emergence of an educated proletariat which they considered "presumptuous and also easily rebellious".[27] Although only a fragmentary education was given, the Germans regarded it as a potential threat to their rule. This fear of the *hosenneger* (the trousered Black) became a recurrent factor in the development of German policy in Cameroon.

It was not until 1906 that the German colonial Government established administrative control over much of Cameroon, although punitive expeditions continued until 1913. It was easier to tempt chiefs to accept German taxation and forced labour. Hence the later rebellions were mostly from non-centralized communities especially over boundary rectifications.[28] The addition of a vast new area *(Neo-Kamerun)* followed an agreement with France to take over Morocco while giving up some of the French Equatorial land to be added to Cameroon. (Map on page xix.)

Resistance to German imperial rule had been wide-spread and the colonial Government devoted more attention to military conquest and economic survey.[29] Lakoswski argues that Germany was determined to build up an enormous colonial empire in Central Africa "as a pillar of German world power".[30] Cameroon must have been ear-marked for that purpose. By 1906, Cameroon rulers had almost all yielded to German military might and were prepared to meet Government demands. Imperial economic activities (trade, plantations, forest exploitation etc.)

---

26 Stoecker., (ed) *German Imperialism in Africa: from the beginning until the second World Wan* translated by Bernd Zollner, London, Hurst Publishers., 1986.

27 GA.ZSTA, EKOLA, no. 4078, p.156. Letter by Mission Inspector Zahn, 25 July 1894.

28 Anglo-German Boundary Commission surveyed and agreed on Yola to Ossidinge (Manyu) between 1912 and 1913.

29 See Rudin H., op cit. 97, for details about Franco-German agreement of 1911 which increased the Cameroon territory.

30 Lakoswski R., in Stoecker, H., (ed) op. cit. pp.379-418.

were developing and the need for Cameroonian clerical and technical assistants became compelling. This required educated Cameroonians. Since education was left only to the Missions and Mission education was found inadequate for such purposes, it became necessary for the Government to consider a frame-work for educational development.

Meanwhile, the appointment of Bernhadt Dernburg as minister for colonies might have contributed to the post-1907 reforms. German colonial policies from the appointment of Dernburg shifted from hard faced exploitation to more progressive development. However, the desire for African assistants coupled with the apprehension nursed about the propensity of educated Africans to revolt, induced the Government to contemplate policies which could control the education provided by Missions. An education conference was held in 1907 which was followed up in 1910 by an ordinance that provided the German colonial policy for education.

The 1907 Conference and 1910 Education Ordinance

The conference marked the actual beginning of German concern for education in Cameroon. It was presided over by Governor Seitz. The issues discussed ranged from the structure of the curriculum, the language of instruction, the harmonisation of standards in all schools, collaboration between Government and Missions, financing, school age, school attendance, and school discipline to vocational education.

The resolutions of the meeting were embodied in the ordinance of 25 April 1910. The ordinance also established Government control over all education in the territory. It was the first legal agreement between Government and Missions for utilizing the institutional structure of Missions to implement Government policy for education in Cameroon. The ordinance ushered in the beginning of Government financing of those Mission schools that satisfied Government regulations. It was the first major attempt by Government to interfere with school curricula, and it imposed the teaching of the German language upon subventioned schools.

All educational establishments were placed under the authority of the governor. This ended Mission autonomy in educational matters, thereby giving Government a means of policing the dangers of a backlash arising from uncontrolled education. This measure confirmed the primacy of political factors in the emergent colonial situation as argued by Memmi.[31]

But the resistance of the Missionaries to the colonial Government's decisions supports the argument that concerted Government/Mission action was not

---

31 Clignet R., 'Damned if you do, damned if you don't. The dilemmas of coloniser-colonised relations in *Comparative Education Review*, 15., 1., 1971.

always possible. The problem of the language of instruction in schools was also tackled. The persistent use of the English language by the military and the traders for over two decades of German rule was now seen as a threat to the regime. Since this was a period of economic and naval rivalry between Germany and Great Britain, the popularity of the English language with its political/cultural ramifications could not be tolerated. The ordinance, therefore, imposed the use of German while forbidding the use of all other European languages. This was aimed at strengthening the political authority of the regime, safeguarding the acquired territory from other colonizing powers and establishing the predominance of German culture.

The administration was also sensitive to the Douala people who occasionally rebelled against the government for not respecting the treaty of annexation. Consequently, the ordinance limited the geographical coverage of the Douala language to the Douala region. The Basel Mission had adopted this language for education and evangelisation in the forest zone. But the Government felt that the spread of the language could eventually instigate the speakers to join them in revolting. Similarly, the influence of Fon Fonyonga I of Bali in the western Grassfields where the Mission was equally using *Mungaka*, the Bali language, posed another threat to the Government. The refusal by the Fon to return 2,000 German guns[32] given to his army, to assist in the conquest of recalcitrant groups in the region, led the Government to believe that the spread of the language could eventually mobilise the region against the regime.[33] An alliance between Bali and the neighbouring kingdom of Bafut was a possibility to be reckoned with. However, although the argument advanced against the use of a local language was to prevent the spread of revolts, it is obvious that a patriotic interest for the establishment of German culture was an underpinning factor.

The language policy promoted by the Government marked the beginning of a serious crisis concerning the language of instruction in Cameroon schools which persists today. It was also the beginning of a disagreement between the state and the Missionary societies. The Missions felt that evangelisation could only be effective through local languages. Some Germans argued that extensive teaching of the German language would lead to linguistic homogeneity of Cameroonians which could be potentially disastrous for colonial rule. They held that

---

32 Chilver E.M., *Zintgraff's Explorations in Bamenda, Adamawa and the Benue lands, 1889-1892*. Buea, Government Press., 1966.

33 The naive response of the Germans to the Douala revolts and the independent attitude of the Bali show how little the Germans knew of language habits in their colony. In the Grassfields multilingualism was common and reinforced by the internal slave trade and marriage into the family of trade partners. Special note can also be taken of the polyglot slaves of the Douala.

...the propagation of the German language could become a threat... as in a manner one rears a conceited presumptuous and easily dissatisfied breed, for the natives learn from the Europeans much that is damaging and are tempted, when they speak the language of the Europeans, to place themselves on equal footing.[34]

Fear of educated Africans having access to information on anti-colonial doctrines, such as the, *Simplicissimus* documents published by the German Social Democrats,[35] influenced the shaping of the policy. German intellectuals are said to have warned that the propagation of European languages in the colonies was a policy with very dubious consequences. They argued that the absence of major uprisings in Cameroon and German East Africa as opposed to the situation in German South West Africa resulted from language heterogeneity which hindered united action. He contended that by introducing a European language, "...not only do we provide the people with the means to reach an understanding..., but we furthermore offer them the best tool for revolutionary propaganda..."[36] These arguments were against the popular concept of the universality of the colonial situation. It becomes evident that there were divided interests and a wide variety of attitudes on the question of educating Africans both in the colony and in Germany itself.

The language policy and the absence of mass education tended to perpetuate patterns of domination while exerting psychological pressures on the people. Learning in an alien language inevitably led to inferiority complex and lack self-confidence and also introduced elements of psychological domination, as Mannoni argued.[37]

The ordinance also emphasized school attendance because of the widely fluctuating attendance of pupils at many Mission schools. The school board had to grant permission before any pupil could leave prematurely. The problem of irregular attendance and early departure from school might seem to contradict the view that Cameroonians welcomed education. But this could be explained by the insecurity created when the administration occasionally recruited school

---

34 Wolfgang H. "Education Policy" in Stoecker EH., (ed), *German imperialism in Africa: from the beginning, until the Second World War,* New Jersey, Hurst and Company 1986, chapter 7., p. 224.

35 ibid p.225. Simplicissmus was a satirical newspaper rather resembling the French, *Le canard enchainé.*

36 ibid. Wolfgang particularly mentioned Carl Meinhof, a linguist. See p. 225

37 Mannoni O., *Psychology of Colonisation* Paris, 1950, translation by Prospero and Caliban, London, Mathuen, 1956. See chapter one.

pupils for forced labour either for the regime or for the German plantations or compelled them to work as porters to the German traders in the hinterland. Some of the pupils and parents were also discouraged by the flogging at school.[38] Furthermore, the regulations for Mission schools receiving Government grants stipulated that in case of departure without permission, the parent or guardian with whom the pupil was identified could be sentenced to a fine of 50 German marks, and in case of repeated absences, the parent had to receive a flogging in accordance with the Imperial decree of 22 April 1896. This typically authoritarian and brutal regulation supports Mannoni's notion that colonial education exerted psychological pressures, in this case by treating "the natives" as naughty children.

The ordinance instituted the administration of German language examination in Mission schools. The examination was used to determine the distribution of Government subsidies to the Mission schools. Schools aspiring for Government subsidies had to conform to the prescribed requirements. An official syllabus was attached which schools had to follow. The ordinance stressed the fact that the amount of subsidies for Mission schools were bound to be in relation to the number of candidates appearing on the pass lists of the official German language, examination conducted at the end of every year.

An examination board was established in each district with a senior Government official appointed by the Governor as the chairman and two non-official members chosen from the Missions. To ensure regular attendance, eligibility for the examination depended on at least 150 days attendance in the school year preceding entry to the examination. The task of ensuring adequate preparation and established eligibility rested on the respective schools.

From the policy prescription, it is evident that the Government deliberately asserted itself in matters of educational development through the attachment of financial incentives and by coercion whenever necessary. These inducements must not necessarily be seen as favour because, besides the desire to train competent Cameroonians for the colonial service, the Government was perturbed by the domination of the English language in a German colony.[39] However, the

---

38 The author's father was refused schooling by his own father because the first son had been flogged at school. As a noble in the community, it was unacceptable that his son should be beaten by a stranger. Hence he prevented all his own children from going to school.

39 Fohtung M., "Self-portrait of a Cameroonian" in *Paideuma*, 38., 1992. Fohtung completed schooling in 1908 and taught with the Basel Mission, before working with two German firms as a book-keeper. He informed the researcher that even the German administration had to use English with Cameroonians. Chilver stated in an interview (March 1995) that a pidgin-English phrase book circulated among officials and German trading agents.

reform also coincides with the positive changes in German colonial policies that have been credited to Bernhardt Dernburg when he became minister for colonies. The role of education in promoting German culture and the impact of the culture struggle, the *Kulturkampf* in Germany at the time, further underpin the rationale for shift in education policy.

The syllabus and curriculum guide that followed the ordinance further illustrate German colonial policy orientation. The syllabus for Mission schools was issued six months after the signature of the ordinance. It was seemingly influenced by Christaller's syllabus proposal of 1892. The five years course for elementary education was maintained. The first year's work was essentially devoted to reading, writing and number work. In the second year, these subjects were retained except for number work, and to them were added grammar or language, arithmetic, factual knowledge and singing. In the third year, speech-training and bible history were added to the subjects brought forward from the second year. Then in the fourth year, they had reading, writing, language, arithmetic, factual knowledge, singing and bible history. In the final year, German, arithmetic, factual knowledge, singing and bible history were taught while drawing and sports or gymnastics were optional.

The first course prescribed six hours a week comprising two hours of reading and writing German speech sounds in German or Latin characters. Two further hours were allocated to self-expression based on objects in the classroom, parts of the body, and pictures. Finally, two hours were allocated to number work or arithmetic based on numbers ranging from one to twenty and eventually reaching 100.

The fifth course, which was the final year, had a week's load of ten hours. Four hours were allocated to reading and writing with practice in the reading of harder German extracts and narrations in German language and dialogue. There was also the memorization of patriotic German poems. Essay and letter writing were taught during this period, together with autobiographical accounts, dictation exercises based on hard passages without punctuation marks and the memorization of grammatical rules. Three hours were allocated to arithmetic or number work based on fractions and decimals, proportions and percentages. One hour was given to history of the German empire since the Franco-Prussian war and German emperors since the war. Then, one hour was given to early-science or geography involving a deepening knowledge of Germany, the importance of Europe, names and locations of the continents, the earth as a planet, the zones of the earth, land and sea, causes of day and night, rainy and dry seasons. The last hour was allocated to natural science covering the importance of minerals, plant and animal kingdoms, the atmosphere, the barometer, thermometer, simple machines or simple mechanical appliances.

Except in the fourth year where one period a week was allocated to the teaching of local climate, local animals and local plants; the entire syllabus neglected environmental studies which ought to have formed the core of the curriculum. Thus, the stress was on Germanic studies ranging from a full coverage of German language, the geography of Germany and Europe, to the glorious histories of German conquest. Inevitably, such a curriculum sought to establish the economic and political supremacy of the Germans. There was nothing on hygiene or health and physical education. Local languages were neglected and the German language was treated as the pupils' first language. The policy of teaching patriotic German songs and memorizing German patriotic poems ultimately aimed at creating and inculcating the notion that the German culture was at a higher level and should replace that of the Cameroonians. This notion was internalized and when the British and the French replaced the Germans, the tendency was for Cameroonians to continuously seek to master European exotic cultures at the expense of their own.

The official syllabus content largely contradicted the objectives of Missionary education and the Missions only reluctantly accepted the syllabus because of the financial subventions. However, the Protestant Missions which had insisted on the, language policy welcomed the regulations on infant education because it suited their desire to prepare their converts to read the Bible. Although Bible studies was left out in Government schools, the Missions were allowed to add religious knowledge to their curriculum. Undoubtedly, given the same duration as other regimes, the German culture would have left a significant imprint.

Government Schools

During the three decades of German rule in Cameroon, there were only five schools provided by the Government. These schools were located strategically at either administrative or commercial towns in order to provide the administrative and technical assistants required. The first Government school was opened in King Bell's town at Bonabela in Douala in 1888. King Bell's readiness to house and assist the first Government teacher Christaller, seem to have influenced the location.

In Douala the two banks of the Wouri estuary had two rival potentates who both requested schools during the signing of the annexation treaty in July 1884. In order to have the collaboration of both rulers, and because the commercial and administrative requirements of the town required more pro-western educated people, it became prudent to open a second school in Douala, but this time at Bonanjo in 1890.

Commercial and administrative reasons also led the Government to open the third school in Victoria about 100 miles west of Douala in 1897. The delay in establishing a Government school in this commercial town until 1897 might be explained by the delayed departure of the British Government and the British

Baptist Missionary society. This Mission already had schools in the area which were handed over to the Basel Mission. Thus the German colonial administration thought it wasteful to duplicate them immediately with another school.

The fourth school was established in 1906 at Garoua in the north of the country. Here, economic interests were not as significant as strategic considerations aimed at forestalling potential expansion of rival colonial powers: the French from French Equatorial Africa in the east and the British from Nigeria in the West (Map on page xix). If those two powers were not blocked, German Cameroon could have lost access to Lake Chad.[40] It was therefore important to establish a Government school in the north to educate a pro-German elite population. In contradistinction to the coastal area where Missionary societies had opened schools, the Government, like the British in Nigeria, had refused Missionaries access to this predominantly Muslim zone.

The fifth and last German colonial school was opened in 1906 in Yaounde which proved to be another potential trading area especially in ivory and had considerable human resources that could serve in a range of economic and military activities. The proximity of this area to the Congo basin where there was serious colonial rivalry by the major imperialist powers required measures to protect German Cameroon from intrusion. Thus schooling here was necessary to create a pro-German interest. The distribution of German schools conformed therefore with imperial interests. The few schools were enough to raise the number of Cameroonians they required to serve the administration.

These Government schools served as models for the Mission schools to copy. Priority was given to the children of the African ruling and trading class. This is evident in the choice of King Bell's town for the establishment of the first school and the priority given to the royal house to register before anybody else. In Garoua the Lamibee's [41] sons were given preference. The priority given to children of the ruling class introduced the idea that education was for those in power and for the rich. This notion attracted those in power to use education in sustaining their positions and encouraged those of low social order to improve on their status. The schools also induced the pupils to appreciate the values of German culture while the Missions upheld Christian culture in general. Indisputably, this strategy established a local bourgeoisie and induced existing influential

40   From the maps on pages xix and xx respectively, British pressure from the west and the French from the east narrowed the territory around the fertile basin of Lake Chad. German decision to surrender Morocco for "greater Cameroon" *Neo Kamerun* was particularly to gain more land around Lake Chad basin., also see more in Rudin, chapters 2 and 3.

41   *Lamibee* is the plural of *Lamido*, a traditional ruler in the predominantly Muslim northern region of Cameroon.

authorities to support German rule and sustain its interests.

Therefore, the interest shown in the education of influential families must not be confused with a desire to prepare Cameroonians for self-rule. The 1910 conference stated that Government schools were not meant to satisfy the needs of the colonized but to train assistant workers to serve as intermediaries between the colonial authorities and the colonized population. Undoubtedly, educated Cameroonians were less expensive to the colonial service than recruited junior staff from the metropolis. The demand for educated Africans caused the Government to request each pupil to sign a service bond.

At the 1910 Colonial Congress 'the consensus was for the colonized to be kept under control and command. It was generally agreed that German colonial education be directed to the imposition of German authority in order to create a peaceful and welcoming atmosphere in which German civilization could flourish. The concepts of obedience, loyalty, devotion to work and respect to the colonial Government could be seen therefore as facilitating principles for exploitation. This was made clear by Dernburg even before he became minister. To, him, German colonial policies had to aim at exploiting the soil and human resources of the colonies for the benefit of Germany in return for the superior culture, moral concepts and improved working system they had to offer. According to him, colonial exploitation was better than slave labour and as such Africans had to be grateful and serve with gratitude.

These attitudes substantiate the argument for political, economic and psychological determinism of colonial situations. Rudin rather perspicaciously remarked that the Germans were franker than others about their objectives. But the fact that a United Germany was a new creation and many were excited with the forms of nationalism and expansionism cannot be overlooked. However, the situation with Government schools was not very different in the Mission schools.

Missionary Societies and the Development of Education

By 1914 when the war started, there were five Missionary societies in Cameroon: Four of them were of German origin while one was from the United States of America. Only one of them, the Gosnier Mission that arrived in December 1913, was not yet involved with the provision of schools. The four Missions with schools following the sequence of their arrival were: the American Presbyterian Mission, the Basel Mission, the Catholic Pallotine Mission and the German Baptist Mission. This section examines the development of education by these Missions to highlight the autonomy they exercised until 1910 and the impact on schooling. It also discusses the disparities in Mission education and the effects of the disagreements between the Missions on the Cameroonian adherents and traditional authorities.

American Presbyterian Missionary Society

The American Presbyterian Mission arrived Cameroon in 1885 and worked mostly amongst the Batanga and Bulu people in the south-west. Some of their chief stations included Batanga, Lolodorf, Efulan, Elat, Fulasi, Metek and Yebe-kole.[42] In these stations they opened schools. At the beginning the educational institutions were slow to develop but there was a rapid expansion towards the war as table 2.1 illustrates:

Table 2.1: Enrolment in American Presbyterian Mission Schools

Year	Enrolment
1901	688
1905	1,113
1909	5,060
1912	9 213
1913	10,827
1914	16,697

Sources: C.B.M.S. Archives, Box 276, File A, "West Africa, Cameroons during the First World War".

A report from the Board of Foreign Missions of the Presbyterian Church in the United States of March 1916 indicates that enrolment in Presbyterian Mission schools at the end of the German rule stood as on table 2.2.

Table 2.2: Number of schools and enrolment per centre.

Station	No. of schools	Enrolment
Efulan	34	2,676
Elat and Fulassi	98	8,152
Maclean	31	6,242
Mete and Yebekole	43	4,227
Total	43	16,697

Source: CBMS Archives, Box 276, File A, West Africa, Cameroons

---

42 Mbala-Owona R., *L'école Coloniale au Cameroun: approche Historico-Sociologique*, Yaounde, Imprimerie Nationale, 1986, p.18.

The Mission developed Bulu which is the lingua-franca of the Beti people of the central African region. Bulu and English were then used as languages of instruction. Till today many English words have become adopted into the Bulu language such as *Kitchen* and *Sunday*. The Mission had a seminary headed by a European for training teachers and evangelists. By 1914 there were three African instructors and 39 student-teachers. They opened the Frank James industrial school in 1908, for vocational training which remained very popular and important until 1945

The Mission developed very good relations with the people but had a major problem of satisfying their demand for schools. The imposition of the German language as the only medium of instruction in schools from 1911 made it difficult for the Mission to recruit competent Missionaries to cope with the provision of schools. The language policy also strained the relationship with the colonial administration. It was not until 1913 that they agreed to stop teaching in English and the local language.

Basel Missionary Society

The Basel Mission was the second to establish following German annexation. It was selected by German Protestants with the approval of the German imperial Government to replace the British Baptist Mission in Cameroon. It therefore inherited all the British Baptist schools and Missionary activities although some of the local Baptists did not take long to pull out and form what became known as the *Native Baptist Church*. The Mission expanded very rapidly and was expected to serve as the main agent for colonial education. Until 1910, the colonial administration relied on them to develop education. Since this Mission will be examined in another publication, it is important here to state just the outline growth as it affected education.

By 1914, the Mission had 19 main stations spread in many parts of the coastal and western regions. There were 384 elementary schools with an enrolment of 22,818 pupils comprising 20,993 boys and 1,825 girls.[43] They also had 16 higher elementary schools with an enrolment of 1,748 pupils. The total number of teachers was 409. They offered vocational and technical education at Akwadorf and Douala. Both centres were headed by European instructors. Meanwhile, teachers were trained initially at Victoria, then at Buea and later on at Nyasoso. At the outbreak of the war, there were 53 student-teachers in training. They improved on the Douala language which the British Baptists had turned into written form and adopted it for school instruction in the forest region. They developed *Mungaka,* for similar use in the western Grassfields. Both languages were used for

---

43 CBMS Archives, Box 276.

education and evangelisation and survived the whole colonial period. Their relationship with the people was good. They intervened very often on behalf of the people against the excesses of colonial agents and labour recruiters. Meanwhile they disagreed with some aspects of the people's culture, such as polygamy and expensive funeral rituals. Finally, they dominated the educational landscape.

Roman Catholic Mission

The Catholic Pallotine Mission followed in 1890. The late arrival was probably because in 1849 the Papacy placed the Cameroon area within Central African territories and assigned it to the Holy Ghost Fathers.

Figure 4: B.M. Middle. School Pupils in Bonaberi by Mr. Spellenberg Gottlieb 1905

Figure 5: Basel Mission School in Bali by Mr. Wilhem Trautwein 1905

The headquarters was in Gabon. They delayed in starting in Cameroon until German annexation. Thereafter, the Germans refused non-German missionaries in the colony. The *Kulturkampf policy* and ban on Jesuits in Germany further hindered them from setting up a Missionary society. The success of the Catholic Party in securing the law of April 1887 which integrated them in educational activities opened the way for activities in the colonies.

In 1889 the Papacy and the German Government agreed on a Berman Catholic Missionary Society in Cameroon on condition that the head of the Mission remained, at all time, a German appointed in consultation with the German imperial Government. Such a condition suggested the search for safeguard on political grounds. It was also agreed that the imperial Government should have the authority to inspect and monitor Catholic schools. The Propaganda Fide authorised the Pallotine Fathers who had a majority of German membership even though the founder was Italian. They were established at Marienberg (1890), Kribi and Edea (1891), Engelberg (1894), Douala (1898), Grand Batanga (1900), Yaounde-Mvolye (1900), Ikassa (1906) Einsieldehen (1907), Victoria (1908).[44] Initially; they faced protest from the Basel Mission not to establish themselves near their existing stations. In fact, their arrival ushered in the inter-denominational rivalry in Cameroon which has outlived the colonial period.

The creation of each Mission station was followed by the establishment of a school. But the number of schools was eventually reduced because of many drop-outs. The Mission even employed Government assistance to control the high rate of drop-out in schools. The head of the Pallotine Mission, Mgr Vieter reported to Van Oertzen, the colonial Administrator for Kribi district, who, in turn, punished the parents of the pupils by requesting them to do heavy unpaid manual, labour *(njongmasi)* on road construction work. It is reported that for the sake of a pupil, the mother's punishment lasted for fourteen days.[45]

Generally, the Pallotine Fathers collaborated better with the colonial administration and were preferred to the Protestants. Unlike the Basel Mission which disagreed with the administration on language policy the Pallotine Fathers, especially under Mgr. Vieter's leadership, considered the inculcation of German language and culture in Cameroon as a German national duty. During a toast in January 1905, he said:

44 Booth B.F., "A Comparative Study of Mission and Government involvement in Educational Development in. West Cameroon 1922-1969". PhD UCLA, 1973. Also see: Ndi, A., "Mill Hill Missionaries and State in Southern Cameroon, 1922-1962" PhD London, 1983.

45 Bureau R., «Ethno-Sociologie des Douala et apparentés» in *Recherches et Etudes Camerounaises*, No.7-8, Yaounde, 1962, pp. 84-85

> ...thanks to the important co-operation between the State and the Church,
> we have had good results in Cameroon. We wish it to continue like that
> in the future and that no misunderstanding should arise between the
> two powers to disturb further achievements.[46]

Their good relation with the colonial administration was expressed especially
on the language policy. This collaboration enabled the Mission to expand rapidly
with the support of the Government. Their relationship with the administration
guaranteed the admission of another Catholic congregation - the Sittard Fathers
or Priests of the Sacred Heart into the territory and gave them the opportunity
of starting Missionary activities in the Muslim dominated north. The Pallotine
Fathers remained in the south where they had 204 schools and a total enrolment
of 19,576 pupils under 223 teachers.

In June 1912, Adamawa was assigned to the Priests of Sacred Heart. The
first Sacred Heart Missionaries arrived in Douala in 1912 led, by F.J. Lennartz.
The party included two priests and four lay brothers. They founded stations in
Shishong, Kumbo and Njinikom. The Shishong Fathers were properly the Sac-
erdotes Cordis Jesu (S.J.C.) and, are distinct from other similarly named orders.
Sometimes they are referred to as the Dehonians after their founder, Mgr. Dehon.
The school in Shishong had 100 pupils while Nkar, Tabinken and Njinikom were
just starting when the war nipped them in the bud.

The Catholic Mission did not promote post-elementary education. They had
only one higher elementary school by 1911. However, they excelled in vocational
education where a wide range of training was given in agriculture, black-smithing,
shoe-making, tailoring, carpentry, brickmaking and bricklaying. By 1914, they
had 259 manual arts instructors in vocational centres and 233 teachers in the
elementary schools.

The German Baptist Mission

The German Baptist Mission arrived in 1891. They had many organisational
and internal problems that prevented them from expanding rapidly in education when compared with other Missions. Their decision to come to Cameroon
resulted from an appeal by Alfred Bell, a Cameroon student in Germany who in
1889 described the problems that Baptists in Cameroon were suffering following the departure of the British Baptists, to a congregation of German Baptists.
He entreated the congregation with a pathetic narration of the schism between
the Basel Mission and local Baptists in 1888. This appeal evoked the sympathy

---

46   Cited in Mbala-Owona R., op. cit. p. 17.

of German Baptists.[47] But although this Missionary society was German, the majority of the Missionaries including the pioneer leader, August Steffens, were Americans of German origin. At their arrival, the Native Baptist Church had 442 communicant members and two schools with 634 pupils.[48]

It was not long after their arrival that a conflict of authority developed between Suvem, one of the Missionaries, and Joshua Dibundi, the leader of the Native Baptist church. The disagreement led to another split in 1897. This affected their educational efforts. The German Baptists opened stations at Bonakwasi (Abo), in 1892, Njamtan in 1907, Ndongongi in the Banen region in 1908, Ngambe in 1910 and Ndumba in 1914. By 1914, they had 57 elementary schools with an enrolment of 3,151 pupils in six main stations located at Douala, Ndumba, Nyamtan Ndongongi, Ngambe and Soppo.[49] They also had three post-elementary schools in Douala, a middle school for girls under two European Missionary school mistresses admitting 10 to 15 girls each year, and another for boys under two European teachers where 50 students were registered in the 1913/14 school year. For a joint training of their teachers and evangelists, they established a seminary.

Although the Baptists did not have many schools, they were more involved with quality education. Of all the early Baptist Missionaries in Cameroon, Carl Bender, an American, wielded enormous influence and recorded the longest serving period. He was the only missionary in the country, who by virtue of his American nationality, stayed during the war until 1919. He served from 1904 to 1919 and 1929 to 1935.

These were the Missionary societies that provided education during the German rule. Each Mission designed its own school structure and curriculum. When compared to Government educational efforts an incredibly wide difference is observed as shown on tables 2.3 and 2.4.

Table 2.3: Mission schools and enrolments

Missions	No. of schools	Enrolment
American Presbyterians	97	6,545
Basel Mission	319	17,833
Pallotine Catholics	151	12,532

47 Weber C.W., *International Influences and Baptist Mission in West Cameroon: German American Missionary endeavour under the International Mandate and British Colonialism*, Leiden, E.J. Brill, 1993. This is the thrust of Weber's thesis.

48 Donat R., *Das wachsende Werk: Ausbreitung der deutschen Baptisten–Gemeinden durch sechzig* Jahre (1849 bis 1909).

49 CBMS Archives., Box 276; West Africa Cameroons during the First World War.

Missions	No. of schools	Enrolment
German Baptists	57	3,151
Total	624	40,061

Source: Kaiserlichen Statistischen Amte: Statistisches Jahrbuch für das Deutsche Reich 1910-1931.

Table 2.4: Number and enrolment in Government Schools

School	Enrolment
Government School Douala	362
Government School Victoria	257
Government School Yaounde	160
Government School Garoua	54
Total	833

Source: Kaiserlichen Statistischen Amte: Statistisches Jahrbuch für das Deutsche Reich 1910-1931

All schools in Cameroon numbered 628 having a total of 40,894 pupils by 1913. The estimated population of school age population for that year was 529,722.[50] Thus the percentage at school was just 7.7 percent. But there was a remarkable increase at the beginning of 1914 when the war broke out. The number of schools increased to 789 and the number of pupils stood at 57,195 with 56,372 in Mission schools alone. Whereas the Government had no higher elementary school, the Missions together provided 24 of such schools with an enrolment of 1,919 under 71 teachers.

There is no doubt that the tempo of educational expansion towards the end of the German regime was accelerated by the financial motivations introduced through grants from 1911 onwards as shown on table 2.5.

Table 2.5: Government subsidies

Years	Amount in marks
1911	20,000
1912	20,000

---

50 GA. ZSTA., Kaiserlichen Statistischen Amte: Statistisches Jahrbuch air das Deutsche Reich 1910-1931.

Years	Amount in marks
1913	30,000
1914	60,000

Source: Rudin H., op. cit. p.358.

The financial assistance enhanced the achievement of the targeted diffusion of the German language. Some of the Missions were initially unwilling to apply the language policy but the grants enticed them. The number of pupils passing the German language examination increased rapidly as illustrated below:

Table 2.6: Successes in German language exams

Year	No. of successful candidates
1910	1,914
1911	4,828
1912	7,284

Source: Shu S.N, op. cit. p.52.

The increasing number of candidates passing the examination also indicated the extent of German cultural influence. In 1913, the increase in the grants to Missions for the teaching of German caused even the American Presbyterian Mission, which had resisted the Government's language policy to succumb. The ban on the use of the English Language on 31 March 1913 finally left the Missions with no alternative. These developments urged the colonial administration to propose yet another increase in the 1914/1915 financial year which unfortunately was aborted by the war.

The role of Government officials in monitoring the application of the Government syllabuses and conducting the examinations had significant impact on education. It stopped the anarchy in Mission schools and made educational provision uniform in structure and in content. This was similar to the state control in Germany. It marked the beginning of collaboration between the Missions and Cameroonian education.

The collaboration had negative effects on Cameroonians because those Missions which had earlier defended Cameroonian interests against imperial impositions and exploitation tended to relent their efforts. All the Missions yielded to the language policy, thereby neglecting the Cameroonian languages they had developed. By and large, Missions became, in effect, agents of the colonial regime.

All Mission schools adopted Government time-tables covering five years schooling with at least 150 days attendance per year at the rate of at least six hours per week on prescribed subjects for the first year, eight hours per week for the second year and 10 hours per week for the last three years as on table 2.7

Table 2.7: Timetable for Mission Schools.

Subjects	Year One	Year Two	Year Three	Year Four	Year Five
German	2 hours	3 hours	4 hours	4 hours	4 hours
Science of Observation	2 hours	2 hours	2 hours	-	-
Arithmetic	2 hours	2 hours	3 hours	3 hours	3 hours
Geography	-	-	1 hour	1 hour	1 hour
History	-	-	-	1 hour	1 hour
Natural science	-	-	-	1 hour	1 hour
Total	6 hours	8 hours	10 hours	10 hours	10 hours

Source: Booth B.., op. cit. p.42.

Each Mission was allowed to fill the blank spaces on the timetable with subjects of their choice. Ultimately, all Missions added religious knowledge and agriculture while some added local languages. Some added crafts such as cabinetmaking, tailoring, cookery, weaving etc.

The length of time allocated to the subjects reflected areas of interests. The German language had maximum time and was taught through a wide range of subjects even in the early stages of schooling. It was taught through reading, writing, drawing, songs and poems. In the third year it was used as the language of instruction. Thus Government's objective to establish German culture became effective.

The general level of education provided was primary. A few graduates of elementary schools continued in vocational schools and teacher-training institutions. Secondary education did not exist. Anybody opting for higher education had to go to Germany or Switzerland. Cameroonians studied in Germany in the fields of medicine, teacher-training, theology and law. For example, Prince Douala Manga Bell and Mpondo Akwa studied general education; Prince Alexander Bell studied medicine and Prince Rudolf Douala Bell studied law. Others included Sosiga of Bali and Joseph Ekolo.

Wolfgang claims that until 1918 not a single African from a German colony was permitted to attend a German university.[51] He states that the Germans did not allow Africans to study in Germany. He quoted a response to an American institution's request for information on Germans' experience in educating Africans in Germany, which stated that "...the influence of civilization was injurious

---

51 Wolfgang M., op. cit. p. 218

to their character and their future existence in the protectorate."

He also states that some Cameroonians of Douala origin and some Togolese who attempted to continue their education in Germany had "a negative assessment by the administration." It is difficult, with the evidence from Cameroon, to believe that Cameroonians were wholly cut off from study travel. However, Wolfgang's statement might refer to university studies and not all institutions *(Technische Hochschukn)*. Moreover, the German officer who replied might have been avoiding a potential debate on "colonial subjects". Nevertheless, the quotations provide further evidence of divided interests and attitudes towards colonial education.

German universities were particularly interested in colonial study and research. The universities of Hamburg and Berlin created chairs for the study of African cultures and languages. Cameroonians were invited to Germany to lecture on their language and customs. For example, Peter Makembe lectured at the University of Hamburg in 1891 on the language and customs of the Douala people. This was probably encouraged by the profound interest and preeminence of the German scholars in philology.

It was in vocational education that the Germans excelled. Technical education was of two kinds. There were trade schools in Douala and Yaounde established by the Missions to teach bricklaying, tailoring, bread-making, and cabinet making and farming. Then there were vocational and agricultural schools opened by the Government in Buea and Dschang. The Buea schools had a similar curriculum to the Mission trade schools where carpentry, printing, and cabinet-making were taught. The structure and theoretical level of the technical education given was not aimed at creative or inventive abilities.

A higher technical centre was started in Victoria in 1910 where graduates of Mission and Government elementary schools were admitted. The duration was three years after which the graduates were bonded to the Government for five years as agricultural assistants. Teacher training was provided exclusively by the various Missions. There was no Government teacher training college throughout the German period. The teacher training centres served the dual purpose of training teachers and evangelists and in many cases the same person was trained to perform both functions.

Adult education was also carried out by the Missions. But it was structured more for religious purposes and organized as Sunday schools for the Protestants and catechism classes for the Catholics. Health centres were also located at the Mission stations which pulled a lot of people and gave the opportunity for the Missionaries to give basic formal and informal education to enhance evangelisation.

Female Missionaries and wives of Missionaries took active roles in teaching Cameroon women about hygiene, domestic science, and house craft and child welfare. The Government did not emphasize female education. The low enrolment of girls in schools was associated with Cameroon culture which allegedly prohibited female exposure. While this might be true in the Muslim dominated areas and in some of the centralized states, it was not in all the societies. The argument that bride price *per se* hindered parents from sending their children to school is not true of all societies because even today, there are communities where bride price remains unknown.

Under the governorship of Puttkamer soldiers were asked to raid and capture people for colonial services. The male were engaged on forced labour while the female were sometimes retained for the pleasure of Europeans and soldiers.[52] Consequently, parents became protective of their children, especially girls. It can also be argued that since the sort of economic activities for which the administrators wanted educated Cameroonians suited only men, female education was neglected. Additionally, distant schools were considered risky for girls.

To conclude, German colonial education policy aimed at strengthening the economic and political ascendancy of the Germans over Cameroonians. Cultural influence through education was minimal because of the late and short-lived imposition of imperial control. The harshness and ruthlessness of the German rule left psychological impact on those who went through the education system and discouraged others. However, German education policy was brief (1910-1914) and the scope of education was, very limited, with just 57,195 pupils in schools by 1914 out of a population of 2,648,610.[53] Besides, the Missions had 56,372 pupils while the Government had only 823 pupils. Thus with less than two per cent of the school age population at school, it was not possible for education to have a significant impact on the people. It is worth noting that when one considers the number of Cameroonians graduating with any knowledge of German culture in terms of those who passed the language examination, it would be noticed that the number was almost insignificant. Apparently, if the German rule had lasted longer, there would have been a greater impact on the attitudes of Cameroonians because of the central role that the Government started engaging in the last two years of the German regime. However, Cameroonians' determination to use education as a means of self-advancement must be considered as an important factor that led to the acceptance of the education provided under the German regime. Interest in education and German culture increased despite the ruthlessness of

---

52 Rudin H. op: cit. pp. 305-306 in 1908 the Catholic Bishop in Cameroon complained about European conduct with Cameroon girls. This followed an earlier petition by Cameroonians to the Reichstag in 1905.

53 This was the population figure of 1913 and school age population of 5+ to 15+ was estimated at 529,722; see Kaiserlichen Statistisches Amte: Statistisches Jahrbuch für Reich 1910-1937.

the regime. Finally, the Missionary societies strengthened colonial education by attracting Cameroonians to this new source of knowledge.

The next chapter will examine the French colonial education policy in Cameroon with the hope of illuminating the impact of its inculcation on the Cameroonians and discussing the effects on contemporary education. The discussion will highlight the nature of the policy and show how it was distinct from other regimes.

CHAPTER THREE

CAMEROON EDUCATION UNDER THE FRENCH COLONIAL REGIME (1916-1960)

The French colonial education policies in Cameroon were adapted from policies developed before the First World War for French dependencies in Africa. Apart from economic exploitation and political domination, the policies aimed principally at establishing the French culture and influence *(Mission civilisatrice)*. The policy imposed a prescribed structure to both private (Mission) and Government schools aimed at producing French citizens from the colonised peoples and discarding all elements of their own institutions. But the duration of French administration in Cameroon (1916-1960) was relatively short, when compared to other French dependencies. The League of Nations mandatory and United Nations trusteeship status also imposed limitations on French administration. It is therefore important to examine whether French policies alone could strongly affect Cameroonians attitudes or other factors may be considered.

This chapter analyses the French colonial education policy within the general framework of the French colonial interests during the League of Nations mandate and the United Nations trusteeship. It assesses the relationship between the Government and the Missions and the impact of the French political and economic interests on the development of education policies to discern the effects on the attitudes of Cameroonians to education. It also examines the impact of other factors that might have influenced the perceptions and behaviours of post-independent Cameroonians towards educational reforms. The role of the French colonial administration in the processes of formulating and implementing colonial education is discussed to show the degree of centralization and the possible effects on attitudes.

French Concept of Colonial Education

The theoretical framework of the policy grew out of the concept of assimilation which was pursued until the First World War. After the war, France shifted more to the concept of association. Thus, French colonial policy in Cameroon, as in other French colonies, oscillated between assimilation and association. The policy of assimilation could be identified with the libertarian views stemming from the French Revolution. It emphasized the political and cultural objectives of the French civilizing Mission as being

> ...la civilisation qui marche contre la barbarie... c'est un peuple éclaire qui va trouver un peuple dans la nuit.[54]

Colonial schooling was therefore, considered to be,

> ...le moyen le plus sûr qu'une nation civilise ait d'acquérir à ses idées les populations encore primitives, de les élever graduellement jusqu' à elle[55].

Assimilation was encouraged by the award of French citizenship to those who acquired and internalized the French language and culture. Such people developed a French life pattern and became known as 'the *assimilés* or *évolués*. They qualified to participate in French political life and formed the capitalist representatives in the colonies.[56] They were trained to perpetuate exploitation during the colonial period and assure its sustenance in post-colonial period by becoming future neo-colonialist collaborators.[57] However, the role of other factors might have significantly contributed in shaping the post-colonial attitudes because, obviously, the conception of the assimilation policy in the 19th century did not foresee the granting of independence. Consequently, the policy could not have been designed initially to guarantee post-colonial French interest.

The policy of association was closely connected with the authoritarian views that gained currency during the 19th century and had paternalistic tendencies. It assumed that most colonized people did not deserve to be treated equally with French citizens. It stressed the traditional colonial objectives of bringing civilization into a primitive and barbaric culture as expressed by orderly and

---

54 "...a move against barbarism...enlightened people seeking to rescue those people still in darkness." Priollaud N., *La France colonisatrice*, Paris, Editions Levi-Messinger., 1983. p. 49.

55 "...the surest means by which a civilized nation can impart her ideas to primitive people, and gradually enlighten them to attain her level." Léon A., *Colonisation, Enséignement et Education*, Paris, L'Harmattan, 1984, p. 24.

56 Cowan L. G., "Britain and France in Africa: A Critical Appraisal" in Piper D. G. and Cole T, (eds)., *Post-Primary Education and Political and Economic Development*. London, Cambridge University Press, 1964, p.182.

57 Altbach P. G., "Education and Neocolonialism: A Note" in *Comparative Education Review*. 15, 1, 1971, p.237.

peaceful society with a well-structured and powerful Government and a good economic structure. Thus even the association policy suggested the recognition of a cultural gap between the colonizers and the colonized.

In Cameroon, aspects of both approaches were applied. The assimilationist policies maintained a demarcation between French citizenship gained by the *évolues* and the vast majority of the society *indigènes or administrés*. The latter were excluded from the French legal system and placed in a separate legal regime known as the *indigénat*. By so doing there was a reconciliation of the differences between the assimilationist and associationist principles. Both policies advocated direct rule and held that France and the colonies were one and indivisible. Thus there was an overlap between them but both concepts sought to serve the same purpose. It can be argued that when the policy of assimilation which preceded association faced attacks and criticisms during the First World War and particularly during the peace conference,[58] France quickly produced the concept of association, which appeared to be more sympathetic to the colonized. But both concepts were ambiguous. Neither of them totally admitted the colonized into the French culture. The school system and structures except at post-primary level never conformed to the concepts of assimilation or association.

Thus the concepts of assimilation and association can be identified as deliberate efforts aimed at entrenching obedience, loyalty and unquestionable service to France. This was strengthened by the development of a highly-centralized system of administration where initiatives came only from above. The centralised system developed the inevitable corollaries of uniformity and subordination that inevitably affected the pattern of education.

French Colonial Administrative and Educational Development

Following the stipulations of Mandate B of the League of Nations' covenant, Cameroon and Togo were to be treated differently from all other French colonies in Africa by not being made parts of the existing French colonies.[59] Cameroon was therefore supposed to be administered differently from other African

---

58 Lakowski R., The Second World War in Stoeker H., (ed) *German Imperialism in Africa. From the beginning until the Second World War.*, London., Hurst and Company, 1986. pp. 379-418. See comment on Lenin's book., *Imperialism, the Highest stage of Capitalism.*

59 Crouzet P., "Education in the French colonies" in Kandel I.L, (ed)., *The Educational Yearbook of the International Institute of Teachers College*, Columbia University, 1931. Columbia University Press. See particularly p. 300, which states, Cameroon and Togo are not markets reserved for French trade. France is to apply to them protective and educational measures which have proved their worth elsewhere... to fulfill "a sacred responsibility of civilization" by assuring the well-being and the development of the primitive peoples who inhabit these territories.

dependencies although the administrative institutions and policies practised in French West Africa *(Afrique Occidentale Française)* and French Equatorial Africa *(Afrique Equatorial Française)* were adopted.

The colonial administration in the two African regions under French colonial rule was coordinated by Governor Generals. Since Cameroon did not belong to either of these blocks, "a specific administration was setup. At the head of the administration was initially, the Commissioner, who later on became the Governor. He was answerable to the minister of colonies. The independent treatment of Cameroon was further re-enforced by the decree of 23 March 1921 which legally separated the territory from the other dependencies.[60] But policy formulation and measures of implementation applied the pattern already in practice in earlier acquired dependencies.

By decree, the Commissioner was appointed at the head of the administration. He was assisted by an advisory council *(conseil d' administration)* made up of heads of central Government departments in Yaoundé and some appointed European residents. There was no Cameroonian representative until 1927 when two were appointed. In 1942, the composition was altered to include four European residents, four Cameroonians, heads of Government departments and the district administrators. It was in 1942 that Christian missions were able to gain representation in the financial and Economic council to which six Cameroonians were also appointed.[61]

The territory was divided into districts. The District Officers *(Chef de circonscription)* were responsible for local administration. They were assisted by Assistant Divisional Officers *(Chef de sub-division)*, who coordinated the council of Cameroon chiefs *(Conseil de Notables)* each of whom represented 5000 inhabitants. The main function of these chiefs was not to advise but to collect tax and assist in the recruitment of community labour. They were either paid salaries, or earned commissions on tax collection. Implicit in this structure was the attempt to control the traditional authorities and make them auxiliaries of the colonial administration. Where the chiefs resisted, like sultan Njoya of Bamum, he was replaced by a subservient person.[62]

The administration of education started in 1916 and was considered temporary since France had not yet acquired legal recognition over the territory. It was only after the peace treaty of 1919 that France organised the administration and

60   NAY. AR. 1921., Government decree of 23 March 1921 in *Journal officiel* p. 151.

61   Mveng E., *Histoire du Cameroun*, Paris, Presence Africaine,1962 p.376.

62   Le Vine VT., *The Cameroons from Mandate to Independence*, Los Angeles, University of California Press. 1964, p. 96.

structures of schools. The Commissioner issued an education regulation on 25 July 1921. Except for a few changes, the regulations were the replica of the 1903 education policy for French West African dependencies. Education was placed under an Inspector but the education service was supervised by the Administrator of the territory. The Inspector only exercised technical and pedagogic roles, by ensuring the implementation of school curricula. He had to visit and report on schools but lacked direct contact with the head-teachers since they communicated directly with the Commissioner through the district heads. The District Officers had more contact and control over the schools.

General Aymerich, who led the French troops and became the first administrator of the territory, converted all the army chaplains into teachers. They started running the schools left by German missionaries 6,363 The Government recruited seven veteran priests of the Holy Ghost Fathers *(Saint Esprit)* of Paris and Sacred Heart Fathers *(Sacré-Cœur)* of Saint Quentin who arrived in Cameroon on 8 October 1916.[64] Negotiations with the French Protestant missions brought a team of the Paris Evangelical Mission in 1917 led by Reverend Elie Allegret, an army chaplain and one of the founding French protestant missionaries in Gabon. Meanwhile the American Presbyterians continued their activities. The church-state collaboration could be explained by government's determination to establish the French culture. The government believed that

> ...le plus sin moyen de franchiser les indigènes, c'est de les convertir au christianisme.[65]

And Missions were considered appropriate agents for French cultural inculcation. This supports the argument that Missions were necessarily arms of the colonial regimes, and explains why the French regime barely tolerated non-French Missions. By 1917 the amount of Government subvention to Missions depended on the number of certificated teachers, Subventions increased in the period before the mandate as shown on table 3.1.

63   Martin J. Y., *L'école et les sociétés traditionnelles au Cameroun Septentrional*, ORSTOM, Yaounde, 1970, p. 23.

64   Van Slagaren J. V., *Les origines de l'Eglise Evangélique du Cameroun: Mission Européen et Christianisme Autochtone*, Leiden, E.J. Brill; 1972. p,133.

65   "... the best way to free the natives is by converting them into Christianity." Statement by René Bazin, in Leon A., op. cit. p. 32.

Table 3.1: Government subventions (francs)

1916	4.000
1917	9.000
1918	15.500
1919	25.500
1920	15.000
1921	26.000

Source: League of Nations Report or 1921.

On 29 August 1916, Ayrnerich issued a circular bearing a school curriculum which gave pride of place to the French language. Programmes for re-training former German trained teachers to teach French started with 40 candidates in 1916. By 1917, the number increased to 70. These efforts aided the schools to start and by 1920, more than 200 schools were revived. On the 24th of November 1918, another order re-established Government schools and 30 were started in nine districts.

Education during the Mandate

The first major policy statement on education was the *Arrêté* of 1 October 1920, regulating the Mission schools. Issues treated related to official authorization to run private schools, the nature of the curriculum, qualifications of head-teachers and teachers, the modalities for keeping school reports, the nature of school leaving certificate examination, school age limit (admission was limited to children of less than 14 years), the French language policy, financial awards and discipline.

Individuals or associations could establish a school on condition that they received official authorization. Such schools were supposed to have satisfactory hygiene and moral conditions with qualified staff. The head-teacher and the staff members required Government approval to teach, and this was granted only on proof of adequate knowledge of the French language. The second article of the *Arrêté* emphasized the exclusive use of French as the medium of instruction.

The prescribed curriculum comprised reading, writing, arithmetic, the metric system, history and geography (especially of France and French Africa), drawing, agriculture for boys and needle work for girls. A school leaving certificate was also instituted to take place once a year at a place and a date decided by the Governor. The examination had to test mostly the French language. To encourage the acquisition of the French language, an incentive of 150 francs per successful candidate was paid to the school. And to discourage the continued use of German and local languages, qualifications of the teachers depended on their knowledge of French. Teachers who did not possess professional certificates from France or a French West African training institution were expected to do written work and an oral test in French to qualify to teach. Head-teachers had up to one year to regularize their qualifications or have their schools closed.

School records were to be kept by all schools and presented to inspectors during school visits. Existing schools were called upon to regularise their situations and conform with the policy within three months of the *arrêté*. From the policy, the Government clearly established state authority over all agencies involved with education for the first time.

It was difficult for the Missions to conform with the policy. Most of their teachers being German trained, were in the process of learning French. Secondly, the policy did not seem to cater for religious instruction which was the principal subject of Mission schools. This marked the first disagreement between the Government and Missions since 1916 and must have affected the quality of education during the early period of the French rule.

The second important policy was issued by Governor Carde in the *Arrêté* of 25 July 1921 organizing Government schools. It treated vital aspects of public education ranging from types of schools, teaching methods, and personnel, organisation of courses, discipline, examinations, and school curriculum. The Government provided the following types of schools:

École du village

They were located in villages and offering folk year courses. From 8 March 1939, these schools became known as *École rurale.* Only pupils below twelve years of age were admitted. Pupils in the first year were taught in the local language by teachers who knew the local language: From the second year teaching was supposed to be in French. The curriculum comprised French, hygiene, agriculture, animal husbandry, reading, writing and elementary notions of arithmetic and metric system.

École regionale

Each of the administrative regions had a central school for children of the regional headquarters and talented graduates of the village schools. Admission priority was to children in the regional headquarters who in most cases were children of Government workers, chiefs, and business people. It was a six-year primary course. Graduates of village schools were admitted in the fifth year. The establishment of a regional school depended very much on the viability of the region and the availability of qualified staff because it had the important role of serving as a model school to the village schools and private schools. The head-teacher was usually a European. Graduates obtained the Primary School Leaving

Certificate or *Certificat d'Etudes Premières* (C.E.P.) at the end of the course. This was equivalent to first school leaving certificate in France and guaranteed the owner to proceed into *sixième* (form one of secondary school) whether in the colony or in France.

The curriculum of the regional schools included French, arithmetic, metric system, notions of physical and natural sciences as applied to hygiene and agriculture, basic notions of history and geography of Cameroon and France and the administrative organisation of Cameroon. In addition, there was practical work in agriculture for boys on the school farm and home economics and needle-work for girls in the domestic science centre. It was hoped that through this practical work, the pupils would be able to improve their environment rather than learn a trade. Regional schools became important as the main sources of educated Cameroonians for employment in the European oriented economy. The attention given to regional schools conformed with the argument that colonial education created interest in white collar jobs and discouraged the development of traditional vocational training.

École Supérieure de Yaounde

Established in 1921, it was the highest institution of learning in the territory during the inter-war years. It was a three years' post-primary institution admitting graduates of the regional schools through entrance examination. It offered multipurpose training for a wide range of roles needed by the colonial service. The first two years concentrated on general education with emphasis on the acquisition of written and spoken French. The third year was devoted to practical training in a chosen career. The three main professions in which training was offered included: teacher training, public administration, and technical training for nursing, agriculture, posts and telecommunications. The practical training was done in the form of industrial training on the job. Many of the nationalists and post-colonial leaders including Ahmadou Ahidjo, the first president of the nation, were graduates of this school.

Government Schools during the period

Education was considered a state responsibility because of its importance to imperial interests. By 1920, the Government was providing 34 village schools enrolling 2,200 pupils. The number increased as indicated on table 3.2

Table 3.2: Number and Enrolment in Village Schools.

Year	No of schools	Enrolment
1921	26	2711
1925	50	2453

Year	No of schools	Enrolment
1930	64	3580
1934	61	5377
1938	66	6639

Source: NAY.AR. Journal Officiel of 1925,1930 and 1938.

There were fewer regional schools than village schools. They admitted only the best from the village schools. However, in 1933 the children of village chiefs could be admitted regardless of their abilities. Consequently, enrolment was relatively slow as table 3.3 indicates:

Table 3.3: Number and enrolment in Regional Schools.

Year	No of schools	Enrolment
1921	4	922
1923	5	1480
1925	9	1666
1927	10	1867
1930	12	2300
1932	9	1953
1935	9	2646
1937	9	3166
1938	10	3470

Source: NAY.AR. Journal Officiel for the respective years.

The restriction on admission into the regional schools was ultimately determined by economic reasons since the objective of these schools was to prepare candidates for employment in the administration to supplement colonial civil servants. Consequently, metropolitan based curriculum was established "to produce people with qualities close to those obtainable in France. Since the nature of work available to Africans was mainly administrative the education policies tended to emphasize literary" studies. Thus the criticism of the transplantation of metropolitan education system, discussed in the introductory chapter can be considered valid and may be explained by the urge to solve specific problems.

Similarly, the growth of the École Supérieure correlated with the rate of economic and political developments since it was a professional training school. The impact of the world economic crisis in the 1930s reflected on the enrolment as table 3.4 shows:

Table 3.4: Enrolment in the Ecole Supérieur de Yaounde

Year	Enrolment	Year	Enrolment
1921	32	1930	147
1922	65	1931	124
1923	72	1932	73
1924	111	1933	77
1925	136	1934	80
1926	110	1935	85
1927	110	1936	79
1928	78	1937	100
1929	150	1938	89

Sources: NAY.AR. Journal Officiel for the respective years

The fluctuations in the École Supérieure resulted from the reluctance of the Missions at certain periods to send their teachers to the school for training because on graduation some of the teachers joined the Government service because of better salaries. Undoubtedly, Mission attitude was conditioned by fear that trained teachers would demand for higher salaries.

Generally, the school produced more teachers than other professionals. Of the 680 who gained admission from its creation until 1938, a total of 415 graduated, amongst whom was a total of 135 Government teachers and 33 Mission teachers.[66] When compared with the large number of schools and pupils, the number of trained teachers was grossly inadequate.

Other Government Professional Schools

The expanding economy caused increased demand for technical and administrative personnel. This necessitated training in various fields. Vocational training and apprenticeship practices were introduced first in some of the regional schools. By 1922, the regional school at Ebolowa became one of the very first schools to start vocational training. It had a workshop for sisal and raffia fibre for making ropes and weaving bags. They also operated a carpentry workshop which helped the pupils to learn how to make the tables, chairs, beds, doors and window frames. The sale of these items enriched the Ebolowa school cooperative. The regional school at Dschang also started vocational training by employing specialists who taught pottery, carpentry, mechanics and iron works to the pupils.

Vocational training was also introduced in the regional schools in the north

66   NAY.AR., «*Statistique de I 'Ecole Supérieure*», in Journal Officiel of 1938, p. 104.

(Garoua, Maroua, and Ngaoundere). Workshops were established in schools from 1927. They concentrated on embroidery which suited the local outfit. However, by 1934, woodwork and metal sections were also introduced. The importance attached to apprenticeship training in the north was particularly because tradesmen were very scarce in the region and those from the south resented working there. Thus training indigenous people became a necessary solution.

Vocational or apprenticeship training was therefore given side by side with the full primary school education in the regional schools. Besides, the desire, to prepare the graduates for the colonial service (administrative and technical), it is evident that vocational training aimed also at eventual self-employment. Apparently, candidates were more attracted to literary education for employment in the administration. The Government realized this and decided to offer incentives to those interested in the technical training. In the north the pupils were motivated with 25 francs per month during their last two years. These motivations were indicative of the failure of the vocational education scheme. Many of the courses aimed at developing skills in local vocations. But schooling was regarded by most parents and pupils as the place for literary studies. They believed that vocational skills could be better acquired out of school.

Meanwhile in Douala, a more formal technical education was established in 1922 where apprentices were recruited from primary school leavers aged between 14 and 17 years.[67] The workshop was placed under the Public Works Department. They had five and a half hours training sessions a day with general education in French, arithmetic, drawing and the particular trade that the candidate had chosen (either woodwork or metal work) because the quality of training was higher. The school closed after three years because of the high demand for successful primary school leavers (with the CEPE) for white collar jobs with regular salaries. The tendency was therefore for pupils and parents to be less interested in vocational education.

However, the school was re-opened a year later as a trade centre for the Railway Corporation. Candidates signed a contract of five years' apprenticeship and had to pay 75 francs per month. The trades available included blacksmith, welding and electricity. At the end of their training, they were, automatically absorbed into the Railway Company.

However, despite all these attempts, technical training remained inconsistent until 1937 when better organised schools with professional staff were established.

Yaoundé High School of Agriculture
This was established by the Department of Agriculture in collaboration with

67 NAY.AR., Governor Marchand in Arrêté of 20 December 1925, p.,181.

the Department of Education. Primary school leavers aged between 14 and 17 years were recruited for a four years' technicians' course in agriculture or forestry or animal husbandry. They also trained trade instructors for the Regional Schools. The school succeeded because the graduates were employed mainly by the Government and private firms.

Douala Professional School

This school started in 1937 with the same objective of training competent technicians for the Railway Company and the Public Works Department. Like the Yaoundé schools, it offered free lodging and promised employment at the end of training. The graduates were more competent and mature when compared to those of the regional schools. They were highly valued by the technical departments.

Ayos Nursing School

Admission was limited to school leavers with the CEPE. The introduction of anatomy and physiology on the curriculum raised the standard to cover full nursing care during the three years training period, and therefore placed the school amongst professional schools in 1934. Until that year 54 people had enrolled and 16 successfully graduated.[68]

Vocational and Professional Education for Girls

Of all the attempts to train technicians and professionals, little attention was given to girls except those preparing as teachers and nurses. Generally, female education was associated with preparation for marriage and motherhood training which the Missions were offering. However, the Government opened vocational centres for training girls in Home Economics at all regional stations. The requirement for a CEPE during recruitment was often overlooked because few girls completed their primary school course. However the Government insisted on French Language arguing that a Gallicized girl at marriage could be instrumental in diffusing the French language.

These Home Economics centres taught house-care, sewing, cookery, needlework and child-care together with elementary knowledge of reading, writing and spoken French. The first centres were opened in the two big towns of Douala and Yaounde in 1923. Thereafter, sections were attached to the regional schools of Ebolowa and Dschang. To attract many girls, the administration recruited the daughters of local chiefs, Cameroonian civil servants and business men. But they

---

68 NAY.AR., *Journal Officiel*,1937, p. 106.

failed to maintain standards since some of these pupils were hardly literate.[69] In some centres, the school mistress had to divide the students into two groups placing the educated ones under a European lady and those without previous education under a local lady who instructed in the local language. When parents realized the importance of schooling in preparing girls for marriage, female education started gathering momentum.

Besides the disequilibrium between boys and girls in education, Government educational provisions also created a regional imbalance. The majority of the schools were in the south, the vast north and much of the eastern areas lagged behind in education. The north and east corresponded also with the Muslim population but more importantly, these two regions were not easily accessible and were not economically viable at the time

These were the educational efforts made during the inter-war period. Education was limited to primary schools with emphasis on French and basic technical skills were given to those needed for colonial services. This pattern of education and the negligible proportion of the population involved does not support the argument that French colonial education during the inter-war years had significant impact on the territory. However, since Mission education affected a larger population and also implied a cultural Mission, it is necessary to examine the impact.

Christian Mission Education

As shown previously, Mission education started in close collaboration with the colonial regime during the war and was making significant progress when Government policies introduced restrictions. Before the 1920 law, all the Missions provided 193 schools with 9,000 pupils and Government subvention for that year amounted to 14,995 francs.

The law proposed grants only to schools teaching in the French Language. The number of pupils in the approved schools passing the School Leaving Certificate Examination (CEPE) also determined the amount of grant. The *Arrêté* of 26 December 1924 modified that of 1920 granting to each Mission the sum of 150 francs for every 20 pupils in those schools headed by a certificated teacher and 300 francs for every Mission pupil in the École Supérieure. The policies therefore determined the quantity, quality and orientation of education through financing. These conditions affected inter-denominational relations as the Missions competed for higher financial awards from the Government.

---

69   NAY.AR., «*Ecole de fils de chefs*», in Journal Officiel 1937, p.106.

Table 3.5: Distribution of grants to approved Mission schools.

Year	No. of schools	Enrol-ment	Total Grants in Francs	Catholic Missions	Paris Evangelical Mission	American Presbyte-rianMission
1921	22	4.067	12.450	5.250	2.100	5.100
1923	36	4.683	7.050	1.800	1.350	3.900
1925	36	6.122	29.100	5.400	8.100	15.000
1926	38	4.915	45.500	10.250	14.800	20.400
1930	51	7.059	87.600	8.400	21.000	57.600

Sources: Compiled from Annual Reports.

Before 1920, the Catholic Mission received a very, high proportion of the subvention when compared to the other Missions. For instance, in 1920, they received 11,072 Francs while the Paris Evangelical Mission had only 1,923 Francs and American Presbyterian Mission had just 1,923 Francs. After the passing of the law in 1923, the amount declined as shown in table 3.5.

From 1926, a block grant of 20,000 francs was included in the subventions for examinations. This relaxed the difficult and tight conditions imposed in 1920. The administration realized that educational objectives could not be achieved without the collaboration of the Missions. The increasing number of trained teachers also contributed to the rapid increase in the number of approved schools. By 1935, the number of approved schools increased to 78, then to 81 by 1937. Changes resulting from the war which will be discussed later, increased the number of approved schools by 1946/47 school year to 1,188.

Unapproved (unassisted) Mission Schools

Unapproved schools included all schools that did not satisfy the regulations stipulated in various Government regulations. They included schools where only religious instruction was taught and needlework classes. But there were occasions when Christians either opened a school in the name of a Mission or revived one of the German Mission schools in anticipation for a Mission or the Government to take over. In all these schools, basic education was offered but generally in local languages. The total number of pupils in these schools outnumbered those attending Government schools and the approved Mission schools as shown on table 3.6.

Table 3.6 Comparison of Government and Mission provisions.

Year	Government School Enrolment	%	Approved Mission School Enrolment	%	Unapproved Mission Enrolment	%	Total
1921	3.633	9.1	4.067	10.2	32.011	80.6	39.711
1925	4.119	7.5	6.122	11.2	44.417	81.2	54.658
1930	5.880	8.3	7.059	10	59.267	84.4	70.206
1938	1.109	10.5	5.351	5.5	81.758	84	97.218

Sources: NAY.AR. Journal Officiel for the respective years.

From the table, Missions made provision for 84 per cent of school attenders by 1938, while the Government provided for 10.5 per cent and subsidised another 5.5 per cent. Individual Missions made various attempts to sustain the schools but the motivating factor to all of them was the desire to gain adherents and establish local churches.

The American Presbyterian Mission

This was the oldest Mission in the territory having started in 1885. It had a difficult beginning with the French rule because of disagreement over the language policy and also because of the earlier connection with German Missionaries. They trained their teachers with *Alliance Française*[70] and perhaps more than any other Mission they endeavoured to satisfy Government requirements. This enabled them to have the highest number of successful candidates at the French examinations and consequently to have the highest amount of Government grants.

Whereas this Mission operated mostly in the Bulu land during the German era, they extended their influence amongst the Ewondos in Yaoundé (1922), Nkol Mvolan (1928) and amongst the Basa in Edea (1930) and the Bafia people (1930) during the French period. They refused to take over the Basel Mission establishments in the British zone probably because they realized that the French were interested in having a French Missionary society to replace the Basel Mission.[71] Table 3.5 above illustrates their achievements.

70   A Cultural and educational association officially approved and sponsored by the French government particularly for the teaching of French in the world since its creation in 1883. See more from Alliance Française, 1 Dorset Square, London NW1 6PU.

71   IMC/CBMS Archives., Box 276 File E. See letter from the secretary. Stanley White, on 15 June 1923.

The Catholic Holy Ghost Mission

The French Holy Ghost Order replaced the German Pallotine Fathers. They were led by the army chaplain, James Dowry from Gabon. In 1922 he was replaced by Mgr. Francois-Xavier Vogt who came on transfer from East Africa. Vogt was in Cameroon from 1922 to 1939 and contributed enormously to the success of Catholic education. This earned him the recognition of many Cameroonians. In appreciation the first Catholic college, located in Yaoundé, was named after him, *College Vogt*.

At the beginning of the mandate period, the Mission had 140 schools with 6,145 pupils, 13 priests and 600 catechists/teachers. By 1930 the number of schools increased to 448 with an enrolment of 19,815 pupils.[72] The relationship between the Mission and the colonial administration was not always cordial since the administration insisted on respect for school regulations while the Mission was interested in evangelical expansion. Apart from schools, the Mission was also involved with social services such as orphanages, dispensaries, and workshops where a variety of trades were taught.

Another Catholic Order that was established separately was the Sacred Heart Order which arrived in Cameroon on the eve of the war in 1914 to operate in the new Apostolic Prefecture of Adamawa. During the mandate period, they worked in the Foumban Apostolic Prefecture which later became Nkongsamba Apostolic Vicarate. They extended their activities to cover Bafang, Bangante, Dschang, Loum, Melong, Ngaoundere, Nkongsamba, and Yabassi. Starting only with one school in 1920, they had 84 schools by 1930 with 3,243 pupils.

The Paris Evangelical Mission Society

This Mission was invited by the French Government to take over the Basel Mission activities in French Cameroon. Although their resources were limited, they found the Mission field so interesting that after reorganising the activities, they embarked on negotiations to take over the Basel Mission field in British Cameroon.[73] Despite this ambition, the Mission was initially not capable of financing all the Basel Mission establishments in French Cameroon. They handed over part of the stations to the American Presbyterian Mission which was then more able. By 1924 the Mission was left only with four main stations at Foumban, Ndoungue, Yabassi, and Douala with six Missionaries, 10 pastors, 22 evangelists

---

72 These Figures represent both approved and unapproved schools. For approved schools, see table 5.

73 «Projet d'accord entre les Société de Bale et la Mission Evangélique de Paris pour l'organisation et la reprise du Cameroun Anglais, 5 January 1925», pp. 1-4., in NAY AR., 1925.

318 catechists and 12,536 pupils. By 1925, they had 25 approved schools with seven European headteachers, 18 certificated teachers, 18 un-certificated teachers and a total enrolment of 1,868 pupils.

An interesting feature of this Mission was the initiative in establishing self-supporting projects, such as the school on a farm at Ndoungue which was maintained from the proceeds of the farm.[74] The Missionaries were also praised for sacrificing their leisure periods to prepare teachers for the Government certificate examination since they could not raise money to train them formally. Further to strengthen the teaching staff, they established a teacher training school *(École Normale)* in Ndoungue in 1929. By 1935 the Mission had 20 approved schools with 1,430 pupils and there were 16,910 pupils in their unapproved schools. Two years later the situation changed. Enrolment in the approved schools dropped to 800 but those in the unapproved schools increased to 19,281 pupils. The decline in the number of approved schools however, affected all the Missions and may be explained by the growing number of Government schools in the territory.

These were the Missions under the French colonial regime during the mandate period. Before the Second World War, the Missions were struggling to cope with Government regulations. By establishing public schools in all districts, the Government promoted competition with the Missions.

In summary, access to schooling during the inter-war period was not available to everyone and was limited to primary level. Even the League of Nations failed in its role to guide the course of educational development as it was required by the terms of the mandate.[75] No measures were provided for the League to oblige the mandatory powers to fulfil their responsibilities. Consequently, education remained low key throughout the inter-war years.

Thus the assumption that France desperately wanted to establish French culture through education is challenged by the rate of educational developments during this period. Quantitatively, education did not involve many people as the statistics on the tables have indicated. In 1921, all educational institutions (public and private) enrolled only 39,711 pupils out of a school age population (6-14) of 566,000 people i.e. seven per cent. By 1930 the enrolment had increased only to 70,206 out of an estimated school age population of 437,203 people which was just sixteen per cent. The last statistics collected (1938) before the war showed that school enrolment had increased to 97,218 out of an estimated school age population of 560,000 which was 17 per cent. Thus the impact of French colonial education during this period was negligible.

74　School Work in NAY.AR., 1923 *Journal des Mission Evàngeliques des Paris.*

75　See more arguments in Rubin N., *Cameroun, An African Federation.* London, Praeger, 1971.

Education during the Second World War and Trusteeship era

The impact of the early part of the war had far reaching effects on the French colonies. When Germany occupied France, it became difficult for the regime to exercise normal colonial administration. Most French administrators were engaged with the war efforts. The priority at the time was to free the metropolis from Nazism. Thus problems ensuing from the war added to the issues brought forward from the inter-war period. This section examines the range of educational issues that confronted the regime during and after the war, and the strategies that were applied to resolve them. It further examines the impact of those strategies on Cameroonians and their outcome on contemporary education.·

During the war, the Government recognized the absence of competent Cameroonian assistants to supplement the limited colonial staff. Yet Cameroon had played a valuable part in the Free French war effort. Douala was the first of the African towns that received General de Gaulle in 1940 as head of the Free French Government and although there was no actual fighting in Cameroon, the territory like all dependencies supplied soldiers to the French troops, and made financial and material sacrifices towards the war efforts. These factors and disturbances in the French Asiatic dependencies coupled with promises made during the Brazzaville conference to influence policy orientations during the postwar period.

The Brazzaville Conference (30 January-6 February 1944)[76]

The first reaction of the colonial Government was shown during the Brazzaville conference. The conference had delegations from all the French African dependencies. It was presided over by Governor Felix Eboué of Chad but General Charles de Gaulle, leader of the Free French Government chaired the opening session. The objective of the conference was,

> to raise the standard of living and improve on education and health of the population because a wealthier, and better educated colonial population would consume a far larger proportion of French manufactured goods.[77]

---

76 PRO FO.371/42216., The Brazzaville Conference of 1944. The influence of British Colonial policy on the Freed French Government of De Gaulle was evident as Rene Pleven, the Commissioner for colonies disclosed to the British representative in Algiers on 22 January, 1944.

77 De Gaulle quoted by Duh Cooper of the Office of the British Representative with the French Committee of National Liberation in Algiers on 22 January 1944., see PRO.F0/4216 of 1944, 78 Gardinier D.E., Cameroon: United Nations Challenge to French Policy, London, Oxford University Press., p.19.

But undoubtedly, Government aim was also to mobilise more efforts to support Free France in the war and in return seek for solutions to African problems. In other words, the French wanted more support from the African colonies but had to promise reforms to satisfy African demands. The reforms included decentralization through the creation of representative assemblies, with limited powers, in each territory. But there was no question of independence for any of the territories. Any idea of autonomy or evolution outside the French empire was specifically excluded. Even the idea of self-government after the war was explicitly rejected:

> ...the aims of the work of civilization accomplished by France in the colonies exclude all ideas of autonomy, all possibility of evolution outside the French bloc of Empire; the eventual formation even distant, of self-governments in the colonies is to be rejected.[78]

Thus France was determined to maintain the colonies. However, African educated elites asked for mass education and the provision of post-primary schools whilst the thrust of French reforms was to prepare the educated Africans to become more serviceable to the colonial regime. This had been expressed by responsible colonial administrators like Eboue, who in 1941 expressed his opinion on African education in a circular entitled, "The New Native Policy".

> ...Education is the very foundation of colonial policy and the value assignable to our overseas possessions is to be measured first of all by the value of the individual in virtue of the instructions he receives.

> Education has as its first effect a large increase in the value of colonial industrial output through multiplying the intellectual abilities and capacities among the masses of colonial workers... as skilled mechanics, foremen, inspectors, clerks to supplement the numerical insufficiency of Europeans and satisfy the growing demands of agriculture, industrial and commercial colonization enterprise..., to train native officials of various categories... to train native non-commissioned officers.... Education should develop in them facilities and capacities necessary for useful collaboration with us... there is urgent need to develop without further delay all the educational institutions which should render our subjects...

---

78 Gardinier D. E. *Cameroon: United Nations Challenge to French Policy.* London, Oxford University Press, p.19.

more capable of playing their part in French civilization.[79]

As an administrator, Eboue was motivated by the dearth of African administrative and technical assistants during the war and therefore proposed that education policy be directed to teach practical things and take initiatives because until then, education had been limited to a minority *évolués*. Members of this group were supposed to become true citizens of colonisation especially as councillors in their territories representing and defending colonial ideas.[80] As conference chairman, his ideas influenced the discussions and resolutions. Education was seen as means to cultivate attitudes necessary for collaboration with France and in the promotion of French civilization.

Furthermore, the socio-economic impact of the war was considerable on the colonies. Since the French Government was in disarray and the 'Free France" faction that gained the respect of the colonies was in exile, the Cameroon economy African criticisms of the socio-economic malaise pointed at the weaknesses of the education system that required reforms. International pressures as indicated earlier argued that if German colonies had not been confiscated at the end of the First World War, there would have been no Second World War. The argument raised by Lenin during the First World War against monopoly and capitalist system in his work, *Imperialism, the Highest stage of Capitalism*, was revived.[81] The presence of Russia in the same camp against Germany exerted pressure on French policies. These observations influenced changes in French colonial polices.

One solution in education was to establish secondary schools. Thus, a secondary school that started in Yaounde in 1944 exclusively for Europeans opened its doors to Africans in 1947.[82] To solve the problem of teachers, a teacher training college was opened in Nkongsamba. On 23 December 1947, an *Arrêté* was published that brought many significant changes. Education was placed under a Director who had to be a French civil servant with a university qualification. The Director was assisted by inspectors for primary, secondary and technical education. A new curriculum for primary schools was also published which reflected the new policy orientation. The professional school in Douala was reorganised and grants to the Mission schools were revised.

79   Crouzet P., op. cit. pp272-276.

80   Madiba P., *Colonisation et Evangélisation en Afrique: L'Héritage scolaire au Cameroun*, Berne, Peter Lang, 1980.

81   Lakowski R., op. cit. pp.379-418.

82   NAY AR., *Journal Officiel*, «Enseignement du second degré classique et moderne» 1948, p.133.

These changes brought rapid growth in school enrolment but did not provide for strategies to monitor the quality of education. It became necessary in 1952 to take measures to control the growth of education and make sure that the curriculum implementation respected Government objectives. This was done by granting the Director of Education the power to appoint, train and retrain teachers. Two assistants were assigned to coordinate primary education and technical education respectively. To cope with the required standard and statistical records, offices were created for statistical data and curriculum within the Director's Office.

These were the policies that guided post-war education in the territory. Constitutional reforms and Cameroonian reactions were very influential. The Fourth French Republic reversed the promise for decentralization made at the Brazzaville conference and decided to maintain strong central control on the colonies. This ignited protests in most of the dependencies. In Cameroon resistance from the *évolue* was accompanied by the *administrés* to produce an anti-colonial ferment in the territory that dominated much of the entire post-war era. Nevertheless, the provision of education by the Government during the post-colonial period made significant progress.

Government provisions

Whereas education during the mandate concentrated on a few primary schools, the trusteeship era witnessed a dramatic expansion in primary education reforms in vocational training and the introduction of secondary education. The new structure of school management and supervision brought efficiency and greater coordination in educational developments in general and particularly in Government schools which had the task of setting a model to private schools. The territory was divided into four zones for closer supervision in contrast to the district system of the mandate period. Each of the four inspectors was assigned a zone.

Primary Education

The aim of primary school education was said to give the child education and knowledge necessary to enhance his/her ability to participate actively in his society and in *modern civilisation*.[83]

These changes led to phenomenal expansion in schooling as shown on table 3.7.

83 NAY.AR., *Journal Officiel.*, "Enseignement Technique" 1956, p.134.

Table 3.7: Government schools during the post-war period.

Description	1945	1950	1953	1959
Number of schools	136	181	364	728
Number of Cameroonian pupils	15.942	26.682	50.258	103.072
Number of European pupils	130	423	506	N/A
Number of African teachers	261	572	889	N/A

Sources: NAY. Services de l'Enseignement et de l'orientation professionnelle ; Annuaire statistique du Cameroun : Service coloniale des statistiques. Vol. II. Also see Report of the Advisory Commission for the development of Higher Education in Cameroon, UNESCO, Paris, 1962; for 1953 to 1959 figures.

Secondary Education

Though lately introduced, secondary education rapidly expanded. By 1956 there were already two lycées (lycée Leclerc in Yaounde and Lycée Joss in Douala). Then three junior or first cycle secondary schools were opened in Nkongsamba, Garoua and one in Douala for girls only. The certificate examinations, whether at the Brevet or Baccalauréat level, were organized by Examination Boards in France, based on French curricula. Until after independence all the secondary schools were headed by Europeans. Table 3.8 illustrates the statistical development in secondary education during this period:

Table 3.8: Statistical situation of Government secondary education:

Description	Years		
	1950	1953	1959
Number of schools	4	5	5
Number of Cameroonian Student	858	1.300	1.833
Number of European Student	70	214	67
Number of European teachers	15	15	N/A
Number of African teachers	30	39	N/A

Sources : NAY Service de l'enseignement et de l'orientation professionnelle: annuaire statistique du Cameroun. Also see, Report of the Advisory Commission for the development of Higher Education in Cameroon, UNESCO, Paris, 1962.

Technical Education

Technical and commercial education were restructured and made attractive to pupils. The students spent the first year for general orientation after which those retained were admitted into apprenticeship in a variety of trades ranging from masonry to woodwork, motor-mechanics and electricity. The course took three years at the end of which the students sat for a trade test comprising theoretical and practical components to obtain Certificat d'Aptitude Professionnelle (C.A.P.)

There was also the establishment of the *lycée technique* structure which offered intermediate professional training. It was a comprehensive system in which the three years were devoted to general education as in grammar schools. Graduates of general secondary education with the *brevet* certificates were also admitted to the fourth year into specialized courses where they studied both theory and practice until the sixth year when they did the *probatoire technique*. Those who succeeded continued to the seventh year where they sat for the *Baccalauréat technique*. This level of training aimed at supplying competent intermediate cadres for industries. Others continued for higher studies in technical field in France. Table 3.9 gives statistical illustration.

Table 3.9: Government Technical Education.

Description	1947	1950	1953	1959
	Years			
Number of schools	1	1	19	34
Number of European students	2	3	12	N/A
Number of Cameroon Student	102	114	880	1.441
Number of European teachers	8	20	34	N/A
Number of African teachers	0	1	1	N/A

Sources: La Documentation Française, La République du Cameroun in Notes et Etudes Documentaire, N. 2741, 1961. Also in Gardinier D.E. "French Policy in the Cameroons, 1945-1959" PhD Yale 1960.

Despite the reform in technical education, it did not expand as rapidly as secondary general education. The slow expansion was firstly, because there was dearth of qualified development of teachers. Secondly, it is possible to believe that the expensive cost involved in the construction, equipment and management of technical institutions when compared to the establishment of secondary general education slowed down, the development of this type of education. Finally, it was also evident that More interest had been developed for white-collar jobs requiring general education. General education graduates had more access to university education where they qualified for managerial posts whereas most technical school students ended up as technicians under university graduates, a practice that has persisted.

Teacher Training

The expansion in primary schools inevitably had implications for teacher training colleges. The Teacher Training College at Nkongsamba replaced the Higher Primary School in Yaoundé. Four more training colleges were established to train teachers in three categories: Grade One Teachers *(instituteur or institutrice)*, Grade Two Teachers *(instituteur or institutrice adjoints)*, and Grade Three Teachers *(moniteurs)*. Thus by 1956, there were five Government Teacher Training Colleges with 12 Grade One student-teachers, 528 Grade Two student-teachers and 30 Grade three student teachers.[84] These were the efforts made in formal educational provisions by the colonial Government. They combined with efforts in the private sector to establish the educational system that was inherited at independence.

Mission/Private education

Besides the Mission schools, secular schools started during the post-war period. By 1952, there were already 22 secular primary schools with a total enrolment of 1,873 pupils and by 1956 secular secondary schools were also established.[85] The emergence of this pattern of schooling may be explained by the improved educational policy that guaranteed initiatives by individual or corporate bodies. It can also be explained by the economic development of the territory that stimulated high demand for educated people. The desire of some people of good will to offer social services cannot also be excluded. There were also inducements from increased Government subvention for private education that might have attracted prospective proprietors of schools. For example, the 1948 budget for education was 116,000,000 francs and Government subvention was 18,500,000 francs making a total of 134,500,000 francs and the following year the budget increased to 334,336,000 francs to which was added a subvention of 78,000,000 francs making a total of 412,336.000 francs.[86] This was unprecedented in Government financing and therefore attracted private investment.

The increased subvention stimulated more rivalry between the Missions as they struggled to build more and better schools. Good results attracted more pupils. More enrolments also meant more school fees. In this light, the Catholic

---

84   NAY.AR. *Journal Officiel*, 1956.

85   NAY, Service de I' enseignement et de l'orientation professionnelle: Annuaire statistique du Cameroun, Service des statistique. vol.11.

86   NAY, AR:, Journal Officiel,1948 and 1949. Also see Shu S.N., *Landmarks in Cameroon Education*, NOOREMAC. Limbe, 1985, p.147.

denomination in particular revised the strategies after the war which paid dividends. All the Catholic Missions united and together, opened teacher training colleges and secondary schools while expanding primary schools. All the Missions had four teacher training colleges with 429 students by 1956, comprising two Catholic colleges at Makak and at Mbanga and two Protestant colleges at Bafoussam and Sangmelima.[87]

The Mission secondary schools included the following Protestants colleges: Collège Evangélique de Libamba, new colleges at Banga, Bagangté, Douala, Elat, Metet and Sakbayémé; and the following Catholic colleges: Collège Modern de Makak, Collège Sacré-Coeur de Douala, Collège Saint Esprit de Douala, Collège Saint-Jean de Mbanga, Collège Saint-Esprit de Yaounde, Collège Vogt de Mvolyé and Institut Libermann de Douala. In 1956, all these schools had an enrolment of 2,725 students.[88]

The Catholic schools were strategically placed and demonstrated an overriding interest to spread Catholic influence throughout the length and breadth of the territory. This followed a strategy developed during an internal reorganisation of the administrative structure in 1949 when a department of education was created to administer, coordinate and supervise all educational activities of the Mission. These innovations ultimately infused new blood in catholic educational activities and enabled the Mission to resist the protestant domination of the interwar years. The predominance of the catholic religion in Francophone Cameroon today began during this period.

Meanwhile, the Protestant Missions did not stop expanding. They collaborated so as to counteract the threat of Catholic expansion. This collaboration started, even before the war when they trained teachers at the École Supérieure and jointly operated a teacher training college at Foulassi from 1936.[89] Thus both individually and jointly they struggled to open more schools and establish both secondary and technical colleges. These efforts were slowed down when the protestant Missions' activities were handed down to local churches.[90]

Notwithstanding the increased efforts made by the Government in the postcolonial period, the contribution of the private agencies remained Very significant. The following table further enhances an understanding of the provision of education during the period.

87   87 NAY.AR., *Journal Officiel*, 1947.

88   88 NAY. *Journal Officiel*, 1956, pp.245-246.

89   NAY.AR., *Journal Officiel*, 1948.

90   The Protestant Missions handed over to the local churches between 1954 and 1956. see more in Van Slageren, J., op. cit.

Table 3.10: Statistics of Schooling by 1959

Description	Government schools				Private schools			
	No.	Boys	Girls	Total	No.	Boys	Girls	Total
Primary	728	72.273	30.799	103.072	2.012	157.511	70.511	227.911
Secondary	5	1.376	524	1.900	11	1.354	359	1.713
Teacher Training	1	36	-	36	14	617	69	686
Supplementary courses	15	1.456	390	1.846	19	1.235	109	1.344
Technical education	34	1.315	126	1.441	29	1.853	983	2.836
Total	783	76.456	31.839	108.295	2.085	16.249	71.922	234.490

Sources: Report of the Advisory Commission for the development of Higher education in Cameroon, UNESCO, 1962.

From the table, the total number of educational establishments at the eve of independence (1959) added up to 2,868. The Government supplied 27.3 per cent while the private, agencies provided 72.7 per cent. Out of the total enrolment of 342,785 people at school, Government schools enrolled 31.6 per cent while the private sector had 68.4 per cent. Consequently, if the impact of French colonial policy is measured only from the education provided by the Government, it will be an overstatement to claim that Cameroonian attitudes were seriously affected by the education they received. However, it has been evident in the discussion of the post-war educational development that the colonial administration had a firm control over all education (public and private). The curricula, school structures, pedagogic methods, teaching aids and all aspects of school life except the teaching of religious instruction were uniform and controlled centrally by Government. Thus the French colonial education was not as peripheral as earlier assumed in this study. Such a uniformity centrally controlled by a regime that had cultural inculcation as an overriding interest could conceivably implant homogeneous values.

It was also presumed in the introduction to this study that the quantitative impact of the educational policy was insignificant, but the statistics of educational expansion during the post-war period refutes that assumption. The phenomenal increase from 17 per cent of the school age population in schools at the eve of the war (1938) to 55 per cent in 1955 and to 71 per cent at the eve of independence (1959) is evidence of the fact that an important proportion of the youths who became responsible adults at independence received this cultural inculcation. This corroborates the assumption raised in the introduction that French colonial education was stronger than that of the other regimes.

Furthermore, the French colonial regime offered the same system of education to French and Cameroonian children, especially at the post primary level, as indicated in tables 3.8 and 3.9. The curricula were the same with those in France. The assessments were by the same examination boards in France. Thus the French colonial metropolis was ultimately more assimilationist and inevitably more influential.

It is however arguable that the Government's action in offering the same education was deliberate. The role of Cameroonians in demanding parity of education with the metropolis was significant because the ultimate aim of most students was to end up in French universities and professional schools. This required the acquisition of the same education as their counterparts in the metropolis. Many Cameroonians also abandoned further studies in Dakar which used to be the citadel for French colonial education in Africa, in preference for studies in France.[91]

Besides the search for diplomas in the French institutions, there was a desperate need at home for qualified people at independence. The qualifications were measured in terms of French education. Expansion in the economy also required competent Cameroonians aware of modem economic theories. Such training was not available in Cameroon. Thus decolonisation factors developed a growing interest in education that attracted Cameroonians to France. By 1948, there were already 194 Cameroonian students in France and by 1953, there were 357 scholarship holders in various fields.[92] At independence, Cameroon had more than 1,000 students abroad with some 504 registered in French institutions alone. Between 1957 and 1959, Cameroon had the highest number of African students in France.[93] The following table illustrates the number and fields of study.

Table 3.11: Higher and Professional education.

Courses	Number of students per year				
	1957/58	1958/59	1959/60	1960/61	1961/62
Medicine	59	64	62	59	70
Pharmacy	18	21	19	16	20
Law	43	52	49	51	47
Veterinary Medicine	2	-	5	6	10

91 Mbono-Samba M, who was one of the graduates of the Higher Primary School in Yaounde, told the author that they left Dakar for France as soon as the war was over.

92 Le Vine V,T., op.,cit. p. 525.

93 Booth B.K.A., "Comparative Study of Mission and Government Enrolment in Educational Development in West Cameroon, 1922-1969". PhD UCLA, 1973. p.298.

	Number of students per year				
Courses	1957/58	1958/59	1959/60	1960/61	1961/62
Science	24	45	59	70	67
Arts and Humanities	29	38	39	46	53
Engineering	1	16	20	5	N/A
Theology	-	4	9	7	5
Higher Professional education	9	15	9	28	N/A
Preparation for higher professional education	13	24	24	28	N/A

Sources: Compiled from Report of Advisory Commission for the development of Higher Education in Cameroon, UNESCO, Paris, 1962. Also see Reports to the United Nations Trusteeship Council.

These statistics do not include the large number of students who proceeded on their own to complete their secondary school studies and the number of nurses and secretaries who were self-sponsored since education in France was without school fees. Exposure to the French educational model further increased the already acquired interest for French educational system.

Most of the graduates in the first two decades of independence were destined for lucrative jobs where they had rapid professional progress. This was further favoured by the relatively strong economy[94] supported by France and other developed nations and international organisations. The relatively good socio-economic climate at independence must have induced Cameroonian leaders to believe that the apparent successes came from the educational system and found no reasons for reforms.

This chapter started with the premise that French colonial education advocated the diffusion of the French culture throughout the colonial period. It was therefore assumed that the inculcation of French culture led Cameroonians to understand education only from a French framework. It was also assumed that the regime unequivocally discarded all African traditions and cultures. But the discussion has demonstrated that until the Second World War, French cultural impact through education was negligible and could not significantly influence the attitudes of Cameroonians. There was also ambivalence in the conceptual framework and practice of assimilation and association that invariably rendered total cultural implantation impracticable. The disparity between those who gained

94 The tropical crop boom of the 1960s and 1970s was followed by oil boom at the beginning of the 1980s.

French citizenship under the assimilation policy and those who were considered under the association policy combined with the differences created between the *évolués* and the *indigènes* to complicate the successful attainment of the policies. The realization of the deceptive status gained by the African elites caused them to rally with the rest of the society against colonial policies.

It was also noted that educational provision created disparity between the northern and the southern regions of the territory. At independence, the political power was dominated by people from the north who found it necessary to raise the standard of education in that area before considering reforms. Furthermore, education at independence ended at the secondary school level. Consequently, the post-colonial Government concentrated efforts on establishing higher and professional education for manpower training and could not devote time for educational reforms.

Evidently, the colonial Government did not apply any coercive measures to implement educational policies. Rather, Cameroonian desires for socio-economic and political mobility apparently urged them to imbibe French cultures and reject alternative proposals to adapt education. As a consequence, most Cameroonians became attracted to this system of education because of the social mobility resulting from it. Additionally, the predominance of Missionary education operating within French cultural background and strongly controlled by the regime also re-enforced the inculcation of French values which became deeply entrenched in all those who went through the school system. These people became the leaders of Cameroon at independence and since "old habits die hard" they find it difficult to accept changes in the education system. Thus the resistance to reform is a combination of several factors and cannot be attributed only to colonialism. This is further supported by the next chapter which examines the development of the British colonial education policy in Cameroon. Since British rule was peripheral the chapter examines why Cameroonians who went through that system resist reforms and remain attached to the inherited system.

CHAPTER FOUR

CAMEROON EDUCATION UNDER THE BRITISH REGIME:
(1916-1961)

B ritish colonial education policies in Cameroon as in all British dependencies were adaptationist. Unlike the French, whose assimilationist policies were implemented through a centralized administration, British education policies were developed and implemented indirectly through Missionary Societies and Native Authorities. Britain considered the acquired Cameroon territories to be part and parcel of their Nigerian colony. The two narrow strips had been acquired to resolve an outstanding boundary problem on the Nigerian-Cameroon border. These territories were therefore treated like all other similar places in Nigeria but suffered more neglect because of the distance separating them from the colonial capital at Lagos. Education policies developed for Nigeria were adapted. Colonial administrators and educators who served in the territories were recruited for Nigeria and never specifically for Cameroon.[95] Therefore, unlike the French, British colonial policies and administrative strategies in Cameroon were peripheral. Yet some Cameroonians, encouraged by Nazi Germany at the eve of the war, and post-war developments held that they were not part of Nigeria and deserved better and direct British attention.

This chapter examines the impact on education of the disagreement between British interest and the determination of those Cameroonians to achieve special attention. It seeks also to understand why, in spite of this peripheral treatment, Cameroonians resist post colonial reforms and retain the inherited British colonial system. The question is whether or not the nature of the British colonial policies and the method of implementation had an impact on post-independence attitudes. British dependence on Missions and the NA school systems for the provision of schools which contrasted with the French centralised system is also

---

95 All the retired British colonial administrators interviewed during this research confirm that they were employed by the Nigerian service and were posted or transferred to Cameroon like in all other parts of Nigeria.

examined to find out the implications for post-colonial regimes. The administrators and administrative system, the structure of schooling and teacher training as well as the curriculum are therefore analyzed to highlight their influences on post-colonial attitudes to education.

British colonial policies before the Second World War and during the post-war periods are markedly different. Before the Second World War, the education policy encouraged vernacular, infant and elementary education to improve on the traditional institutions and to prepare some Africans to assist the colonial services. But the socio-political and economic ramifications of the war on both the colonizers and the colonized necessitated a change in the formulation of the post-war policies. The thrust of the new policies was to educate competent people in secondary schools and professional institutions for responsibilities in self-government. Thus this chapter is sub-divided into two major parts to take account of the differences between the two periods.

British concept of colonial education

British colonial education policy in Africa was adaptationist.[96] Adaptation policies were supposed to encourage mass education through schooling but with the desire to relate this education to the traditional, political and economic cultures of the Africans so that traditional institutions could be developed and socio-political harmony enhanced. Adaptationist policies were also said to encourage local and national socio-political identification and were supposed to secure the needs of the rural masses and reduce the social differences between the educated elite and the rest of the colonized population. These contrasted with the assimilationist policies which sought to create a minority elite imbued with colonial culture (see chapter three).

The implementation of these adaptationist policies was generally left to local colonial administrators, who controlled the development of curricula, the training of teachers, the supply of resources such as textbooks and the conduct of examinations. The provision of schooling facilities supposedly aimed at universal education whilst the curriculum policies encouraged teaching in African languages and the teaching of African history and geography. Local institutions and local agricultural needs were also to be encouraged by the curriculum policies which were also expected to enforce inter-relations between schooling and activities in local communities.

The content of elite education under the adaptationist policies was supposed

---

96 Advisory Committee on Education in the Colonies, Memorandum on the Education of African Communities, Comd. 2374, 1925., p. 4. Also see Mumford W.B., "Comparative study of native education in various dependencies" in *The Year Book of Education*, 1935., p. 824.

to be related to the local life of the community and selection to advance education had to be based partly on social status and contributions to the community and partly on ability. Thus by adaptation, mass education could be acquired without much risk of social division. At the same time, a substantial degree of local political self-determination could encourage local political stability and boost African cultures.

However, as educated Africans evolved, they felt that the practicality of the adaptationist policies was invariably aimed at maintaining the Africans in their perceived primitiveness. These elites felt that the limitation of the scope of curricula reduced the hope for scientific and technological education considered essential for acquiring Western knowledge for development. The African perception of education was therefore shaped by the introduction of relationship between educational achievement and socio-economic advancement. Thus any insistence on adaptation was regarded by Africans as a constraint on development and African opinions on the type of education they wanted were never sought. Therefore, there was a conflict between the British concept of colonial education and African perceptions. Such contradictions ultimately affected the realisation of all educational policies.

The demand for educated Africans to serve in the colonial services also required the acquisition of a more literary education than that available via an adaptationist education. Missionary societies also required well educated Africans to eventually become responsible for the Christian church. The type of education required to train such people was ultimately different from the education proposed by the adaptation policy. Since those who had this pattern of education enjoyed economic mobility and enhanced social status, most. Africans tended to be more attracted to it than to adaptationist schooling. Meanwhile, the content of his pattern of schooling was a replication of the metropolitan practice meant to ensure the suitability of the recipients for colonial service. Thus it was assimilationist and British colonial education could therefore not be consistently adaptationist. But how did the pursuit of the educational aims, the administrative, provision, curriculum and teacher training policies affect educational development and what impact did that leave on post-independent education?

Educational Development from 1916 to 1939

As stated earlier, British Cameroon Became part of Nigeria from 1916. The northern part (British Northern Cameroon) was merged with the provinces of Northern Nigeria while the southern part (British Southern Cameroon) became a province within Southern Nigeria and placed under a Resident.[97] Most authors on British colonial rule in Cameroon hold the view that the territory was neglected. They argue that British Cameroon should have been treated like other dependencies. These contentions underpin Cameroon peoples' understanding of the colonial situation and suggest their readiness to internalize British education. However, British administrative design gained international support in 1922 when the League of Nations mandate over the territory authorized the administering power to "...constitute the territory into a customs, fiscal or administrative union or federation, with the adjacent territories under their sovereignty or control".[98]

The immediate British colonial education policy was thus adapted from Nigeria. It had been proposed in 1914 by Lugard, Governor General of Nigeria.[99] It became the 1916 education code for Nigeria.[100] It matured for implementation just when British Cameroon was subsumed within Nigeria. Hence, the nature and pattern of implementation had inevitably, to depend on the administration's attitude to British Cameroon.

As a colonial administrator, Lugard's interest in colonial education ultimately aimed at raising capable Africans to fill vacancies in the colonial service and in private colonial enterprises. Thus the policy aimed at inculcating obedient and respectful attitudes in Africans, for the sake of discipline. It emphasized character formation in school pupils. The administration further pursued this objective by insisting on the teaching of religious and moral instruction in all schools.[101] Ultimately, the importance attached to the education of colonial support staff led to elitist education and defeated the design for adaptationist education.

The 1916 education code for Nigeria authorized the award of Government grants was to approved schools. Inspectors had to award marks for teachers' efficiency, teacher/pupil ratio, school sanitation and school buildings. The code further suggested the adaptation of education to African culture.[102] This implied emphasis on education for the development of the rural sector and the improvement of the socioeconomic conditions of the mass of the population. The British

97 NAB. BA. 1916/1., Annual Report. Also see, BA.Sd/1916/1 , Intelligence Report on Bamenda.

98 See Article 9 of the Mandate covenant in appendix 4.

99 Lugard F.D., *The Dual Mandate in British Tropical Africa*; London, Frank Cass and Co., 1965, pp. 425-466.,

100 NAI. CS0.1/1., Lugard's dispatch to the Secretary of State for the colonies.

101 NAI.CSO 26/03527., Governor to Secretary Southern Provinces, 1923.

102 NAI CSO 26/1 19524., Lugard's address on Educational Development in Nigeria.

considered land to be the natural vocation of the African and education had to enable the African to benefit from that vocation. It has been argued that the British aimed at avoiding the over production of unemployed educated elites.

However, the need for some educated Cameroonians to assist in the colonial services as clerks, nurses, teachers, police officers, technicians and warders necessitated the establishment of literary education. This led to the categorisation of colonial education into literary and rural schools.[103] The few Government schools provided literary education, while most Mission schools, provided adaptationist education.[104] The inevitable consequence of categorisation was the introduction of a new social order. The educated class was eventually to compete or rival the traditional elites because of their acquired, economic and social status in the colonial service.

The literary schools used English for instruction since the graduates had to work eventually with the colonial administrators and European entrepreneurs. The rural schools were conducted in local languages in order to reinforce the adaptation policy. Here the objective was to improve on local craftsmanship and to inculcate the love for manual labour while being initiated into basic literacy. For any school to survive however, the literary content was required to attract the pupils. In the final analysis, none of these schools was exclusively assimilationist or adaptationist.

The notion of literary education should not be misconstrued for post-elementary education. The duration of schooling throughout the pre-1925 period varied between three and five, years and the curriculum emphasized English language acquisition. Compulsory subjects included: reading, writing, English composition and grammar, English dictation, colloquial English and Arithmetic.[105] This was the nature of British colonial policy during the pre-1925 period.

Educational provision during that period was equally limited in scale. Schools re-started in 1917. Besides the former German school at Victoria, the British administration opened other schools in Buea, Kumba, Nyassosso and Ossidinge. The first year of schooling was conducted in the vernacular, followed by two years of infant school, then four years of elementary school and two years of primary school. Up to 1922 the highest class in the province was standard four and the level of the pupils' achievement was said to be lower than that of equivalent

---

103 Fajana A., *The Evolution of Educational Policy in Nigeria* (1842-1939), PhD, Ibadan, 1969.

104 NALCSO 26/03527., Education Policy in Southern Provinces.

105 NAB.Ba.1925/5,, Report on Education to the League of Nations for 1924. NA13.13a.1923/1 Annual Report p.12. (elementary schools).

standard in all of Southern Nigeria.[106]

During this period private schools in Cameroon were either nonexistent or barely thriving under the initiatives of enthusiastic Cameroonian Christians in what became known as "hedge schools".[107] They could hardly attract, government grants because of irregular attendance, especially during planting and harvesting seasons. They were unorganised, ill-equipped and had unqualified staff.

The teacher-catechists, unlike the Missionaries suffered antagonisms from local rulers. It is probable that if the Government had shown interest in what the teacher-catechists were doing the conflicts could have either been avoided or minimised. They were accused of opposing the traditional cultures because of the acquired Christian influence. Further reports associated events from Christian practices to ethiopianism a phenomenon that threatened colonial regimes in East and South Africa during the period.[108] But a close examination will point to syncretism rather than ethiopianism because no significant political issues were raised during the period. Rather, it was a poor understanding, interpretation and practice of the scriptures by ill-informed Christians.[109]

It has been argued that since the early British administrative officers such as Major Ruxton, Captain Denton, Captain Duncan, Captain Buchannan Smith and Major Smith[110] were mostly retired army officers they did not show much concern for the efforts made by Christian Cameroonians to sustain Mission education. Even Brayne-Baker and Cardote, who were sons of parsons, are said to have made little efforts to encourage the Cameroonian teachers. But Brayne-Baker, whom the author of this study met in Exeter on 25 April 1995, argued that local administrators in the province were faced with many problems,[111] particularly the lack of communication system both within the territory and with Lagos and the absence of social facilities. However, the annual reports also reveal that these local administrators including Lugard made commendable efforts, 'first to

106 NAB.Ba.1923/1,, Annual Report p.12. (elementary schools).

107 NAB.Sd.1921/5., Basel Mission handing over to United Free Church of Scotland Mission, 1921, p.2.

108 Ayandele, E.A., *The Missionary Impact on Modern Nigeria 1842-1914. A Political and Social Analysis*, London, Longmans, 1966., pp.177-178. It was a nationalist expression of anti-British feelings.

109 NAB.Sd.1920/1, Rutherford J.W.C., op. cit.

110 Annual reports of the period starting from 1916.

111 Bryne-Baker who served in the Nigerian colonial service, was in Cameroon during several tours starting in 1928 to the eve of independence.

replace the German Missions and subsequently to bring them back. [112] The efforts made can only be fully appreciated when Cameroon is seen as part of Nigeria.

In 1922, three significant events in the provision of schools were initiated. Firstly, the Mill Hill Catholic Mission was permitted to enter the territory and establish schools.[113] Secondly, there was the establishment of 10 NA schools. Finally, H J. Davidson was appointed as the first inspector of schools.

The appointment of an inspector of schools, introduced positive change. Davidson was enthusiastic and hard-working. He appointed three third grade schoolmasters, three assistant teachers and six pupil teachers, in the Government schools. He insisted on the use of printed handbooks and schemes which he compiled to improve teaching. Thus as shown in table 4.1., there was improvement in schooling by 1924.[114]

Davidson organized regular vacation courses for teachers of public and private sectors. In July 1923, he arranged for W.E. Hunt, the acting Resident, Dr. Hanington, the Medical Officer, and E. Garnar, the curator, to give lectures to the course participants. The problems of distance and transportation warranted the organisation of a similar course in Mamfe under Hay for the two northern divisions. The successes recorded at official school examinations in 1923 may be attributed to his efforts. Hyde-Johnson, the director of education for Nigeria unhesitatingly acknowledged Davidson's contributions when he visited the province.[115]

Davidson's efforts can be further appreciated when the enormous difficulties he encountered are considered. He was alone except when relieved by W B. Stimson from Nigeria. There was no transportation, and the diversity in climate and vegetation combined with the difficult landscape in the territory to hinder him. However, he surmounted the difficulties because of his zeal for the profession and the cooperation with the Missions, the teachers and the administration. His dedication caused him to catch pneumonia in the cold dry weather of Kumbo where he died in April 1924.[116] He was replaced by Stimson who in 1924 upgraded

112 Most reports from 1921 at both divisional and territorial levels contain appeals by administrators to the authorities for the resumption of Mission activities.

113 NAB. Ba. 1922/1., Annual Report. Also see Ndi A., op. cit 1983. This thesis has treated the arrival and development of the Mill Hill Fathers; while Booth B.F. "A Comparative study of Mission and Government involvement in educational development in West Cameroon, 1922-1969" UCLA, Ph.D. 1973 has examined Catholic Mission education during the period.

114 NAB.Ba 1924/1. Annual Report.

115 NAB Ba.1923/1., Annual Report by H J. Davidson

116 NAB Ba.1924/I., Annual Report pp.53-59.

two of the Government schools to standard six level and four others to standard five levels. From these efforts, there was a marked improvement in schooling in the province which convinced the regime to consider the approval of a secondary school in 1925 as shown in table 4.1.[117] The increased number of schools and enrolments from 1922 may be attributed not only to the creation of the N.A. Schools but also reflects the criticisms and pressures that British colonial policy was facing. These reproaches suggested the need for a broad-based policy to guide the development of education in the colonies. This section discusses the background of the policy.

Table 4.1: Number of Schools, enrolment and school age population.

Year	Gov't Schools	N.A Schools	Catholic Schools	B.M. Schools	Total Enrolment	Total Population	School age Population
1971	6	-	-	N/A	279	-	-
1918	5	-	-	N/A	596	-	-
1919	10	-	-	N/A	614	-	-
1920	10	-	-	N/A	658	-	-
1921	7	-	-	N/A	465	645.174	129.035
1922	7	10	3	1	1610	551.321	110.264
1923	6	12	3	1	2150	632.303	126.461
1924	6	12	3	33	3662	660.024	132.005

Sources: Annual Reports and Mission Reports.

Background to the 1925 Education Policy

A growing concern had been expressed even before the war by colonial Governments for a common guiding principle for colonial education.[118] Lugard's concern was just one of many. Although colonial governments needed educated African support staff, they were worried about the implications of Mission education. Mission education was elitist and therefore a potential source of unemployment. They also doubted the relevance of the pattern of education

---

117 NALCS0.26/09767., Report on the establishment of a Secondary school in Cameroons Province., 1923.

118 Whitehead C., "Education Policy in British Tropical Africa: the 1925 White Paper in Retrospect", in History of Education, 1981 vol.10. No.3, pp. 195-203.

to the needs of the colonial service. Thus, control over Mission education was considered necessary.

Meanwhile, Missionaries were also apprehensive of colonial Governments' control and intended to circumvent such policies that might restrain their educational objectives. Unlike the situation in India where the Educational Dispatch of 1854 guaranteed effective co-operation between Government and private initiatives, Mission education in Africa had no security.[119] Thus they wanted co-operation with the Government, so as to provide safeguards against the rigidity and uniformity characteristic of bureaucratically managed schools. Such collaboration could encourage experimentation and initiatives. An atmosphere of collaboration between the state and the Missions could easily accommodate schools of special and distinctive types within a national system, which could help to fulfil Missions' objectives.

This concern was discussed during the Edinburgh Missionary Conference of 1910. The Protestant Missions agreed to co-ordinate their activities in Africa by means of a continuation committee charged with the responsibility of negotiating with the Government on the future of African education.[120] Under A.H.L. Fraser as chairman and J.H. Oldham as secretary, the committee proposed a memorandum on the future of education in West Africa which was presented to the Colonial Office on 5 April 1914. They asked for a general policy on education in the African colonies, general policy outlining the role of the colonial Governments and the establishment of a commission to examine the policy.

The response from the Colonial Office in 1914 asked the Missions to suggest the policy but rejected the idea of a commission because the colonial Governments were supposedly, fully aware of their educational needs. The Government preferred each Mission in each colony to formulate proposals to the local administration. The war disturbed further discussions.

In 1923, the education committee of the Missions presented a memorandum on education to the Secretary of State for Colonies. It requested the Government to invest in colonial education if Africans were expected to advance in the scale of European perceived civilization and also in moral and material prosperity. And that:

> the Secretary of State lay down the broad principles by which each educational policy in the African colonies will in the future, be directed. Such a declaration made... will help to ensure the consistent carrying out of

119 Whitehead C., op. cit. p.197.

120 Memorandum on Education in West Africa IMC/CBMS archives, Box 263.

whatever broad lines of policy, the imperial Government might desire.[121]

Thus, the 1925 Memorandum was strongly influenced by Missions. However, other forces were also involved in the process that eventually produced the 1925 White Paper. Severe criticisms of the colonial policies in general and particularly of the general welfare of the colonized during the Versailles Peace Conference influenced the establishment of an educational policy.[122] Colonial powers were blamed for doing little to alleviate the ignorance of the colonized in Africa. The limited scale of literacy achievement was considered the bases for the continued backwardness in the colonies.

The American Baptist Foreign Missionary Society also accelerated the process by requesting the Phelps-Stokes Fund to sponsor research on African education. Earlier research on Black American education had led Caroline Phelps-Stokes in 1911 to start the Fund as a philanthropic organization which in collaboration with the International Education Board in 1919 investigated the needs of the Africans with special reference to social, hygiene, religious and economic conditions.[123] During their first trip to Africa the commission was in Cameroon from 19 to 25 of December 1920.[124]

Dr. Jones' report raised cogent arguments for policy formulation.[125] Agreeing with Lugard's earlier proposal, the report highlighted the need for the adaptation of African education in order to integrate the citizens into the process of development. It also proposed the need for the training of an elitist group from the existing leadership class who would be conscious of their responsibilities and commitment to the development of their societies and who would be entrusted with social, economic and political developments. This was at variance with that of colonial administrators such as Lugard who saw the elites more as supportive agents for colonial rule. It also differed from the objectives of the Missions which

---

121 Oldham J.H., "Education Policy of the British Government in Africa" in International Review of Missions,1925, p. 422.

122 Roger-Louis, W.M., *Great Britain and Germany's lost colonies. 1914-1919.*, Oxford, Clarendon Press, 1967, p. 78. Also see Smith, W.D., *The German Colonial Empire*, Chapel Hill, University of North Carolina Press, 1978., pp.232-234.

123 See "Phelps-Stokes Commission to West and South Africa 1920/21: Documents" in IMC/ CBMS Archives, Box 263. Also see Lewis L.T., *Phelps-Stokes Reports on Education in Africa*, London, Oxford University Press., 1962.

124 See Jones T.J., Private Journal, August 1920 to March 1921, "Liverpool to West Equatorial and South Africa" in. IMC/CBMS Archives, Box 263.

125 Cowan L.G., "Education Policy in British Tropical Africa" in *Education and National Building*, London, 1965, pp. 45-52.

expected an elite group to enhance the establishment of local churches. However, similarity was found in the desire for a small elite group.

Unlike Lugard's proposal, the Phelps-Stokes report recommended mass education as a way of improving sanitation and adherence to Government law and order. It argued that the tiny percentage of educated population and the limited scope of infant vernacular education that was generally provided, could not guarantee the desired change. It recommended a close collaboration between the colonial Government and Missionary bodies because of the Missions' widespread and significant involvement in African education.

The chairman of the Advisory Committee for Education established in 1923, was, the Parliamentary Under-Secretary of State for Colonies, Ormsby-Gore, who warned against a repeat of British errors in India. Lugard and Oldham were both retained as members of the committee while Hans Visher, former director of education in northern Nigeria, was the secretary.[126] The role of the committee was to advise the Secretary of State on matters relating to African education and also to assist in advancing the progress of education in the dependencies. The report of the committee's deliberation that emerged after two years (1923-1925) was submitted in a memorandum to Secretary of State for Colonies and became the 1925 White Paper on education in British Tropical Africa.[127] It is evident from the range of people and the diversity of the pressures involved that the British colonial regime was a reluctant colonizer when compared to others.

The 1925 Policy and implementation[128]

The White Paper guaranteed Government support to Missions that conformed with the policy. The principle of co-operation between Government and the Missions was endorsed. Financial support through grants-in-aid to schools was established. Through the aid package, aided schools became possible replacements for Government schools. Thus criticisms of the British regime for leaving the provision of education to Missions ignored this agreement. Education boards involving Mission representatives were established in the colonies to advise local Governments.

The importance of the policy has been debated by scholars. Fanfunwa argued that the policy was crucial and pertinent because it served as a useful frame of

---

126 NAI CSO 26/03527/v01.11., Minutes of the Advisory Committee of Native in Tropical Africa, pp.1-4.

127 Advisory Committee in Education in the colonies. Memorandum on the Education of African Communities, Colonial No.103.

128 Colonial Office., Education Policy in British Tropical Africa., (Cmd.2374) London, 1925.

reference until 1945[129] Perham considered the policy guidelines as an important document.[130] But the success in Cameroon can only be assessed within the context of its implementation.

A Nigerian education ordinance of 1926 was enacted from the framework provided by the policy and became law in May 1926. It focused on the Nigerian society including Cameroon. A Federal Education Board was established in Lagos (without representation from Cameroon). The only opportunity available to Cameroon was at the level of the Provincial Education Committee. But the first provincial education meeting in July and in September 1926, had no Cameroonian representative.[131]

Following the meeting, schools were structured into infant or village schools (provided by NA and Missions), then primary or central schools in administrative headquarters (provided by the Government and covering both elementary and primary sections) and finally secondary sector (covering middle school and Normal classes in the Provincial headquarters only). The complete primary school course covered nine years. Indiscriminate opening of new schools was stopped. The Government had to train teachers, supply textbooks, inspect and supervise all except religious schools. Infant classes were permitted to use local languages and the Missions were allowed to continue with the use of Douala and Bali languages in their schools. All NA and village schools and infant classes of Government schools had a common curriculum comprising: Reading, Writing, Arithmetic, Nature Study, Moral Instructions, Singing and colloquial English. Meanwhile English was recommended for all post-infant education.

The problem of untrained teachers (in 1926, only 26 of the 228 teachers were trained, and over 90% of them were Nigerians) was also addressed. Teacher training which started in Victoria in 1925, was transferred to Buea in 1926 for closer supervision. In September 1927, there was another Nigerian Education Code aimed at raising the standard of teaching and enabling teachers to guide their pupils not to alienate themselves from their society and cultures. The Governor had observed that:

> ...pupils turned out by Nigerian (Cameroon inclusive) schools in the past regarded themselves too much as a special class or craft equipped

129 Fanfunwa A.B., *History of Education in Nigeria*, London, George Allen and Unwin Limited. 1974 pp. 125- 126.

130 Perham M., *Lugard: The Years of Authority: 1895-1945, The Making of Modern Nigeria.*, London, Collins. 1960 p.660.

131 NAB. Ba 1926/1., Report to the League of Nations, p. 70.

to use pens, ink and paper as if they were the implements of trade.[132]

Therefore, the policy aimed at training teachers to become agents of adaptation. All teachers had to register with the Director of Education for Nigeria, who could refuse or strike off unsuitable teachers. All teachers had to be trained and inspected. The standards of the teachers' examination were raised and the number of passes to obtain teaching certificates increased from two to three subjects. Those who were teaching were given at least six years to obtain teaching certificates. Uncertificated teachers could not teach beyond standard three. Pupil teachers were allowed only 16 hours weekly in order to do private studies under the supervision of qualified teachers. Infant class size was limited to 45 and in primary classes to 33. No new schools were to open without the authorization of the Director of Education who had to certify that the requirements of the Board of Education were satisfied and particularly that the school was sufficiently equipped and staffed.

The bulk of Cameroon teachers were in Mission service and did not possess the required professional qualifications for registration. The Missions had barely reopened since their expulsion during the War. The Catholics restarted in 1922, the Basel Mission in 1925 and the Baptist Mission in 1927. The failure to include Cameroonians on the Education Board at the Federal and Provincial levels combined with the difficult measures taken against Mission schooling to raise a joint opposition to the policy. Consequently, Mission representatives on the Provincial Board mounted pressure for a change. The policy was intended to provide guidance against any rapid detribalization and disintegration of the African society. This guidance was perceived and prescribed for Africans regardless of their opinions. The process involved blending what the regime considered necessary in European culture for Africans to know with what were local ways so as to prepare the African pupil to be an agent of change as stated below:

> ...education should be adapted to the mentality, aptitudes, occupations and traditions of the various peoples, conserving as far as possible, all sound and healthy elements in the fabric of their social life, adapting them where necessary to changed circumstances and progressive ideas as an agent of natural growth and evolution. Its aim should be to render the individual more efficient in his or her condition of life, whatever it

132 NAB Ba.1927/1 Annual Report.

may be and to promote the advancement of the community as a whole.[133]

The assumption underlying the formulation of the policy was that the African society had to remain static in order to adapt the European prescribed education to suit the mentality, aptitude, occupations and traditions. But the rapid socio-economic changes during the inter-war years combined with international developments to overwhelm European expectations. As such, the policy proved unadoptable in Cameroon.

The introduction of the NA Schools within the framework of Indirect Rule may also be interpreted as an aspect of decentralization following the local Government pattern in England. Government and Mission schooling were considered alien to the people while the NA schools were closely in touch with local interests. Yet the ethos of the English education system was to develop the pupil's character and intelligence in order to enable him/her to fit in the existing society. Thus education could not serve as a cementing factor to strengthen those elements in African society which would have enabled it to adjust to the rapidly changing world system.

The Government failed to allocate finances for policy implementation. The financing of the new policy depended on the resourcefulness of the local colonial Governments. But these Governments hardly allocated adequate funds for education. As Hussey, director of education for Nigeria argued in 1931, the Education department was treated as "the Cinderella of Government departments".[134]

Furthermore, whereas Nigerians and Missions operating in Nigeria were represented on the Federal Education Board Cameroon had no representation. It is possible that available funds might have been distributed first among those represented and Cameroon could only survive on the crumbs. The financial problem was heightened by the World Economic depression of the 1930s. The increasing scarce resources and rising costs led to severe cuts in Government revenues. The implications of such severe financial problems for social services were numerous. There was a slow increase of grants to aided schools and an increasing large number of unaided schools. (See table 4.2).

Limited Government spending heightened the regime's determination to exploit local resources to finance education. Thus there was insistence on the Native Authorities managing their own schools and also raising subventions

---

133 Advisory Committee in Education in the colonies. Memorandum on the Education of African Communities, Comd. 2374, 1925 P. 4. Also see Mumford W.B. op. cit. p.824.

134 Hussey E.R.J. "Education policy and Political Development in Africa," in *Journal of African Affairs*, vol.44 of 1945 p.73

for the Mission schools in their districts. They had to build and maintain their schools; employ, pay and train their teachers, while awarding scholarships to competent children for further studies.

For all its weaknesses, the policy did develop a self-reliant attitude in the territory which was a tremendous asset to the sustenance of education. This continues today in the form of assistance from the Parent-Teachers Associations.[135]

Teacher training continued to pose problems. In 1931, the training school was transferred from Buea to Kake, a rural area in Kumba, to reflect the adaptation policy and option for ruralization of education. It was intended to develop teachers' interests in rural life. But teachers from urban areas tended to return only to similar environments. This further weakened the implementation of the adaptation policy. However, enrolment in the teachers college remained low. With all the reforms and pressures carried out in 1931, the enrolment at Kake was just 24 and by 1939 it was 33.[136]

Another dimension of failure associated with teacher training was the problem of retaining trained teachers in education. When trained teachers were forced to teach in rural environments against their will, they tended to abandon their work for other colonial or commercial jobs. Since the teacher training college offered the only post-primary education in the territory during the inter-war period, all commercial and administrative services looked to it for a supply of better educated people.

The implication for the training of teachers for the NA schools was even more profound since these schools aimed more specifically at providing education for the rural masses. Most teachers declined to serve in those rural areas. By 1936, only seven out of 18 NA schools where there were 14 trained teachers, had attained elementary grades. The rest were infant schools[137] (See table 4.2) The argument for the slow development of NA schools was that opportunity existed in Government schools for the NA school children to continue their education. However, as all six Government schools were all located in urban areas the transferring of pupils from the rural areas to urban centres contradicted the policy of adaptation. In addition; it was not convenient for pupils and parents "...owing to the paucity of elementary schools, many children had to travel a considerable distance through difficult country to attend them. The parents are not ready to

135 Tembon M.M., "The Financing of Secondary Education in Mezam Division, North West province Cameroon; An uneasy partnership between family and state." PhD London, 1994.

136 Reports to the League of Nations and Annual Reports for the respective years.

137 NAB. Ba. 1937/5., Report to the League of Nations, p.101.

allow their children to do this."[138]

Another implication of the NA school system was the antagonism that erupted between Mission schools (particularly the Catholic Mission) and traditional rulers. It is argued that: "Catholic opposition to the NA schools was given its official declaration in 1929 when the Western Cameroons (British Southern Cameroon) was being administered by Shanahan's vicariate."[139]

Catholic opposition to the NA school system was supported by Catholic Missions all over tropical Africa. The Catholic ordinaries of Nigeria and British Southern Cameroon adopted the resolution of the Nairobi Mission Education conference which regarded the growing influence of the NA schools as a betrayal of the state-Mission cooperation established by the 1925 policy. They considered the traditional elites responsible for NA schools to be rivals and obstructionists to evangelical work. These rivalries and disagreements ultimately affected educational development. More significantly, seeds of social crisis resulting in disrespect for traditional order as well as the disintegration of social setting were planted. The Government did not intervene because it was felt that the Missions should have taken the initiative to establish collaboration with the local councils in order to have access to evangelization.[140]

Another problem of the NA school system was instability. The unstable evolution of the NA schools can be explained by the weaknesses in some of the appointed leaders who in some places were forced onto the communities. This generated resistance to education policies and created tensions in the society, which was not healthy for educational development. The tension was inherited by the post-colonial Government and contributed to the early disappearance of the NA school system.[141]

Table 4.2: Government and N.A. teaching staff.

Year	Certified Government Teachers	Uncertified Government Teachers	Certified N.A. School Teachers	Uncertified N.A. School Teachers	Total
1923	8	25	-	14	47

138 ibid.

139 Omenka N.I., *The School in the service of Evangelisation, the Catholic Education impact in Eastern Nigeria 1886-1950*, Leiden, 1989, p.231.

140 Perham M., *Native administration in Nigeria*, London, Oxford University Press, 1937, p.284.

141 In 1962 all N.A. Schools were converted into Government schools by a presidential decree.

Year	Certified Government Teachers	Uncertified Government Teachers	Certified N.A. School Teachers	Uncertified N.A. School Teachers	Total
1924	16	19	-	N/A	N/A
1925	18	29	3	27	77
1926	21	28	3	27	79
1927	21	29	N/A	N/A	N/A
1928	28	23	N/A	N/A	N/A
1929	32	12	5	43	92
1930	36	15	5	31	87
1931	40	12	5	28	85
1932	36	11	5	28	80
1933	34	10	7	23	74
1934	37	14	13	18	82
1935	38	14	14	14	80
1936	38	13	14	20	85
1937	42	12	20	21	95
1938	44	18	20	28	110

Sources: Compiled from annual reports and reports to the League of Nations.

The dearth of trained teachers also affected the development of schools, because the policy for granting aid to private schools insisted on the availability of at least one trained teacher. But there was only one training school, with limited places for Mission teachers. By 1927, there were only three assisted schools out of 258 private schools and by 1937 there were just 15 schools out of 227 private schools receiving Government assistance. (See table 4.3.)

Table 4.3: Schools, enrolments and Government assistance.

Total	Total No of Schools	Aided Mission Schools	All aided Schools	Grants in £	Boys Enrol-ment	Girls Enrol-ment	Total Enrolment
1925	133	1	18	-	6.250	355	6.505
1926	150	5	13	184	6.439	537	6.976
1927	274	3	13	169	6.724	863	7.587
1928	216	3	20	472	6.910	877	7.787
1929	219	3	20	360	6.977	921	7.898
1930	220	3	18	360	7.249	879	8.128

Total	Total No of Schools	Aided Mission Schools	All aided Schools	Grants in £	Boys Enrolment	Girls Enrolment	Total Enrolment
1931	195	3	19	700	N/A	N/A	N/A
1932	156	15	19	1.600	6.150	910	7.060
1933	158	14	20	1.224	6.340	936	7.276
1934	162	14	20	1.152	6.610	1.149	7.759
1935	190	15	18	1.775	7.093	1.196	8.289
1936	234	15	23	1.775	8.957	1.179	10.136
1937	252	14	24	2.360	9.989	1.490	11.179
1938	251	16	N/A	2.310	9.211	1.510	10.721
1943	327	16	366	6.020	15.400	2.093	17.493
1944	354	22	332	8.361	18.011	2.470	20.481

Sources: Annual reports and Mission Reports.

The Government was not unaware of these problems. The Director of Education, E.J.R. Hussey, with the assistance of the four European staff- Messrs. W.B. Stimson, W. Plant, G.R. Oake and E.A. Cadle embarked on a series of reforms to adapt the policy. Hussey's reforms of 1931 reconsidered the Government's role in controlling education. State-Mission relations were re-examined. The teaching profession, school structures and school administration were reorganised.[142]

The policy on teacher's registration was amended and the criteria for registration based on age and good character rather than on qualification. The duration and structure of teacher training was extended from one to two Years. The reform limited the village school to two years, then two years of infant school, four years of elementary schooling and two year of senior primary schooling. Thus full primary education was, reduced from nine to eight years. In 1933, Camerooni-ans were appointed into the local advisory board of education. This marked the beginning of Cameroonian induction into British educational administration.

In 1935, the Advisory Committee on Education in the Colonies issued a memorandum on mass education.[143] It emphasized the educational significance of the inter-relation of all the factors in community life. This was in recognition

---

142 Hussey E.R.J., "Education policy and political Development in Africa," in *Journal of African Affairs.*, op. cit. Also see NAB. Ba 1931/1 and NAB. Ba 1932/1., Annual Reports.

143 Colonial Office., Memorandum on the Education of African Communities. (Colonial No. 103) London, 1935.

of the intimate connection between educational policy and economic life, and the need for a close collaboration between the different agencies responsible for public health, agriculture and school.

There was also a steady increase in grants to private schools from 1932 (See table 4.2). McCowan, the new director after Hussey, also showed interest when in 1937, he promised members of the Cameroon Welfare Union that he was going to post three highly qualified and experienced teachers from Yaba College to help in the training of teachers in Cameroon.[144] He also promised the opening of a secondary school. In 1939 the secondary school, St, Joseph's College, Sasse, was opened by the Roman Catholic Mission with Government assistance. Thus despite the impact of the World Economic Crisis, school provision and enrolment improved remarkably. (See tables 4.3 and 4.4).

Table 4.4 Development of schools

Year	Government Schools	N.A Schools	Mission Assisted	Mission Unassisted	Total
1922	7	10	-	-	17
1923	6	12	-	4	22
1924	6	12	-	36	54
1925	6	10	-	117	133
1926	6	10	5	255	150
1927	6	14	3	255	278
1928	6	12	3	193	214
1929	6	13	3	198	220
1930	6	13	3	198	220
1931	6	13	15	161	195
1932	6	14	12	124	156
1933	6	13	14	124	157
1934	6	18	14	132	170
1935	6	18	15	151	190
1936	6	18	15	195	234
1937	6	19	15	212	252
1938	6	19	16	220	251

Sources: Annual Reports, Inspection Reports and Reports to the League of Nations.

144 NAI CS0.16/40435., Education in Cameroon Province.

These were the educational developments before the Second World War. Despite the limited scope of educational provision, the schooling system introduced attractive British cultural elements that the pupils imbibed. For instance, musical drill in some of the schools became very fashionable while English football was reported everywhere to be popular. The Resident watched with amazement a concert and play acting of English drama by the staff and pupils of Government school Kumba. After the show he remarked:

> ...it came as a revelation to me. I had no idea that these children could undertake so ambitious a play and perform it so well....The home made stage and costumes were most effective. All enjoyed it hugely and seemed to wish the play continued on indefinitely.[145]

These attractions urged many people to seek a literary education and reject the agricultural curriculum which was the basis of the adaptationist policy. The pupils and their parents could not compromise education with manual labour because they were farmers without education and they did not want their children to become farmers after acquiring education.

During the inter-war period, the admission of Germany into the League of Nations had implications on British rule that affected education. It guaranteed the return of German business people and Missionaries who repossessed their properties.[146] They had huge plantations and factories in the territory employing over 25,000 people. The rise of a totalitarian Government in Germany awakened revisionist claims for German lost colonies. Various German societies federated 1933 to form the *Reichskolonialbund* in favour of the return of the German colonies.[147] The leading propagandist in the territory was Luppe who headed the local *Landesgruppe* of the Nazi party until his internment in Lagos 1939.[148] They instigated a pro-German sentiment, and assured Cameroonians of a better future under German rule.

The great number of Germans (300) as against the British (90) nationals in

---

145 NAB Ba.1925/5., Report to the League of Nations, 1925.p. 48.

146 The Mandate order of 1922 had excluded all nonmembers of the League from entering and transacting business in mandated territories. See appendix 4, p. 267.

147 Henderson W.O. *Studies in German Colonial History*, London, 1962 p. 120. Also see Lakowski "The Second World War" in Stoeker H., German imperialism in Africa: From the beginning until the Second World War., London., Hurst and Company, 1986. pp. 379-418.

148 Epale S.J., *Plantations and Development in Western Cameroon, 1885-1975: A Study in Agrarian Capitalism*, New York, 1985. p. 116.

the territory was threatening to the British regime.[149] All the Missionary societies had German nationals, varying from seven in the Mill Hill Mission to over 60 in the Basel Mission (including their families) while the German Baptist Mission was essentially made up of Germans. Resident F.H. Ruxton had stated in 1925 that even though the Germans were numerically superior to the British, the regime was competent to deal with any eventuality.[150] But towards the beginning of the Second World War, the regime regretted having allowed so many Germans into the territory.

Their influence was much more felt than that of the ruling regime.[151] Following the *Anschluss* of March 1938 between Germany and Austria, the fragility of British rule in Cameroon became even more delicate. The Germans residing in Cameroon retorted by hoisting the German flag in Victoria and indicating their preparedness to regain the colony.[152] The impact on education was incredible as pupils, teachers and parents puzzled about the future of the territory. The idea of a reunification of the former German Cameroon was also born, an aspiration which eventually materialized at independence and may be considered the bedrock of the post-colonial reform impasse.

Education during the Second World War and Trusteeship era

The war marked a turning point in British imperial, policies.[153] It threatened the collapse of the empire and weakened British control over the colonies. The need to adjust postwar colonial policies to regain the confidence of the dependencies and adapt to the new realities of world politics became crucial. Nothing in 1945 could be quite the same as in 1939 in a range of subjects coming under the general rubric of British colonial policy.[154] Opposition to colonialism by the U.S.A and Russian Governments also had a significant impact.[155]The military breakdown

149 NAB, Ba. S2/1938., p, 93.

150 PRO.CS026/15844., Recognition of ex-enemy Missionaries admission to Cameroon.

151 Le Vine V.T, *The Cameroons from Mandate to Independence*, UCLA, 1964, p,38.

152 NAB. Ba. 82/1938., p.3. of 10 May 1938., Dispatch by Resident to the Chief Secretary of the Colony in Lagos.

153 Whitehead C., "The impact of the Second World War on Education in British Colonial Empire" in Lowe R, (ed) *Education and the Second World War*. London, Palmer Press, 1992, p.151.

154 Killingray D, and Rathborne R, (eds), *Africa and the Second World War*, London, Macmillan, 1986).p.1

155 Ngoh. V. J. *Constitutional Developments in Southern Cameroons 1946-1961*.Yaoundé, CEPER., 1990.p.42

in South-East Asia gave Britain a profound shock. British imperial policy was henceforth marked by a series of efforts to come to terms with the changes as their implications were perceived combined with a British determination to maintain world power influence except where the pressures were irresistible.[156]

In Nigeria (including Cameroon) the Richard's constitution of 1946 set the pace for other post-war policy reforms to follow.[157] There was an administrative re-structuring of Nigeria into three regions; in the East with the capital at Enugu, in the North with the capital at Kaduna and in the West with the capital at Ibadan while Lagos remained the Federal capital. British Southern Cameroon fell under the Eastern Region and was sub divided into Bamenda and Cameroons provinces. The Federal Board of Education and the Director of Education were at the Federal headquarters in Lagos while deputy directors of education were in the regional capitals. Southern Cameroon educational problems fell under the supervision of the Deputy Director and Regional Board of Education at Enugu. A Provincial Board and a Chief Education Officer were established at Buea for the two provinces[158] while each of the two provinces had an Education Officer.

Although the new structure aimed at decentralizing decision making, Regional Boards still referred their problems to Lagos for final decision. It was not until the Macpherson's Constitutional change of 1951 that power was extended to the Regional Assemblies. Thus matters affecting British Cameroon's education were referred to Enugu. From 1954 the territory gained a quasi-regional status and the Provincial Board of Education received some autonomy but continued to refer their problems to Lagos. In 1958 they gained full regional status. This was the political and administrative structure in which education evolved during the postwar period.

The first post-war education policy was developed in 1947 and became law in 1949.[159] Following subsequent constitutional changes, the policy was revised in 1952 and in 1954. The Government objective in the policy was defined as

> ... not merely the training of the intelligence or the acquisition of the means of livelihood but the raising of the general level of the life of the whole people and the provision of adequate facilities for their

156 Darwin, J. *Britain and Decolonisation: The retreat from Empire in the post-war world.* London, 1988, p. 333.

157 NALCSO., Richard's Constitution of January 1946.

158 Southern Cameroon became two provinces: Bamenda Province and Cameroons Province. See more in chapter nine.

159 NAI.FRI/B. Col.262., see Sessional Paper no. 20 of 1947.

development, physically and spiritually.[160]

From the report, the aim was "to bring a basic primary education within the reach of every child and make such a provision for secondary and higher education and post-primary vocational training to educate for the economic and social development of the country." The failure to achieve this goal in the mandate period had been blamed on the lack of economic development, geographical remoteness and poor communications. Measures were taken to overcome some of these impediments. For example, in 1947 the road linking the two provinces was opened.

The broadened scope of the educational programme provided by the policy, reflected its objectives. Education was not confined to schooling but re-emphasized its adaptation to rural life, the extension of teacher training, the development of secondary education, the encouragement of female education and literacy amongst adults and work with women in villages and compounds.

The school system was restructured to provide eight years of primary education, six years of secondary school, two and three years of teacher training. The scope of the curriculum began with a Nursery section which taught good physical habits and how to be socially cooperative. No precise curriculum was prescribed at this level but the teaching of storytelling, games, simple handwork and activities suitable for the age were suggested. This was followed by the Infant section which taught numbers, writing, speech training, dictation and conversation in the vernacular or simple English as well as nature study, hygiene, religious knowledge, physical education, drawing, colour work and singing. In the Junior Primary (standard I and II) speech-training, dictation, oral composition in vernacular (where one was approved) and English (reading; writing, written composition), arithmetic, religious knowledge, handicraft, music, drawing and colouring were taught: finally the Senior Primary: (standard III to VI) had to teach oral and written composition, reading and grammar in English and any approved African language (where there was one), writing, arithmetic, religious knowledge, rural science, domestic science and needle work (particularly for girls), history and civics (citizenship), geography, drawing and colouring, handicrafts, physical training and organized games, singing and music.

The curriculum of Teacher Training Colleges reflected school subject content in addition to some secondary school subjects. While in training the teachers had external examinations in English Language, Arithmetic, Principles and Methods of Education organised from the regional headquarters. Practical teaching was also assessed by a team from the headquarters and oral English was tested.

160 Report to the United Nations General Assembly for 1948, p. 97.

Practical and theoretical Rural Science; Physical Education and preparation of teaching aids together with real classroom teaching were also tested. The internal examination curriculum comprised history, geography, English literature, Religious Knowledge and for some students, further work in Mathematics, Rural Science and Handwork.

The secondary school curriculum was guided by British overseas school certificate examinations boards (especially the Universities of London and Cambridge External Examination Boards). The subjects were; English language, English Literature, Mathematics, Natural Sciences (Biology, Chemistry and physics), Agriculture, West African Language (usually Hausa, Yoruba and Ibo with none from Cameroon) classics (Latin and sometimes Greek) and modern foreign languages (French, German, Spanish), History (British, European, British Empire and Commonwealth) Geography (with stress on Physical Geography), Handicrafts, Mechanical Drawing, Religious Knowledge, Physical Training and organised Games, Arts, Music and Domestic Science subjects.

The role of the voluntary agencies, particularly the Missions, as an educational force was strengthened. New conditions for granting financial aid to private schools included the local community's share. School fees were instituted. Primary schools were classified into *junior* (four-year course) and *senior* (four-year course) sections and Government aid varied according to these levels. The amount of grant payable to primary schools consisted of the recognised expenses of running the school less the assumed local contribution which was based on varying figures multiplied by 35 in the case of urban schools and by 25 for rural schools.[161] This was in essence the structure of education in the post-war period.

From the curricula for all the different levels of schooling described above, including Teacher Training Colleges, it is evident that apart from a few subjects (local languages where they existed, African history and geography taught from books written from Euro-centric perceptions), the rest of the educational content and practices together with the implied philosophies and ideologies remained alien to African frameworks of reference and tradition. It may be argued that Africans asked for this pattern of educational[162] but there is no doubt that the new socio-economic order introduced by colonialism motivated the demand. Besides the search for certificates to enhance social mobility, there was an inevitable psychological factor urged by Cameroonians' determination to attain equality and share in the socio-economic and political status which the British colonizers

---

161 Report to the United Nations :1948-49 Supplement to the laws a Nigeria, Lagos,1952, p.216.

162 Foster, P., *Education and Social Change in Ghana*, Chicago, Routledge and Kegan Paul., 1965.

and Nigerian civil servants were enjoying.

Government Provision of Schools

The Government continued to provide only the five primary schools started during the mandate period. These were located at the divisional capitals of Bamenda, Buea, Kumba, Mamfe and Victoria. The NA schools increased from 27 in 1946 to 35 at independence.[163] There were no Government secondary schools. The Government Teachers Training College opened since the mandate period was upgraded in 1944 to train higher elementary teachers for all agencies. The Government further supported the Missions to open and run their own teacher training institutions. In 1952, the Government opened a trade Centre in Ombe for the training of skilled tradesmen and artisans who were supposed to acquire "sound practical training with the allied theory but with emphasis on apprenticeship rather than studentship".[164] Courses were taught in motor mechanics, electricity, carpentry and joinery, bricklaying, and welding.

Mission Provision of schools

Government assistance to Missions resulted in faster expansion in the development of Mission primary schools as shown on table 4.5.

Table 4.5: Postwar development of schools

Year	Gov't & N.A	Mission Unast.	Mission Ast.	Total
1946	33	159	36	228
1947	33	159	36	228
1948	34	174	35	243
1949	32	86	141	259
1950	32	83	148	263
1951	30	84	152	266
1952	31	93	161	285
1953	37	112	170	319
1954	30	116	173	319
1955	28	133	196	357
1956	31	149	205	385

163 Report to the United Nations,1948-1959. See table 4.5. At reunification, N.A. schools became Council Schools and subsequently became public or Government schools.

164 Report to the United Nations General Assembly, 1955 p. 171.

Year	Gov't & N.A	Mission Unast.	Mission Ast.	Total
1957	31	141	222	394
1958	31	116	302	449
1959	35	94	298	427
1960	35	-	-	-
1961	35	-	-	499

Sources: Compiled from reports to the United Nations.

The total number of Mission schools was nearly doubled from 228 in 1946 to 427 in 1959. The number of pupils enrolled increased from 25,174 in 1947 to 64,076 in 1959 within which were 16,833 pupils in unassisted schools in 1946 and 49,012 in 1959 as shown on the next table. The fluctuations in number and enrolment in the unassisted schools indicated continued expansion and attempts to meet Government required standards. From 1953 to 1959 female enrolment grew from 6,769 to 15,834 while male enrolment increased from 27,189 to 48,242.

Table 4.6: Trained teachers

Year	Gov't. & N. A		Mission Assisted		Mission Unassisted		Total
	Male	Female	Male	Female	Male	Female	
1948	268	22	243	62	488	8	1.091
1949	248	35	504	52	243	12	1.094
1950	175	36	597	71	226	1	1.106
1951	158	32	670	70	128	2	1.060
1952	241	97	761	93	140	3	1.335
1953	174	38	709	132	145	4	1.202
1954	172	38	1.142	171	31	6	1.560
1955	169	33	894	168	239	8	1.511
1956	193	48	950	163	289	15	1.658
1957	213	55	1.085	156	320	19	1.848
1958	86	24	1.477	162	157	24	1.720
1959	129	19	-	-	-	-	1.930

Sources: Compiled from reports to the United Nations

Teacher Training

Government support enabled the Basel Mission and the Catholic Mission to establish teacher training colleges in 1944 at Nyasoso and Muyuka respectively. The Njinikom school was finally established at Bambui in 1947 while that of Nyasoso was transferred first to Bali (1946) and finally to Batibo in 1949. The Catholic Mission also opened the first female teacher training institution in Kumba in 1949. The Baptist Mission opened a training Centre at Great Soppo in 1954. It was temporarily in Belo but was brought back to the permanent site in Great Soppo. In 1955, the Catholic Mission started one college in Muyuka which moved to Bojongo and another in Bambui which was transferred to Tatum in 1957. These institutions helped to improve the number of trained teachers as indicated in table 4.7.

Secondary Education:

Secondary education was provided only by the Missions but with a strong support and encouragement from the Government. After the first secondary school was opened at Sasse by the Catholic Mission in 1939, the Basel Mission opened one in Bali in 1949. The Catholic Mission opened the first girls' secondary school in Okoyong-Mamfe in 1956. These were the three secondary schools until the eve of independence in January 1961 when the Catholic Mission opened another boys' school in Bamenda, Sacred Heart College.

Figure 6: St. Joseph's College, Sasse started in 1939

Figure 7: Cameroon Protestant College, Bali started in 1949

Figure 8: Queen of Rosary College, Okoyong started in 1956

The Missions' contribution to the development of education was therefore quite significant, but the importance of an increasing Government financing (table 4.7) must not be ignored. The rapid expansion during the trusteeship era may be explained by the regular visits of the United Nations Trusteeship Commission and their reports on the postwar education development from 1949.

Inherent in British policies were also weaknesses that rendered colonial education vulnerable. The neglect of female education had serious disadvantages for educational development in Cameroon as in Britain. By 1935, only one girl had successfully completed primary schooling. It is possible that an earlier emphasis on the education of girls could have enhanced a wider acceptance of education. However, schools were often far away from most homes and involved long daily trekking distances and sometimes required accommodation near the schools. Parents found the risks involved unacceptable for their daughters.[165] Also, since colonial education aimed primarily at educating those who on graduation would be employed in the colonial services the targeted population were boys.

Female education did constitute part of the principal concern of Cameroon elites that resulted in the appointment of Dr. Phyllis Kaberry to investigate the status and functions of women in the territory. This was followed by the appointment of a Woman Education Officer. The establishment of a Teachers Training institution and a secondary school for girls gradually motivated many parents.

Table 4:7: Expenditure and Enrolments.

Year	Expenditure (£)	Primary School Enrolment	Secondary School Enrolment
1947	42.943	25.174	151
1948	62.039	25.810	160
1949	117.000	26.331	239
1950	149.000	28.860	267
1951	181.000	29.790	322
1952	190.000	30.240	330
1953	202.000	34.345	394
1954	244.055	33.850	426
1955	256.000	44.600	450
1956	274.000	46.800	468
1957	330.000	50.600	460
1958	338.000	54.900	513
1959	380.000	64.000	571
1960	418.475	73.000	660
1961	502.170	86.257	780

Sources: Annual Reports. Reports to the Trusteeship Council for the respective years. Estimate of the Southern Cameroons, 1960-61, 1961-62, p.21.

165 Interview with S.N. Njinimbam and Z.N. Memoh, in August 1993.

There was also a neglect of the less able or handicapped children. No policy was developed to cater for children presenting special social, physical, mental or psychological needs, nor did the teacher training curricula provide training skills towards these needs.

Through grants the Government kindled inter-denominational rivalry that sowed seeds of discord which are still traceable. The freedom accorded to Missions to educate and evangelize at will and the competition to gain adherence as fast as possible led to conflicts between the Missionary societies which affected their followers. Some zones were declared exclusive areas for particular denominations. Sectarian dissent, sometimes of serious magnitude was noticed between Protestants and Catholics. These rivalries affected education since children could only attend schools provided by their denomination,

This chapter began by arguing that although the British colonial education policies were adaptationist and peripheral, and depended on voluntary agencies for its provisions, it might have been strong enough to influence the attitudes of Cameroonians. A study of the NA school system and Government collaboration with missionary societies, reveal the development of common education educational cultures characterized by communal collaboration and local initiatives. The policy favoured decentralization of education and therefore gave power to local authorities and church leaders to manage education. Attempts by post-colonial regime to seize the power through reforms aimed at centralization under Government control are inevitably resisted.

The Mission schools imbued their pupils with common Christian virtues which are ignored by the post-colonial reforms. Since Mission education was dominant and was received by almost all those who are parents today, the tendency is for these people to regard their period of schooling as "the good old days" and to resist any change that disregard particularly the moral content. The contemporary Church leaders who replaced the missionaries would inevitably oppose any reform that disregards religious education and introduces strong central control as it has been proposed.

In conclusion, it is evident that although the British education policies were peripheral, the circumstances of their development and the strategy applied, had deep rooted impact on Cameroonians. The development of local initiatives for school provision and the liberal latitude towards Missions, contrasted with the centralized state controlled French system (see chapter three). The implications of these differences for post-independence reforms cannot be under-rated.

The next chapter examines the development of education under independent re-unified Cameroon regime. The main thrust is on the difficulties faced by the new government to redress the inherited problems and harmonize the educational legacies bequeathed by the French and the British regimes.

CHAPTER FIVE

CAMEROON EDUCATION DURING EARLY INDEPENDENCE PERIOD

Independence in Cameroon, as in many other African nations, marked an important turning point in the history of education. Africans felt for the first time that they could determine the form of education that suited them. Earlier attempts had been restricted by the colonial masters. The decolonization period in Africa had been characterized by ceaseless attacks on the inadequacies and the irrelevance of colonial education for African development. Christian Missions and colonial Governments had been blamed for providing education that neither integrated the individual in the society nor enhanced development. As discussed in chapter one; critics saw colonial education as the underpinning factor in the slow rate of African development. Colonial education systems in particular, were accused for being used by capitalists to exploit the underdeveloped world and subjugate their peoples[166] whilst Missionaries were accused of being the lackeys of imperialism.

These attacks were consistent with the accusations levied against Colonial rule by the new African leaders at independence. These leaders considered colonial education to have separated the recipients from their society through the teaching of Christian European civilization.[167] They maintained that where colonial and Mission education prepared the individual for life it was life outside the mainstream of the African society, life as a servant of the colonial Government, European firm or Mission.[168] Nyerere particularly blamed colonial education for being elitist, designed to meet the interests and needs of a very small proportion of those who entered the school system. The 1961 Addis Ababa Conference

166 Watson, K., (ed) *Education in the Third World.*, Croom Helen., London, 1982,

167 Ukwu, I U., "Education for Self-reliance and National Development"- *Education for Self- Reliance*, Enugu, 1989.

168 Nyerere J.K., *Education for Self-Reliance*, Government Press, Dar es Salaam, 1967, p. 22.

questioned the relevance of the inherited colonial education for African development. It was proposed that African education should produce men and women interested in technological development.[169]

These criticisms led to reforms or what became known as the *Africanisation* of education.[170] Some nations changed their school curricula and teaching/learning material. In Cameroon, these concerns were widespread in both the French and the British trusteeship territories during decolonization. There was anxiety, hope and expectations that a unique Cameroon education system would be established from a Cameroonian perspective. But to what extent did the reforms differ from the colonial systems? What was the influence of the inherited policies? What were the post-1961 influences of the two colonial powers and what influence did the Missions continue to exert?

This chapter examines the attempts made by independent Cameroon Government to *Africanise* and unify the two inherited educational systems following the re-unification. The objective is to find out the impact of the two legacies on reforms. The scenarios at both the national and regional levels are discussed to show the impact of internalized colonial attitudes and the continued influence of former metropolis through financial assistance and supply of expatriates. The continued impact of Mission education on the reforms is also discussed. A brief introduction to the new political setting is important to place educational problems in perspective.

Independence / Reunification and Education

On 1st January 1960, French Cameroon became independent. On 1st October 1961, British Cameroon was also granted independence. British Northern Cameroon became integrated in Nigeria while British Southern Cameroon re-unified with the former French Cameroon to form a federation. The former French Cameroon became the Federated State of East Cameroon, and the former British Southern Cameroon became the Federated State of West Cameroon.[171] At this stage, two major aspects of educational reforms became evident. The first was to *Africanise* each of the two inherited systems and the second was to unify

---

169 O.A.U. "Outline of a plan for educational development: Conference of African States on the development of education in Africa", Addis Ababa, 15-25 May 1961.

170 Afari-Gyan, K., "Nkrumah's Ideology" in Arhin, K., (ed.) *The Life and Works of Kwame Nkrumah*, African World Press, New Jersey, 1993. p.164. For more on Africanisation, see Mwereria, G.K., *Re-Africanisation of Knowledge; The roots of the African politics of education*, Kenyatta University Press, Nairobi, 1987.

171 Government of Southern Cameroon., Fact Sheet of the Southern Cameroons, Government Press, Buea, 1961, p. 1.

both systems. But on the accession to independence, East Cameroon had signed bilateral treaties with France for economics, military and cultural cooperation.[172] Whilst Britain ceased to have any direct relations with West Cameroon except through the Federal Government.[173] These relationships signalled the pattern of future support and influence of the metropolis.

Disagreement during the constitutional conference on the structure of institutions in the new Federation focused on centralization or regionalization and indicated the difficulties of unifying the inherited systems.[174] Education in East Cameroon had been maintained at independence under the Ministry of Education, Youth and Culture in a centralized structure as inherited from the French colonial administration. Meanwhile, West Cameroon had fought and gained the cherished decentralized education system by achieving regional status in the Nigerian federation.

However, the 1961 Constitution partially resolved the problem by establishing a Secretariat of Education in each of the Federated States, to be responsible for primary education while the Federal Ministry of National Education, Youth and Culture at the national capital became responsible for all post-primary education in the nation, Although the Constitution specified the levels and types of education falling within the competence of the Federal authorities and the regional Governments, the limits of the regional Governments remained unresolved and the West Cameroon Government seemed determined for decentralization. This disagreement was manifested in the reforms they carried out respectively and underpin the present stalemate.

The Federal Ministry of Education, Youth and Culture

The decree of 12 March 1962 established the Federal Ministry of National Education, Youth and Culture. The structure and attributions of the ministry remained the same as it was inherited from the colonial administration. There was no innovation to reflect the new political reality of the nation. The internal service of the ministry was structured into departments, *directions*, headed by directors. The department of administration was responsible for all matters of personnel, accounts and equipment related to secondary, technical and higher education and the administration of the examination board. The department of

---

172 PRO, CO 554/1745., Movement for unification of Cameroon under trusteeships of United Kingdom and France.

173 PRO.CO 554/1661., Report on the Separation of Southern Cameroons from Nigeria.

174 PRO.CO/1662., Terms for unification of Southern Cameroons with East Cameroons. Also see Ngoh, V.J., *Constitutional Developments in Southern Cameroons 1946–1961.*, CEPER., Yaoundé, 1990., chapter one.

higher education was responsible for coordinating and applying Government policy on higher education with particular attention to the development of university education. The departments of secondary and technical education were responsible for the administration of all public and private institutions of those levels. Meanwhile, the department of youth and sports coordinated and applied Government policy on youth and sport, culture and mass education (literacy).

The Bureau of Educational Research and Curricula[175] was responsible for curriculum development, teaching methods *(Pedagogy)* and evaluation and the educational and administrative inspection of secondary education. It was also responsible for bilingualism and the coordination of the curricula in the two states of the Federation. It produced the lists of school textbooks recommended by ministerial circular for all schools in East Cameroon. The Bureau had inspectors (none of whom was Cameroonian until 1976) for French, English, mathematics and physics, natural sciences, history and geography.[176] Until 1976 teachers were inspected by inspectors from France (under a bilateral co-operation and technical assistance agreement).

The Minister appointed an officer, "the cultural delegate", to represent him over all matters relating to secondary education, technical education, youth, sports, mass education, and after-school and out-of school centres in West Cameroon with a resident in Buea. These delegates represented the Minister in their respective regions on all post-primary education while each of the Federated states had the "Secretariat for Education" for primary education. Although the functions of the Federal Ministry were apparently different from those of the Secretariat of State at the regional level, there were overlaps which led to confrontations.

The ministry controlled all private schools including Mission schools. They received instructions from the Minister and the award of grants depended on reports of inspections by Government inspectors. All the Protestant Missions were represented at the Board of private education by one representative while the Catholic Mission also had one representative. Ministerial authorization was required for any new school. This required teachers to have certain minimal qualifications. As discussed in chapters three and four, private education was very significant in Cameroon at independence (60 per cent of the primary and 45 per cent of secondary schools in East Cameroon and 95 per cent of primary and 100 per cent of secondary education in West Cameroon). Thus the new measures were

---

175 This is the office that is represented today by L' Inspection Générale de Pédagogie, which is responsible for all curricula development and assessment and the training and retraining of teachers.

176 The major problem posed at this level was for the French inspectors to inspect schools in the Anglophone zone which had a different educational system.

bound to affect particularly the Mission schools in West Cameroon where an appreciable measure of autonomy had been allowed during the colonial period.

The Federal Government also took measures to unify the two educational systems. Law No. 63/COE/13 of 19 June 1963 organized secondary and technical education; and law No. 64/CE/11 of 26 June 1964 specifically reformed private secondary and technical education.[177] Secondary schools were reformed to have two levels comprising a junior section of five years and a senior section of two years. Secondary schooling in East Cameroon had therefore to change from a four years secondary education where students could be educated in the two systems junior section and three years senior section to five years and two years respectively as in West Cameroon. The *Probatoire* examination taken in the sixth year of secondary education was dropped.

To experiment with the possibility of a bilingual system of secondary education where students could be educated in the two systems concurrently, a bilingual secondary school was proposed to start with effect from 1963 with 35 students from each of the two states. Teachers appointed to this school came from France, Britain, Canada and Cameroon to ensure absolute bilingualism.

Higher education had been introduced by the colonial Government in East Cameroon in 1959 with the establishment of the Cameroon School of Administration. This was followed in 1960 by the National School of Agriculture. In 1961, France and UNESCO helped in the establishment of Higher Teacher Training Institute (ENS). The Federal University was established in July 1962. With the assistance of *Fondation Française* the courses of the Faculty of Law and Economics leading up to the *licence en droit, licence en science économiques* and, *certificat de capacité en droit* started on 16 June 1962, while the degrees conferred by the Faculty of Arts and Humanities started on 8 October 1962.

Therefore, France made valuable contributions in kind and cash to enhance a successful beginning of the university. The administrative hierarchy of the university and its institutions were headed until 1975 by French expatriates.[178] The different faculties and institutions were linked to French universities and institutions of higher education. But, until the creation of the department of English Language in the Faculty of Arts and Humanities (1968), and the department of English Law in the Faculty of Law and Economics, the courses and assessment systems were all based on French precedents. Yet as a meeting point of two cultures, the university was undoubtedly seen to occupy a unique national position.

This structure gave the ministry central control over education in the entire nation. The French influence remained dominant until the appointment of

177 UNESCO., World Survey of Education, UNESCO Publications., Paris, 1971: p. 257.

178 Jean Wilbert (Rector, 1971-1975) was the last French expert to head the university.

Cameroonian directors and inspectors. Their presence and contributions during the move to reform ultimately contributed in sustaining the inherited French colonial education system.

Meanwhile, the British intervened only when invited by the Federal Government. For instance the British Council in Cameroon was requested to organise English Language courses at the Linguistic Centre and also to supply teachers for the English Department at the university. Eventually they trained Cameroonian teachers to replace the British expatriates. They also supplied British Volunteers to serve as sciences and English Language teachers in secondary schools.[179] These interventions also served to rekindle interests in the British inherited system.

This was the situation of the educational development as a result of the reforms by the Federal Ministry of Education. It was a reflection of the inherited French system. Inevitably, the overlaps of ministerial prerogatives over regional control were bound to create tensions between the Federal Government and the West Cameroon Government and differences in the perceptions of the two groups on the issue of reform were unavoidable. Furthermore, reforms by the respective regional Governments were bound to strengthen the disagreements and reduce the hope of unifying the two systems.

Reform attempts in East Cameroon

Primary education including the training of teachers for primary schools was left to the Governments of the Federated states and placed in each region under a Secretary of State for Education. The decree of 7 June 1962 organized the Secretariat of State for Education. Each of the Secretariat of State had inspectors of schools.

Reforms in East Cameroon, although part of Federal reforms, were a continuity of reforms started during decolonisation in preparation for independence. Priority was given to mass education at the primary level where the stated aim of primary education was to give the child the necessary knowledge required for everyday use and for "modern civilisation" while avoiding the separation of such an individual from traditional society. Implied in this objective was the French understanding of "civilisation" as contained in mission civilisatrice? Civilisation in this context stood for "modernity" which meant everything European and a disregard for all traditional cultures.

To attain mass education, the East Cameroon Government's objective was to establish schools in all localities so that every child could have access to primary education. Large classes were to be reduced and the plan was that more teachers were to be trained or retrained. This was not successfully achieved.

179 Information from Manley, who was responsible for the Volunteer Service.

Another important objective was to confront the delay in developing female education. This goal was considered urgent because the évolués felt that the inequality in male-female education did not reflect "modernity". Consequently, there were plans to build specialized schools for girls and to add Home Economic sections to teacher training schools so as to increase the number of female teachers. It was also proposed that the girls leaving school at the end of primary education should be assisted in the process of integrating themselves in their communities, in order that they could motivate others and also become the agents of change in their societies.

The most important and urgent task was that of expanding education in the northern region which had been neglected throughout the colonial period. Most of the schools in the north had remained only at the stage of "bush schools" until 1956 when the primary sections were progressively introduced.[180] There was need to accelerate the change. But the major problem was the lack of educated people (particularly teachers) from the region. Another problem was that of the settlement pattern. Most of the villages were sparsely populated and widely dispersed. Consequently, the reforms could only be effective if boarding, schools were established to bring the pupils together.

It is important to mention the significant role of the Pitoa pilot boarding school near Garoua. The aim of this school was to recruit and train the future leaders of the region. The boarding facilities gave opportunities for children from remote villages to attend school. An attempt to blend the cultural diversity of these pupils through living together could have resolved part of the social problems of the region. But this was never fully addressed. The establishment of a teacher training course in the same site should have given the opportunity for the teacher trainers to use the local resources to adapt the training to the realities of the region. The student-teachers received general and professional education and had the opportunities of having their practical teaching not only on the campus but in some of the village schools.

In spite of attempts to make education more relevant to the environment, the French language and French culture dominated the Pitoa scheme. There was a disagreement between the Muslims and non-Muslims which pre-dated the colonial period. The Muslims were considered invaders who had seized the land of the original inhabitants. These Muslims, who were mostly Fulbe of Semitic origin, considered themselves overlords to be served by the conquered non-Muslims. This had been the practice since the conquest of Fombina during the raids of

180 NAY.AR., *Journal Officiel* of 1956.

the central Sudan and the establishment of Othman Dan Fodio's Empire.[181] The colonial regime had neglected the problem and the post-colonial Government reform failed to redress it. However, the school administration and training core were French and had to maintain the same colonial policy.

If the Pitoa scheme had considered this historical disagreement and made attempts to introduce a balance between the rival factions, the reform would have solved a major social problem. Instead, the school recruited mostly Muslims of the Fulbe background to the disadvantage of the indigenous tribes. As such, the Fulbes dominated the new elite role. Therefore, it can be said that the educational reform in the northern region perpetrated the division between the Muslims and the non-Muslims which colonial rule left unsolved.

The Pitoa scheme also failed to solve the problem of female education in the region. Both traditional practices and the Muslim religion restricted the freedom of women and female education remains a cause for concern until today.[182]

Primary school duration in East Cameroon was maintained at six years. At the end of which the pupils sat for the *Certificat d' Etudes Primaires Elémentaires* (CEPE). The age limit for schooling in primary schools ranged from six years of age to sixteen years. Children of six to ten years were accepted in the initial class *(section d 'initiation au langage)*. Those from seven to eleven were accepted in the preparatory class *(section préparatoire)*, those for the elementary class *(Cours élémentaire)* were from eight to thirteen years of age while those for the senior primary *(Cours Moyen)* were between ten and sixteen years. It was also officially stated that all instruction had to remain in the French language.

The school curriculum as reformed since 1956 was maintained, reflecting former metropolitan system although some aspects of the History and Geography of Cameroon were incorporated. The syllabus on Hygiene included studies on tropical diseases and the rules of hygiene which could cultivate the prevention of such diseases. The syllabus on observational sciences paid attention to the fauna and the flora of the locality. The civics instruction subject was supposed to introduce the children to an understanding of the political structure of the nation and provide them with basic notions of economics. They were also supposed to know, about the importance of international organizations such as the United Nations Organisation (UNO).

There were no qualified teachers to implement the changes. Nor were there in-service training for the new orientations. The Government had also to depend

---

181 Njeuma, M.Z., Fulani Hegemony in Yola, (Old Adamawa) /869-1912, CEPER., Yaoundé 1978.

182 Brok C, and Cammish N.K., Factors affecting Female Education in Developing Countries, O.D.A. Occasional Papers on Education., 1991. pp.38-47.

on France to provide teacher trainers and supply the necessary finances. This combined with the persistent departure of teachers leaving to take up other careers to create a Problem. The solution was to revise teachers' salaries. The civil service salary scale was used to upgrade Government teachers and also to award them "inducement allowance." Elementary teachers and assistant primary teachers were classified in the same category as skilled and highly skilled workers. Meanwhile, primary and secondary teachers were classified as technicians, while primary inspectors, secondary teachers holding degrees or the *agrégation* were classified in the Managerial and upper managerial grade.

This led to a rapid increase in the number of people opting for the teaching profession and expansion in training colleges. Between 1966 and 1971, the shortage of elementary teachers and assistant primary, teachers could be regarded as negligible if *moniteurs* (untrained but experienced teachers) were considered. However, for the same period, the shortage of primary and secondary teachers, 18 per cent was to be met by French teachers supplied through technical cooperation. At the level of higher education with *agrégation,* the shortage for the same period was reckoned at 27 per cent of the strength planned in East Cameroon. These gaps had to be filled by foreign teachers ultimately from France.

Primary inspectors and inspectors for mass education, youth and sports were trained in France and at the Secondary Teacher-training College in Yaoundé by French teacher trainers supplied under technical aid. Those recruited had the *baccalauréat* and five years teaching experience. They were given a specialized training for two years after which they sat for a qualifying examination. *(Certificat d'Aptitude aux fonctions d'Inspecteur de l'enseignement Primaire,* CAIP). Besides inspecting teachers, the inspectors were also responsible for the administration of primary education at divisional levels where their presence further spread the French influence.

These reforms combined with rapid school growth to stimulate expansion in schools as shown on table 5.1. From 246,223 pupils in primary schools in 1956 and 377,089 at independence in 1960, there were 602,463 pupils in schools by 1966[183] in East Cameroon. At the level of secondary schools, enrolment grew from 6,100 in 1956 to 8,688 at independence and by 1966 that number tripled to 29,059. Technical and commercial education also experienced rapid development. From 5,667 students in 1962/63, there were 8,186 by 1966. The university which started with 85 students in 1962 had 1,646 by 1966/67 school year.[184] The involvement of French aid and experts maintained post-1961 colonial influence.

183 Cameroun. Economique, Paris, 1967/68.

184 Shu S.N., *Landmarks in Cameroon Education*, NOOREMAC., Limbe, 1985

Reform attempts in West Cameroon

The West Cameroon Government considered itself a full state preparing for inter-state institutional integration with East Cameroon. It also expected that the situation in Nigeria where regional Governments reformed their educational systems could be practiced in Cameroon. Therefore since the educational system practiced till independence was more related to Nigeria, the Government embarked on a more comprehensive reform and educational planning. The reforms were not limited just to the primary level as stipulated in the constitution. An education policy and planning encompassing primary, secondary and tertiary education was developed. The feeling of acquired autonomy over policy was expressed in the statement that:

> Government (West Cameroon) believes that education is an investment in human material which can reap rich dividends. No policy for education can be relevant unless it takes into account all the economic, social, political and spiritual factors of our time and circumstances.[185]

The immediate intention was to accelerate the rate of educational expansion so as to attain universal primary education in West Cameroon by 1970. But this depended on the regular supply of trained teachers and the availability of school structures. The existing schools could not accommodate all the children of school age. Consequently, plans were proposed for opening more schools and expand the existing ones.

Following the law No.63/COR/5 of 1963 the time spent at primary schooling in West Cameroon dropped from eight to seven years in 1964 and was supposed to drop further to six years by 1965 so as to have the same level as East Cameroon. The Main objective here was not only to implement the Federal law but to create room for mass education. It was estimated that primary school enrolment had to increase from 95,000 in 1962 to 120,000 by 1964 and to 150,000 by 1966 if the target of universal primary education was to be attained by 1970.

Related to this growth was Government concern for female education. While the number of boys in school doubled from 35,516 in 1955 to 67,454 in 1962, that of girls had tripled from 9,050 in 1955 to 27,705 in 1962 but still lagged behind that of boys. The government was urged to establish Domestic Science Centres and vocational schools for those who did not want to follow a secondary course or become teachers. They could follow courses in cookery, needlework and general housecraft.

185 Ministry of Education and Social Welfare., West Cameroon Policy: Investment in Education, Government Press, Buea, 1963 p.1

Growth in school enrolment ultimately required extension of school buildings and their equipment. The Government was determined to assist communities and voluntary agencies to improve school buildings through grants. As evidence of this intention, the sum of ten million francs was placed on the draft estimate of 1963/64 for approval by the West Cameroon parliament.

Since the length of primary education had been reduced, a proposal was made for diversification of post-primary education to cater for vocational and general education in order to make education beneficial to the individual and the society. The Government requested UNESCO to advise on a three year junior secondary programme to be followed by two years of vocational education aimed at agriculture, technical and commercial training. The intention was to give opportunities to graduates of primary education who were gifted academically to continue in secondary schools, whilst those talented in farm work or artisan skills transferred to Farm Institutes, technical or vocational schools. In this connection, the West German Government agreed to start a Commercial school in the territory in September 1964.

On the challenging bilingual reality of the nation,[186] the policy cautioned against hasty introduction of French in schools within the region. It was suggested that the teaching of French had to be intensified at the post-primary level until such a time when the teacher training colleges could have turned out sufficient teachers proficient in French to permit the graduation and harmonious placing of French on the primary school curriculum. The West Cameroon Government and also Federal Government planned for a bilingual secondary school where students could be educated concurrently in the two systems.

The policy for secondary education aimed at making places available for all primary school children who proved able to benefit by further academic qualification. This needed an urgent preparation for 985 places and required at least '14 more secondary schools by 1965. This required more support to the Missions to open the schools. Secondary school examination was to change from the West African School Certificate Examination Board to London University General Certificate of Education (G.C.E.) Examination Board with effect from June 1964, because of the inhospitable atmosphere caused by the separation of West Cameroon from Nigeria. The subjects prescribed by the examining board dominated the curriculum and destroyed the hope of Africanisation and thus consolidated British educational pattern.

Unlike the East Cameroon Government; Mission education was held in high esteem in West Cameroon. This may be explained by the fact that all members of

---

186 Article 1 of the Constitution made English and French the official languages, see appendix 6.

the Government were educated by Missions. But more importantly; it might be explained by the inherited tradition from the British. Hence, the policy strongly supported a continuation of the type of collaboration that existed between the Missions and the colonial Government.[187] The policy stated that

> Government appreciates the fundamental influencing of sound religious training in the formation of character and it is our intention to see that religious instruction takes its rightful place in the curriculum of schools.[188]

This contrasted with the Federal Government's view on Mission education. However, the policy also supported the creation of non-Christian schools but maintained religious instruction in the Government schools of West Cameroon. It is worthy to note that religious instruction was not offered on the official, curriculum under the French and the Federal Government. Even now, certificates in religious knowledge are not accepted by the Government. On the contrary, the West Cameroon Government was determined to sustain the collaboration system with religious organizations started during the colonial period.

The reform also recognized the importance of technical education. There was only one inherited trade or apprenticeship school at Ombe which was up-graded and expanded into a technical college to enable the production of competent technicians and give opportunities for the talented graduates to further their education abroad. Meanwhile the development of technical/commercial schools, by enterprising Cameroonians which started timidly during the decolonization period, started to expand and the Government decided to encourage them through the award of subventions.

Teacher training was inevitably linked to the proposed scheme for expansion in primary education with the aim of providing 100 percent trained teachers in all the schools to cope with universal primary education in 1970. This required the urgent establishment of more training colleges and the expansion of existing ones so as to increase the number of trained teachers from 360 Grade III and 180 Grade II per annum to 600 Grade III and 300, Grade II annually. This would require the establishment of four more Grade III and Grade II colleges by the Missions and at least one Government teachers training Centre capable of an extension to provide a Grade I course

A proposal was made to start a teacher training programme of one continuous

187 Ministry of Education and Social Welfare, Education policy for West Cameroon Buea, Government Press., 1963

188 Ibid.

course of five years for Grade II teachers to provide a better theoretical background based on a secondary general education programme for the first three years and followed by two years focused on pedagogical training and practice, Furthermore, the policy proposed a combined Grade II and Grade I certificate course which previously had been obtained only from Nigeria or from the United Kingdom.

A request was also made to UNESCO for advice on a training scheme for teachers for the junior classes of the secondary school while maintaining that the upper classes could only be taught by university graduates. Meanwhile the policy envisaged a diversification of the curriculum of the Cameroon College of Arts and Science on the lines of the model in Nigeria to train teachers for junior secondary schools.

The policy proposed the expansion of Cameroon College of Arts and Science to include Technology. It was hoped that it could become a decentralized college of the Federal university, offering intermediate courses. An appeal was made to the U.S. Government for assistance towards this goal, considered crucial in the development of the required manpower.

The impact of these reforms on educational expansion was tremendous as shown in the table 5.1. The number of training institution increased to 12 by 1964 and to 14 by 1966. The number of student teachers enrolled in these institutions also increased from 396 in 1961 to 1,379 in 1966.

The expansion in primary schools had a direct effect on the Secondary and Technical education sector during the period. From three boys' secondary schools and one for girls in 1961, the number increased to 16 by 1966 and enrolment rose from 780 students in 1961 to 3,388 by 1966/67 as shown in table 5.1. The number of technical/ commercial colleges also increased from just one in 1961 to 16 by 1972 and the enrolment increased from 1,401 in 1962 to 3,400 by 1966/67.

Table 5.1: Enrolments (1960-166)

Year	Primary Schools		Secondary Schools		Technical Schools	
	West	East	West	East	West	East
1960	73.400	377.089	660	8.688	-	-
1961	86.200	330.393	780	10.840	-	-
1962	95.200	427.129	1.401	18.403	1.401	5.667
1963	160.100	489.808	1.658	19.173	1.658	6.104
1964	116.900	551.880	2.481	21.974	2.481	6.387
1965	124.300	576.416	3.008	25.767	3.008	7.328
1966	152.300	602.463	3.388	29.059	3.400	8.186

Sources: *Cameroun Economique 1968/69: Annual Statistical Report of West Cameroon*

1965/66-1966/67.

The demand for manpower to replace the departing colonialists was the motivating force behind the reform. Sydney Phillipson's report had indicated in 1959 that only 50 per cent of the colonial civil service was Cameroonians.[189] The departure of expatriates in 1961 created 410 vacancies at the administrative and technical levels of the public service. The implication of the dearth of qualified staff had immediate consequences for education. Starting from the Prime Minister, J N Foncha, a former Mission headmaster, the cabinet was dominated by former teachers. Since teachers were the most qualified people at the time, the tendency was for the Government to pull out many of the experienced teachers from their classrooms to fill the empty posts in the administration. Furthermore in the absence of adequate number of secondary school leavers many primary school leavers were employed to fill the lower ranks as clerical officers. This sustained the old notion that literary education was good because of the availability of employment opportunities. Consequently, any reforms proposing changes on the literary pattern is resisted.

The policies hardly reformed education because both states focused only on the situation in the respective territories without considering the wider implications of the union. Neither a specific policy was formulated to address the important issue of national unity through education nor was there a policy in respect of the content of the syllabuses. All the reforms failed to consider the education of children with special needs which never figured on the agenda of the colonial regimes. There was no planning for the development of teaching/learning resource materials. Thus education had to continue to depend on foreign assistance for the production of teaching aids.

The idea of setting up a bilingual school in Buea embracing the cultures of the Francophones and the Anglophones could have created a nucleus for national integration and thus contribute enormously to the socio-cultural understanding of the nature of national integration and the pattern of education. But the policy did not provide any mechanisms to motivate those who became interested. Consequently, the students tended to revert and re-focus on their original educational systems. Thus the school and subsequent ones have failed to fulfil the objectives of developing strategies for harmonising the two systems. They have all become two schools representing the two systems in the same campus.

The rush to train manpower accounts significantly for the inadequacies of

---

189 Phillipson S., Financial, Economic and Administrative consequences to Southern Cameroons of separation from the Federation of Nigeria, Federal Government Press, Lagos, 1959, p. l. Also see, PRO.00 554/1661., Report on Separation of Southern Cameroon from Nigeria.

the reforms. The pressure to open many schools and enrol more pupils without provision for funding encouraged the Government to depend on foreign aid: All proposals for change sought for the assistance of France, Britain, West Germany or UNESCO. West Cameroon's separation from Nigeria marked the end of financing from the Colonial Development Fund and the Commonwealth trade preference.[190] This placed the economy of the territory in a limbo at the beginning of independence[191] and obliged the leaders to depend on the Federal Government to negotiate for foreign aid. It cannot be denied that foreign-aid programmes of many industrialized nations foster interdependence. Thus, by appealing for their assistance, the policy was openly declaring its continued dependence on the industrialized world and accepting their influence.

Seeking foreign aid implicitly committed the educational system to foreign influence because as it has been argued, "foreign aid, particularly intellectual assistance, cannot be separated from the policy goals of the donor country or for that matter from the policies and orientations of the recipient nations' Government."[192]

Post-independence relations with France and French speaking' countries further widened the gap between the two systems and forestalled the reforms. The influence of France in all educational institutions in East Cameroon after independence and the assistance in expatriates and educational materials perpetuated their influence. Their policy against Mission education was upheld by the Federal Government and contradicted with the West Cameroon policy. Whereas reforms in West Cameroon were implemented by the Missions, those in East Cameroon were by the Government. Hence, while the Missions were gaining more influence in West Cameroon, those in East Cameroon were marginalized. As such the Missions in West Cameroon hesitated to support reforms that will hinder their educational efforts,

Relations with Francophone African countries have also affected reforms in Cameroon. After the 1963 law introducing a uniform structure of schooling in Cameroon, the Federal Minister of Education participated at an all-African French speaking ministers of Education conference in Dakar, Senegal in 1966 during which curriculum reforms for all French speaking African States were

---

190 PRO.FO 371/161618., Agreement to keep West Cameroon in Commonwealth Preference Area.

191 Booth, B. F., "A Comparative Study of Mission and Government Involvement in Educational Development in West Cameroon, 1922-1969". PHD, UCLA, 1973, p.273.

192 Altbach, P. G. "The distribution of knowledge in the third world: A case study in neocolonialism" in Altbach P. G. (ed.) *Education and the colonial experience.* Transaction Books, New Brunswick, 1984. P.273

adopted.[193]The structure disagreed with the 1963 law.[194] The Dakar structure was implemented in East Cameroon in defiance of the decision taken by the Higher Council of Education following a meeting presided by the Vice President of the Federal Republic. The meeting had resolved that all foreign names of school certificates (G.C.E., B.A.C., etc.) had to be dropped and replaced by Certificate of General Education (C.G.E.).

West Cameroon started implementing the 1963 law by reducing primary education from eight to seven years in 1964, with the intention of dropping to six years by 1966. But the adoption of the Dakar reform[195] indicated East Cameroon unwillingness to implement the law. Henceforth, the West Cameroon Government stopped the implementation. This accounts partly for Anglophone resistance since then and explains why they have a seven-year primary course.

The dilemma of educational reform in Cameroon seems to be a general problem in most African countries. However, some degree of success has been achieved, where some socio-economic or political forces have been placed in motion. For instance, in Ghana, the expansion in educational provision was in part the outcome of the economic policy which had been planned to cope with educational expansion.[196] The Ideological Institute of Nkrumah provided a strategy which enabled the state to prepare the minds of the citizens for the outcome. The Government of Ghana was in dialogue with the people to encourage their participation in the effort to improve upon their standard of living through education. The inclusion of a large number of artisans and tradesmen on scholarships to study abroad raised hopes in the policies and encouraged acceptance of the change that Nkrumah introduced even though it was not very different from the colonial package.[197]

However, the eventual failure of the Ghanaian experience can be attributed to the economic programme which did not expand fast and far enough to absorb the growing number of graduates. Other factors including political instability and world economic order account for the failure. However, with an academic

---

193 Ministère de l'Education Nationale., *Programmes de l'enseignement général.*, édition 1982/83., CEPER, Yaoundé, 1982.

194 Law No.63/COR/5 of 3 July 1963., op. cit.

195 See curent copy by Ministère de l'Education Nationale., Programmes de l'Enseignement General., Edition 1982-83., CEPER, Yaoundé, 1982.

196 Arhim K., op. cit. pp. 53-79.

197 Ibid., p. 63. In 1952, Nkrumah sent 107 artisans and tradesmen to the UK for further training. This motivated other people to develop interest in apprenticeship education.

hindsight, some Ghanaians have argued that Nkrumah's reforms were not mere rhetoric because many people gained from it.

Neither the preparation of the people's minds nor the incentive in apprenticeship education ever occurred in Cameroon. The cultural diversity and the split in colonial allegiance (British and French) combined with economic and political forces to make it difficult for the policies to succeed. The State bureaucracy which employed graduates and stimulated the demand for higher education, contributed to the problems that prevail now.

Similar to the Ghanaian reform, was that of Tanzania where Nyerere introduced education for self-reliance.[198] The theoretical implication here was the suggestion that classroom work and extracurricular activities should be linked through a transformation in teaching and learning methods that emphasize experimental and actual experience. In so doing, it confronted in an integrated way many of the socio-political problems that education was creating or reinforcing in the post-colonial period.[199] Nyerere's concept of *Education for Self-Reliance* had a well-founded cultural foundation, the *Ujamaa* social setting which invokes the African extended family system. All Tanzanians were made to see themselves as members of a single family where each individual had to contribute to the general welfare of all. It involved a common indigenous language to which the people could identify.

Although Nyerere's strategy was socialist and had a striking similarity to the Marxist philosophy of education which posits that once a socialist revolution has occurred, schools must be transformed to provide knowledge of the class struggle, and the struggle for production, it is arguable that his attempts to use education for social and political ends necessarily conforms with that of Marxist-Leninists. Morrison argued that his socialism was strongly tinged with liberal humanitarianism. This is true because Tanzania remained relatively opened to foreign influence which is not the case in socialist states. Thus the approach was based more on moral grounds and was less powerful than those applied by Marxist politicians. Nyerere had a well prepared and favoured background which combined with the respect he commanded in Tanzania to gain him the support he needed to implement the policies.

Unfortunately, neither a favourable cultural philosophy nor a clearly defined conceptual framework was developed in Cameroon to re-state the education policy in relation to the general development of the nation. Although Ahmadou Ahidjo, the first president of Cameroon echoed the tone introduced by Nyerere

---

198 Nyerere J.K., op. cit. 1967.

199 Morrison D. R., *Education and Politics in Africa: The Case of Tanzania*. C. Hurst., London, 1976, p.259.

when he declared for *Development Auto-centré* (Self-Reliance Development), he neither suggested the role of education, its implementation nor did he suggest the implication of the policy for education. Rallying all political parties into a single party (Cameroon National Union) in 1966 could have afforded the opportunity of developing a common ideological base if the influences and ramifications of the inherited colonial diversity were not allowed to dominate.

The difficulty in resolving the differences between the two systems has also hindered the reforms of the individual systems. Neither of the two systems offers a curriculum that respond to national goals in content and in structure, both systems maintain the inherited colonial patterns that no longer give satisfaction even to the needs of the former metropolis.

The current world economic order that has so much affected African economies has had two significant implications for Cameroon education. Firstly, the Government can no longer fulfil the financial obligation to education as required by the inherited systems. Consequently, the financing policy should be reformed. Secondly, pressure from the World Bank and International Monetary Fund to downsize the civil service has affected the teachers who in the majority are civil servants.

This chapter has shown that post-colonial education reform in Cameroon has remained at a standstill. The inherited colonial education systems left by the French and the British have not changed. Hindsight reveals that reforms since independence have been geared towards improved access to education rather than to the relevance of education to the new socio-economic and political demands of the new nation. Teachers, pupils and parents became increasingly used to the type of education and attempts to change are resisted. Thus the greatest achievement of the post-colonial Government has been the expansion of schooling leading to the attainment of a high rate of literacy. The unresolved disagreement on the structure of state institutions (central or regional) has also delayed the harmonisation of the two systems and given room for more people to become permeated by the inherited systems. Following improvements in the economy and expansion in the civil service at independence, certificates guaranteed socio-economic and political mobility, which many people attributed to the success of the education system. Consequently, post-colonial education has failed to fulfil the dreams at decolonization.

CONCLUSION

This book illuminates a historical view of those factors that have caused the current stalemate in attempts to reform education to include African values. The question that this research addressed is why Cameroonians resist educational reforms and remain interested in the inherited colonial systems? It is clear to note that Cameroon's unique colonial experience and post-colonial ramifications are responsible for the deadlock. It is certain to note that the resistance to unify the two inherited systems (British and French) and to reform each of them could not be attributed only to the colonial situation but might also be a result of Cameroonians' perceptions and attitudes to the pattern of education developed since the pre-colonial period amplified by colonial and post-colonial experiences. The predominance of Missionary education during the colonial period was also considered to have had significant impact on inter-group relationships and perceptions of education. Finally, the traditional human resistance to change is an important factor to be considered.

To explain how attitudes to education and development were acquired and how they have combined with post-colonial factors to hinder reforms, educational motives and policies of the different colonial regimes and Missions were examined. Some approaches used in analyzing colonial situations that emphasize economic, political and psychological determinism were discussed to gain insight into a similar analysis of the Cameroon situation. But in as much as they were inspiring and reveal many convincing factors that must have developed to influence attitudes during the colonial periods, the framework was found to be biased because they emphasized only the colonialists' interests and impact on the colonized. When the interests of the colonized were analyzed, they were viewed with empathy, on the assumption that the latter were always in a subordinate position and never allowed to contribute to educational development. As such, the interests of the colonized were not seen to have influenced the colonial situation. It was assumed that the links established between education and the rest of society was predetermined by the interests of the metropolis while the colonized were the silent oppressed. The role of the colonized in determining the development of the colonial situation was therefore ignored.

It is therefore considered important that for effective and acceptable reform, there will be need to reflect on precolonial African educational systems and examine African motives for Western education before, during and after colonial rule so as to discern how attitudes to education were derived and sustained. While accepting economic, political and psychological determinism as an important basis for understanding the colonial situation, this research suggests that such an analysis can only be useful if a balance is maintained by also analyzing the traditional values of the colonized. This conforms with the strategies and orientations proposed by Altbach (1971) for analyzing post-colonial problems but further stress the importance of the economic and political factors.

Whereas earlier studies were based on single situations that evolved common traditions less than one colonial regime, the present study is unique because of the varying traditions that were developed under three colonial regimes and a wide range of Christian Missionary cultures.

By examining the respective colonial and Mission education policies it is possible to assess the impact generated by the respective policies on Cameroonians. The Government's relations with the Missions and Cameroonians in educational development were also analyzed to understand the nature of tensions or partnership/connivance in the development of education. By examining the reactions of the Cameroonians, a better understanding of the development of attitudes to education was derived.

The study found that initially, all the colonial regimes had a common interest in education. They wanted to provide education just for the few who were required for services within the European framework. The nature of the services determined the pattern of education. These activities required more literary and humanistic education and less vocational and technical skills.

This explains why literary education prevailed over all forms of education. But literary education was also the predominant system of education in the metropolis. Consequently, the policy of transplantation or assimilation in education could not be blamed for shortsightedness at the time because literary education was regarded as a universal panacea for social, moral and economic ills. Europeans could only offer what they knew and practised. Besides, the authorities found it justifiable to transplant their educational system which because of the perceived moral content was considered beneficial to Africans. But by so doing, the cultural patterns of traditional societies were implicitly destroyed, largely because many of their essential features prevented traditional people from subordinating social and spiritual imperatives to the short-term economic ends served by participation in the colonial economy. In addition, the employment of educated Africans into the European service enhanced the socioeconomic status of the individual and therefore encouraged all others to seek the same type of education. As such all proposed alternatives for adaptation were looked upon with skepticism.

After the Second World War, the emphasis was on widening the scope of primary education and introducing secondary schooling, particularly because of the pressures mounted by the educated elites since the 1930s and during the war. The curricula of secondary education were transferred from the metropolis and the final examinations were conducted from there. Thus, the structure, curriculum, content, and evaluation maintained the same standard with schools in the metropolis.

Cameroonians who graduated from these secondary schools gained respectable positions and became opinion leaders of their people. Hence the premium placed on book learning and the neglect of any other type of education weaned Cameroonians from their traditional education. Parity in the certificate with the European masters implied that they could eventually replace the Europeans and this led many to involve themselves in the decolonization politics. As representatives of Cameroonians, their contributions to education during self-government were guided by their acquired experiences. Therefore any blame on the colonial regimes for introducing literary education must take cognizance of Cameroonians' contributions to its establishment and sustenance.

This study also found that the colonial policies especially under France and Britain were adapted from policies developed for other dependencies. Yet for any meaningful educational achievement, any curriculum developed specifically for Cameroon, ought to have considered the multicultural setting. The ethnic diversity, varying from the pygmies and Bantus of the coastal forest through the semi-Bantus and the Sudanic peoples of the savannah to the Semitic and Hamitic groups in the Sahelien belt of the extreme north offer a wide range of cultural variations, world views, systems of traditional education and languages that could provide such knowledge-based values that could be extracted and incorporated in the educational system. Moreover, whereas the French set out a direct system of implementation, the British relied on an indirect approach. Both policies failed to share the view that education should aim at ensuring the cultural continuation of the people and transmit knowledge, skills and values from the elders to the young through the school.

The study also identified a similarity in the pattern of geographical distribution of colonial schooling under the respective regimes. Education was largely provided in the coastal region that corresponded with the area with intensive European activities involving Missionary work, European plantation exploitation and a range of commercial activities. The northern region inhabited predominantly by Muslims, hardly received European (Missionary, business people and colonialists) attention. In quantitative terms therefore, there were striking differences in levels of educational diffusion between Muslim and non-Muslim areas.

These variations could further be explained by political and economic reasons. The colonial Governments profited in Muslim areas from the centralized and highly hierarchical political structures to limit expenditure on extensive administration by establishing indirect rule. This could not be obtainable in the acephalous societies of the coastal region. Additionally, access to the Muslim region was difficult because of the mountainous landscape of the territory. But more importantly, the Muslim area lacked the economic attraction that was central to European interest, and did not offer the Missionaries the opportunity to evangelize. Therefore, economic interests and administrative ease combined with evangelical interest to determine the location, rate and scope of educational diffusion.

Besides the similarities that characterized colonial education, there were specific characteristics that distinguished the impact of the colonial regimes on schooling. Education under the imperial German Government was provided predominantly by the Missions with Government support. The German policy emphasized the importance of Western civilization, the dignity of work, respect and reverence for the German Kaiser and his representatives. The respect and loyalty assigned to the German Kaiser and his representatives imposed the superiority of the Germans over local dignitaries. Since educated Cameroonians were subsequently recognised in their new working status as assistants to the German authorities, the presumption was that their education had elevated them into power, and so was derived the notion that education is synonymous to power. This explains why some of the teachers abandoned classrooms in pursuit of political careers at decolonization.

In addition, the respect given to the imperial Government inevitably re-enforced the notion that European culture and institutions were superior and could better replace the local culture. This was further strengthened by the Missions whose educational views associated education with the learning of those things which the Missionaries deemed important in their perceptions of the good, pious and economically productive life.

It was also shown that actual direct German education policy was brief (1910 -1914) and the scope of education was very limited because only about two per cent of the school age population was at school at the eve of the war. Thus German colonial influence on Cameroonian attitudes was inconsequential although the cultural input by the Missions was significant because it fortified Cameroonian perceptions and attitudes. This argument is further supported by the efforts made in sustaining education during the war period by some enthusiasts. Cameroonian speculation for a better and more prosperous post-war period was apparently the motivating factor for the educational activities that were undertaken during the non-Missionary period (1916-1925) because if the efforts of those Cameroonians were purely for religious reasons, then they could have avoided the social conflicts that involved them with their traditional leaders.

This study also found that French colonial education policy was different from that of the Germans and the British and had more profound impact on Cameroonians. From the beginning the French Government vigorously insisted on the diffusion of the French language and culture through education. Emphasis

127

was on French culture, educational certificates and diplomas. These certificates qualified the individual for French citizenship. French was made the only medium of school instruction. The use of French ultimately implied the use of metropolitan educational materials. The French language became the unifying factor for the educated elites and this class of people became identified with proficiency in French and was jealously looked upon by the younger generation as the ultimate goal in education. Therefore the youngsters see reforms as attempts by the elders to stop them from attaining this goal.

French interest for Cameroonian assistants also led to the development of a more literary education, although primary education was combined with agricultural and practical schooling in the period before the Second World War. This was a great deviation from metropolitan curricula and precipitated Cameroonian protests. The establishment of *Ecoles Rurales* and *Ecole Primaire Superieure de Yaounde* with practical curricula based on manual labour and vocational training, which adjusted education to administratively determine political and economic framework contradicted the principle of assimilation which the education system promised. Protest led to the changes that re-established a more literary curriculum. Meanwhile the metropolitan practice of integrating education with economic activities led to the elaboration of secondary vocational training in the post-war era. This was favourably received by Africans because it maintained parity with the metropolitan school system.

To achieve the policy of diffusing French language and culture the regime distinguished itself from the others by operating many direct state schools. At the eve of independence the French Government provided direct state education to 46.18 per cent of the overall total enrolment in all the schools as against less than five per cent by the British and two per cent by the Germans. Therefore, direct French impact was much more deep-seated and widespread. This direct involvement had a deeper inculcation of French culture on those who went through the schooling system.

In addition, the French Government collaborated at the very beginning with the Missions but after establishing a firm hold on the territory, a central control was established over all schools (including Mission schools). The centralized structure and strict state control which was said to avoid disruptions in Mission schools were but a replication of metropolitan practice aimed at consolidating firm Government control following the divorce between the state and the church in France in 1905. The post-colonial Government found it necessary to maintain the system to check against the excesses of education on the regime. This practice contrasts sharply with that of the British.

It was found that the British colonial education policy was peripheral, without any specific interest in Cameroon. British interest focused on Nigeria and as such, involvement in Cameroon was for the convenience of the administration of Nigeria. Cameroon was treated as a province of Nigeria. British educational policies in Cameroon were therefore policies developed for Nigeria. But even in Nigeria, the structure, standards and curricula were fragmented until 1926, since all those who were providing education (mostly Missionary societies) had autonomy in taking decisions. The establishment of the Nigerian educational ordinance of 1926 required many adjustments for effective implementation although Government control remained limited. Rather, a community spirit (through Education Committees) was introduced that contrasted with the centralized Government control under the French regime.

The British policy again introduced local initiatives by encouraging the participation of local business corporations in the management and financing of education as well as in the training of labour in the territory. Therefore companies like the Cameroon Development Corporation (C.D.C.), Elders and Fyffes, United African Company (U.A.C.) and Southern Cameroon Development Agency were involved either by operating their own schools or in awarding scholarships. British strategy might have been considered one of aloofness aimed at minimizing expenditure but it left Cameroonians with a cherished attitude of involvement in their educational matters compared with the French system that imposed strict state control. These opposing attitudes conflicted in the post-colonial era to produce the current educational deadlock.

The British regime also introduced the Native Authority school system that helped to involve Cameroonians in the provision, and the management of schools; an experience that has become invaluable in the post-colonial era for solving school problems. Even more significantly, the regime delegated education almost entirely to the Missions. Throughout the colonial rule, there were only five Government primary schools, one teacher training institution and one technical college. The freedom accorded to the respective Missions to educate and evangelise at will differed from the French system. By involving the entire community to support the Mission schools alongside the local Christians the British regime further strengthened communal cooperation between Christians and non-Christians in matters of education: This further explains the development of the collaborative attitude that is currently manifested in the efforts of the Parent Teachers Associations and contrast with the French system.

The 1926 Nigerian ordinance prescribed an educational system that was adaptationist and avoided book learning. This encouraged the establishment of infant schooling, It was also reinforced by the 1935 memorandum on mass education. But Cameroonian educated elites protested against this pattern of education and opted not just for mass education but also for more literary education involving secondary schooling. Post-war education improved on the pattern as many more full primary schools were opened to replace the vernacular and infant schools. Secondary education was introduced but it was almost wholly metropolitan in theory and practice.

This study found that the Missions in general and the Basel Mission, in particular, were actively involved in the provision of education under all the colonial regimes but that Government/Mission relations in education, varied with the regimes. The differences could be explained by the state-church relations in the respective countries. However the differences between the French and British treatment of the Missions left noticeable differences in the attitudes of their educated subjects that remain visible in post-colonial period.

The relationships between the Missions and the respective regimes also influenced the behaviour and perceptions of their adherents. For example, Government tolerance and encouragement of Mission predominance in education under the British regime conditioned most Anglophones to believe that the best education can only be obtained from a church related school. On the contrary, the emphasis on state schools 'under the French regime led Francophones to believe that education other than in a *Lycée* was incomplete. The inhibiting role of these contradictory opinions on the establishment of an agreed common education system for all Cameroonians cannot be underestimated.

It was also noted that Missionary societies served as stabilizers in the relations between Cameroonian societies and the colonial Governments especially under the Germans and the British regimes. At certain times Missionaries acted as the defenders and even as representatives of the people against Government oppression and urged the Government to amend or change unpopular policies. At other times, they intervened to encourage the achievement of Government policies especially in education. That moderating influence no longer exist because, under the present circumstance the local churches that replaced the Missions are not allowed to intervene on policy issues.

The general involvement of Cameroon rulers in particular, with the request for schools also suggest the possibility that they found in education, a means to consolidate power. Evidence can be found in the Fons of Bali and Bamum who did not hesitate to enroll themselves and their children as pupils of the first schools in their kingdoms. They also realized the value of having enlightened people in their kingdoms and this is shown by their active participation in the establishment of the first schools and in the recruitment of pupils from near and far.

Cameroonians also reacted against the adaptationist policies of all the colonial regimes. These reactions were intended to manifest their own understanding of education. They demonstrated their desires in two ways. Firstly, that they wanted parity with the educational system in the metropolis. Secondly, they wanted more schools so that many more people could be educated. These interests were not adequately addressed by the missionaries and the colonial administrators.

Finally, it was found that after gaining autonomy, solutions to the problem of having more schools and increasing enrolment were applied. Although the independent Government seem finally to have understood the need for reforming or *Africanizing* education, resistance persisted because of the derived attitudes. One of the questions asked by students and parents has always been to know if the reformed standard will be accepted by London/Paris and if the certificates will have international recognition. This is an indication that the desire for parity in educational standard with the former metropolis is still upheld.

Yet changes consistent with those in the former metropolis are also resisted. It is therefore also plausible to argue that the resistance to reform is intrinsically identified with the traditional conservatism associated with humans' general unwillingness to change. Ultimately, reform is more about people than about policies, institutions and processes. And since most people tend to change slowly when it comes to attitudes, beliefs and ways of doing things, teachers, students and parents are skeptical about any changes and rely on their acquired views and experiences. Any attempt to change such views must be accompanied by clearly stated alternatives to which they are also committed. This explains the resistance to reforms better than the notion that resistance is because of continuous dependence on former metropolitan systems.

This study also noted that the over centralization and direct Government control of education has rendered post-colonial educational restructuring more, bureaucratic and excluded grass-root consultation. Those involved in planning reforms are only the inspectors and "policy makers" in the central administration. Occasionally, a few members of the provincial services are informed of the reform processes but hardly are their opinions considered. Teachers and parents are not consulted. Nor are there any efforts to educate the public about the need for change. Thus school reforms imposed from above on teachers and parents cannot escape protest. If teachers are not convinced of the merit of the proposed changes, they are unlikely to implement them energetically. If they are not sufficiently prepared to introduce new control and Ways of teaching, the reform measures will inevitably founder. This is one major reason accounting for the failure of reforms.

But although teachers and parents are central to school reforms, all other educational experts responsible for writing textbooks, developing curriculum, and sensible testing policies should also be co-opted. The support of community leaders and business people should be considered necessary to reinforce parents convictions about the proposed alternatives. In other words, educational reform must be seen as a shared responsibility, which means that the entire nation must be educated to see the need for change. These measures have never been undertaken in Cameroon.

Another weakness in the Cameroon reform approach has been identified by this study to be the piecemeal approach taken to bring change. Quick fixes rarely succeed in education. Attempts in the past to reform secondary or primary education in isolation without considering them as components of one educational system proved less demanding but less related in terms of the continuity of the curricula. For example, the IPAR project which aimed at reforming the primary school curriculum failed to consider the need for change in teacher training. Similarly, the American Support to Primary Schools project was concerned with the retraining of teachers but did not consider the curricula that were already fragmented, outdated and overburdened. And the ODA/British Council INSET project for Anglophone Cameroon secondary school mathematics, physics and English language neither considered implications of the link with the primary curriculum nor the relations with other subjects on the curriculum. Comprehensive reform should address all aspects of the system. It must also consider the preparation of teachers, content of textbooks and other learning materials, the use of technologies, the nature of testing and the organisation of schools. However, comprehensive reform does not necessarily imply immediate total reform. It demands a careful systematic planning for a step by step action and also a careful deployment resources based on well, thought out priorities. Comprehensive reform should also consider every strand of schooling, both vocational and general.

Political, economic and cultural developments in post-independent Cameroon also contributed to the difficulties of effecting meaningful change in the educational system. At independence, many aid agencies and developed nations offered diverse financial assistance to Cameroon. Investment in education focused attention more on the expansion of schooling facilities in conformity with UNESCO advice on mass education and the peoples' understanding that education is a solution to development.

The political climate at that early stage of independence was also allowed both sectors of the Federation to develop independently. As such they evolved no common cultural concept for a common national identity. English and French languages became the liaison for the respective groups. The traditional ethnic and cultural diversities in both zones became subsumed within the cultures of these two official language groups. Thus two cultural groups developed and re-enforced common identities through the educational cultures of the respective systems. They developed distinct common values and attitudes respectively. These developments added to the acquired values derived from the colonial masters to widen the differences between the two groups. It is possible that if attempts were made to evolve a common cultural concept, such as *Ujaama* in Tanzania, whereby both the Anglophones and the Francophones could identify themselves as people of the same nation, then reforms based on that notion could have been more easily acceptable.

The post-colonial relations between Cameroon and the former colonial rulers have also impeded reforms. After independence, France particularly maintained good relationship with Cameroon and offered assistance to Cameroon education through the supply of educational experts and finance. The predominance of French experts *(corperain)* in the Ministry of Education and in all levels of Cameroon schools sustained French influence in Cameroon education. These experts were usually actively involved in elaborating the projects for reforms and, naturally their proposals reflect the French educational system. Such reforms were supported by parents of students aspiring to study in France because the Government still considered French certificates and diplomas as the measurement on which all other certificates have to be equated. Therefore post-colonial relations have strengthened French influence.

Cameroon also became a member of French speaking African states at independence and shared in the formulation of policies relating to economic and cultural developments of the francophone African region that are often Coordinated by France. Cameroon currency like that of the other members of the francophone community is tied to the French franc. Its value therefore depended on the French franc. This dependence subsumes Cameroon and the other Francophone states sharing the same currency to a common economic control. Thus, because of the relationship between education and economy, it is impossible to rule out French interests in any educational reform in Cameroon. A recent example was the devaluation of December 1993, which had enormous impact on Cameroon economy and seriously affected individual incomes as salaries were reduced by more than 50 per cent and redundancy reached a historic level. Many students had to drop out of schools because of their inability to pay school fees. Under such an economic difficulty, attempts to reform will hardly be accepted.

Furthermore, the association of Cameroon with the other Francophone African countries led to joint participation in discussions on issues of development such as education. In 1966, the conference of ministers of education in all Francophone African states held in Dakar revised the secondary school curriculum. A common school structure and syllabuses were developed for all the countries including Cameroon. Based on this new structure common textbooks and teaching materials were developed in France for the entire Francophone region. While such collaboration encouraged regional cooperation, evidently the uniqueness of Cameroon with two educational systems was ignored. The application of the curriculum in the Francophone zone of the country further perpetuated the distinction between the two linguistic groups and placed any hope of harmonising the two systems into jeopardy.

In conclusion, this study has shown that no single factor can be blamed for the current stalemate in Cameroon educational reform. Cameroonian attitudes and perceptions of education derived since pre-colonial relations with Europeans and reinforced by Missionary and colonial educational provisions have contributed significantly to the current deadlock. The several changes in colonial regimes and Missions developed varying attitudes to education and obstructed the development of a consistent education system.

The multiculturalism of Cameroon society and the wide range of ethnic diversity that failed to develop the concept of nation-state during colonial rule make it difficult for the Government to find a common ground on which education reform can be based. The peripheral system of colonial administration inhibited the possibility of developing a common ground on which the integration of national institutions can be achieved. Furthermore, the post-colonial relations of Cameroon with France in particular and with francophone African states in general, have strengthened the differences between the inherited legacies of the French and the British to render reforms difficult. The absence of a political visionary, conscious of the socio-cultural diversity, aware of the wide range of intervening factors that militate against the achievement of national unity and determined to restructure the institutions of state has exacerbated the problem of reforms. Finally, reforms have remained largely a bureaucratic monopoly and neither the masses have been educated in the desirability of reforms nor have the opinions of the grassroots been sought.

It is therefore clear that for any effective and meaningful reform to be undertaken, the Government should educate the population on the need for change. This should establish an awareness of the weaknesses of the present educational system (systems) and create a desire for a new system.

It is also argued that for an education system that will have Cameroonian values, a national education philosophy must be developed that will take cognizance of the diversity of the wide variety of Cameroon cultures. In this relation, the need for the inclusion of national languages becomes very important.

Thus an overall comprehensive reform project should be established. From the master plan different sections can then be considered for change at different times. This will allow room for evaluation of the different aspects of reforms and enhance accountability. It will also avoid the problem of repeating the reform project many times over.

Finally, while the central control that is presently in practice is good because it can enhance uniformity and equity, it is clearly advantageous to decentralize the educational system. There should be decentralization so that provincial services and local communities can be much more committed to the provision of education in their environments. This will enhance commitment and enable people to understand the need for reform in the educational system.

POSTCRIPTUM

This reprint is felt to require a postscript. For one thing, there is a close relationship between the current Anglophone crisis in Cameroon and the systems of education that was detailed in this work more than a decade ago. It is partly due to the failed attempts at reforming and adapting education to the socio-political needs of Cameroon that an avalanche of upheavals cascaded over the entire English speaking Cameroon. Although protests were begun by English speaking lawyers, it is when the English speaking teachers protested the educational marginalization of Anglophones that the formidable force of the educational sector was clearly manifested and spilled over to generalized political dissatisfaction from the Anglophones about their status and treatment in the bicultural union with Francophone Cameroon. Their grievances have been manifested in the observation of ghost towns during which economic activities are stalled and in operation no-schools since November 2016. The phenomena are expected to draw the sympathies of the international community and bring in the United Nations to arbitrate in the general terms of the union between the English and French speaking parts of Cameroon.

Narrowed to education, the sustained imposition of one of the inherited colonial educational cultures upon another in a system that was constitutionally bicultural at the onset was bound to stir up dissatisfaction at some juncture, notwithstanding the minority status of the resisting group. A nation with such a checkered history of development required that decision making be preceded by retrospection into the political evolution if disaster is to be avoided. The reunification constitution that established the Cameroon Federation in 1961 recognized the two educational cultures and sought to adapt their developments to the realities of the nation. Indeed, from 1962 reforms were initiated to merge the respective cultural trends to suit national needs. This agreed policy began to fail within less than five years because one system ignored the national demands and hooked onto neo-colonial strings that economically advantaged its earlier metropolis.

Attempts in subsequent years failed to redress the situation which was further worsened by a unilateral revision of the constitution that disrespected the equality of the two cultural legacies. Thereafter, the majority culture imposed itself overwhelmingly on the minority set. Culturally, privileged educational and professional establishments were established with the technical and financial assistance of France to train managerial cadres for posts of responsibilities. The French speaking cultural group had the advantage from the training. As such management became the monopoly of one cultural heritage. For the other cultural heritage, extra sacrifice or corrupt practices became the only means of penetrating the circle. This practice obliged many of the minority English speaking Cameroonians to flee the country to the diaspora from where they have formed poignant clusters protesting against the injustices and corruption in their fatherland. They profited from the opportunity offered by the home-based protests against the legal and educational injustices in October and November 2016, respectively.

Any upheaval could have been avoided if the two cultures were given equal attention and the graduates of both systems received equal opportunities to train. But the ties with France abrogated treaties made at independence and sustained this abrogation by other enactments after independence between France and Francophone Africa. Expatriate advisers have largely been French and political leadership has perpetually been culturally French, thus predicating a tilt towards these forces. Policy making and implementation are the exclusive prerogative of the oligarchy comprising people of a single cultural bent with only a few puppets from other ranks. To keep this going, disorder, corruption, nepotism and sectionalism takes precedence over equitable development and peaceful coexistence.

Actually, the French speaking section of the country has assumed an assimilationist tenor towards the English speaking component. It can, to a greater extent, be submitted that French Cameroon treats or perceives English Cameroon as a subject people and with the same condescending attitude that the French colonial master had exercised towards all Africans – *"peuple éclairé qui va trouver un people dans la nuit"*. In this context, with very few exceptions, political and professional ascendancy for English speakers is pegged not only to their level of francophonization but to such corollaries as their being lackeys of the political regime and collaborators in the further dehumanization of their fellow English speakers. Veritably, such English personalities snuggle themselves into positions of influence by being assimilé or évolué to francophone habits, practices and mentality. Such Anglophones, to the not so "privileged", are seen as virtual neocolonialist collaborators or even quislings. Which explains why in the raging upheavals since October 2016 to the time of writing this postscript (September 2017), social media is awash with labels of treachery and threats for them.

Whatever the case, at the very least, there is a systemic deep-rooted assumption that Anglophones do not deserve equal treatment with Francophone Cameroonians. And just as the colonial French masters had made it a song to maintain that they and their évolués and indigénât were one and indivisible through direct rule, the highly Frenchified government also considers their nationhood with those of the English speaking part of the country (whether collaborators or not) as "one and indivisible". This perception is ingrained in the highly centralized system of government which perpetrates Anglophone subjugation, subordination and unquestionable submission to the dictates of a system of ruling by decree rather than by consultation. The impact of such marginalizing and exclusivist tendencies on education persist a deep worry, while the divisive implications certainly go beyond the scope of education only.

Yet, the roots of these disheartening outcomes are in education. The development of an appropriate educational curriculum to prepare the nation for its development needs must take into account the economic, social and political evolution of all inherited traditions from the pre-western and colonial legacies in order to craft appropriate policies to foster growth. This of course, in no way blunts the crying need for holistic and accommodating national policy, with a stridently just system to ensure unity and the patriotic participation in development by all.

November 2017

SELECTED BIBLIOGRAPHY

A) Primary Sources

NAB. Ba., Annual Reports, National Archives, Buea.

Sd/1916/1., Intelligence Report on Bamenda.

Sd/1916/8., German Missionaries in Cameroon Province.

Sd/1921/6., R.C.M. A complete report for 1921.

Sd/1922/2 No.574/1922., R.C.M. Handing-over order, Article 438 of the Treaty of Versailles.

Sd/1933/5., Spheres of Influence of Missionary Societies.

Sd/1939/6 No.84/39., German Baptist Mission: Control in time of war.

National Archive, Yaounde,

NAY.AR., *Journal officiel.,* Annual Reports., Government regulations.

National Archive, Ibadan.

C.S.0.19/9 No.5397/1921., Education in Cameroons Province.

C.S.O. 26/03527., Education Policy in Southern Province.

Basel Mission in Cameroons: Correspondence with United Free Church 1920-1930.

C.S.0.26/09377 Vol. 1., Visits of teachers from Provincial Schools and Colleges to Lagos, Cameroon: and other parts of Nigeria, 1922 1927.

C.S.O.26/09767 Vol.11., Establishment of a Secondary Schools in the Cameroons Province, 1923.

C.S.0.26/44249., Cameroon Report to the League of Nations, 1944.

NALCSO., Annual Reports. NAI.FRI/B. Colonial Papers.

Public Record Office, London

CO.554/1658-1661., Report on separation of Southern Cameroons from the. Federation of Nigeria and Movement for Unification of the two Trust Territories of the Cameroons.

CO.554/1741-1745., Developments in Cameroon

FO. 371/2812., The British and French in Cameroon during the First World War.

F0.371/2818., Condominium and partition of Cameroon by Britain and France.

F0.371/42216., The Brazzaville Conference of 1944.

B.M.A.E., Basel Mission's Cameroon Archive

BMA. E-2., Letters and Reports from Cameroon until the First World War.

BMA.E-4., Correspondence during the non-Missionary years.

GA. ZSTA., German Sources.
GA2STA. EKOLA. Council of German Protestant Missions
GA.ZSTA., Missionstatistik des Apostol.
GA.ZSTA., Kaiserlichen Statistischen Amte

Printed reports

British Government report, to the League of Nations on the Cameroons under United Kingdom Administration (1923 -,1939) H.M.S.O. London.

British Government Reports to the United Nations for Cameroons under United Kingdom Trusteeship (1948 - 1959) H.M.S.O. London.

Commission on higher Education in West Afriea.,H.M.S.O:, 1945, (Cmd. 6655)

Colonial Office:, Advisory. Committee on Education in the Colonies.

Education Policy in British Tropical Africa, Cmd. 2374 of 1925.

Memorandum on the Education of African Communities, Colonial 103 of 1935.

Memorandum on Mass Education in African Society, Colonial No. 186, of 1944.

Ministere de l' Education Nationale., *Programmes de l'Enseignement General,* edition 1982-83., CEDER, Yaounde, 1982.

Ministry of Education and Social Welfare, *Education policy for West Cameroon,* Buea, Government Press., 1963.

Nigerian Ten Year Development Plan, Lagos. 1942.

Petitions from Cameroon to the U.N.T.C., Series (T/PET/) Covering 1946 61.

UNESCO *Report of the Advisory Commission for the development of Higher Education in the Federal Republic of Cameroon,* Paris, 1962.

UNESCO Statistical Yearbook., UNESCO publication, Paris, 1991, p. 1- 12.

B) Secondary Sources

Books

Ajayi J.F.A., (ed) *The Education Process and Historiography in Contemporary Africa,* UNESCO publication, Paris, 1985.

Altbach, P.G, and Kelly GP, *(eds) Education and Colonialism,* New York, Longmans, 1978.

Altbach, P.G, and Kelly GP, *(eds)Education and the Colonial Experience,* New Jersey, Transaction Books, 1984.

Arhin, K., *The Life and Works of Kwame Nkrumah,* New Jersey, African World Press., 1993.

Atogho, D. T. (ed), *Basel Mission Schools became Presbyterian Schools,* Victoria, Presbook., 1966.

Ayandele, E.A., *The Missionary Impact on Modern Nigeria 1842 -1914: A Political and Social Analysis,* London, Longmans. 1966.

Beaver; R.P., (ed), *'Christianity' and African Education: Conference papers at the University of Chicago,* Grand Rapids, William B. Berdemans Publishing Company., 1966.

Berman, E. H., (ed), *African Reactions to Missionary Education,* New York, Teachers College Press.,1975.

Bowen J.A., *History of Western Education vol. III. The Modern West, Europe and the New World,* London, Methuen., 1972.

Brok C, and Cammish N.K., *Factors affecting Female Education in Developing*

Countries, O.D.A. Occasional Papers on Education., 1991. pp.38-47.

Brown, G, and Hiskett M., (eds), *Conflicts and Harmony between Traditions and Western Education in Africa*, Conference at SOAS, University of London, George Allen & Unwin Ltd. 1973.

Brunschwig, H., *French Colonialism 1871 1914: Myths and Realities*, London. Pall Mall Press. 1966.

Bude, U., *Primary Schools, local community and Development in Africa*, Baden-Baden, Nomos Verlasgeseuschaft; 1985.

Buell, R.L, *The Native Problem in Africa*, New York, Macmillan., 1928.

Cameron J, and Dodd W.A., *Society, Schools, and Progress in Tanzania*, Oxford, Pergamon, 1970.

Carnoy O, M., *Education as Cultural Imperialism*, New York, McKaey Company., 1974.

Carson, G. and Chau Ta Ngoc., *Disparités régionales dans le développement de l'éducation*, UNESCO Publications, 1981.

Chilver, E. M., *Government* Press.;1966,

Chilver, E. M. Zintgraff's *Explorations in Bamenda, Adamawa and the Benue lands 1889-1892*, The Government Printer, 1966, Buea.

Clatworthy, E.T., *The Formulation of British Colonial Policy, 1923- 1948*, Michigan, Ann Ardor/ Malloy LithPrinting.;1971.

Coleman, IS., *Nigeria: Background to Nationalism*, Berkeley, University of California Press, 1971.

Crowder, M., *West Africa under Colonial Rule*, Evanston, North Western University Press;1968.

Courade, G. C., *L'École du Cameroun Anglophone, 1915-1975.*, Yaoundé, ONARE ST., 1977.

Darwin, J. *Britain and Decolonisation: The retreat from Empire in the post–war world, Basingstoke*, Macmillan. 1988

Debrunner, H. W., *A History of Christianity in Ghana*, Accra, Watersville Publishers., 1967.

Delancey, M.W, *Cameroon: Dependence and Independence*, London, Westview Press, 1989.

Dodd, W.A., *Education for Self-Reliance in Tanzania*, New York, Teachers College Press., 1969.

Dugast, I., *Inventaire ethnique du sud Cameroun*, Yaoundé, IFAN., 1949.

Dumont, R., *False Start in Africa.*, Translated by Phillis Nants, London, Earthscan, 1988.

Donat, R., *Das wachsende Werk: Ausbreitung der deutschen Baptisten Gemeinden durch sechzig* Jahre (1849 bis 1909

Ejiogu, A.M., and Ajeyalemi D., (eds) *Emergent Issues in Nigerian Education*, vol 1, Lagos, Joja Educational Research and Publishers 1987.

Ekechi, ER., *Missionary Enterprise and Rivalry in 1gboland*, 1857-1914, London, Frank Cass., 1972.

Epale S.J., *Plantations and Development in Western Cameroon, 1885-1975: A Study in Agrarian Capitalism*, New York, Vintage Press, 1985.

Eyongetah, T., & Brain, R., *A History of Cameroon*, London, Longman, 1974.

Fafunwa, A.B., *History of Education in Nigeria*, London, George Allen and Unwin Limited., 1974.

Fajana A., *Education in Nigeria, 1842:1939, An Historical analysis*, Ife, University of Ife Press., 1982.

Fanon F., *The Wretched of the Earth.*, translated by Constance Farrington, Paris, Harmondsworth: Penguin, 1967.

Fanon F, *Towards the African Revolution*, New York, translated by Haakan Chevalier., Monthly Review Press., 1967.

Foster, P., *Education and Social Change in Ghana*, Chicago, Routledge and Kegan Paul.,1965.

Gardinier, D E, *Cameroon: United Nations Challenge to French Policy*, London, Oxford University Press. 1963.

Gann, L.A., & Dugan, Peter., *Colonialism in Africa 1870-1960.* London, Cambridge University Press., 1969.

Glennie, R., *Joseph Jackson Fuller, An African Missionary*. London, The Carey Press., undated.

Guifford, P. & Louis WR., *(eds) Britain and Germany in Africa Imperial Rivalry and Colonial Rule*, Yale University Press, New Haven, 1967.

Goodall, N., *A history of the London Missionary Society, 1895-1945*, London, Oxford University Press., 1954.

Graham, C.K., *The History of Education in Ghana: from the earliest times to the declaration of independence*, London, Frank Cass, 1971.

Gwanfogbe M.B., and Melingui A., *Geography of Cameroon*, Basingstoke, Macmillan., 1983.

Halldén, E., *The Culture Policy of the Basel Mission in the Cameroons, 1886-1905*, Lund, University of Upsalla Press., 1968.

Hansen, J.W., and Bremback C.S., *(eds) Education and the Development of Natives*, New York, Holt, Rinehart and Winston, 1966.

Hazelwood A., *(ed)African integration and disintegration: Case studies in Economic and Political Union*, London, Oxford University Press., 1967

Henderson W.O., *Studies in German Colonial History.*, London., Frank Cass & Co Ltd. 1962

Hilliard, F.H.A., *A short history of education in British West Africa*, London, Thomas Nelson and Sons., 1957.

Holmes, B., (ed) *Education Policy and Mission Schools: Case studies from the British Empire*, London, Routledge and Kegan Paul., 1967.

Idowu, E. B., *African Traditional Religion; A Definition.* Ibadan, SCM Press., 1973.

Johnson, W.R., *The Cameroon Federation: Political integration in a fragmentary society* Princeton, Princeton University Press.; 1970.

Jones, T.J, *Education in Africa: A study of West, South and Equatorial Africa*, New York, Phelp-Stokes Fund, 1924.

Joseph, *Radical Nationalism in Cameroon: social origins of the U.P.C. rebellion.* Oxford, Oxford University Press., 1977.

Kaberry, P. M., *Women of the Grassfields: A study of the Economic Position of Women in Bamenda, British Cameroons.* London, H.M. Stationary Office. 1952.

Keller M., *The History of the Presbyterian Church in West Cameroon*, Victoria, Presbook, 1969.

Killingray, D., and Rathbone R., (eds) *Africa and the Second World War*, London, Macmillan., 1986.

Kirk-Greene, A.H.M. (ed)., *Africa in the colonial period. The transfer of power: The colonial administration in the age of decolonization*, Oxford University Press., 1979.

Kitchen H., (ed) *The Educated African: a country by country survey of educational development in Africa*, New York, 1962, Praeger.

Kofele Kale, N., (ed) *An African Experiment in Nation Building: The Bilingual Cameroon Republic since Reunification*, Boulder, Colorado, Westerview Press., 1980.

Kwast, L.E., *The Disciplining of West Cameroon; A study of Baptist Growth*, Michigan, Berdmans Publishing Company., 1971.

Leon, A., *Colonisation, enseignement et éducation: étude historique et comparative*, Paris, L'Harmattan., 1991.

Lewis, L.J., (ed), *Phelps Stokes Reports on Education in Africa*, London, Oxford University Press, 1962.

Lloyd, P.C., *Africa in Social Change: Changing traditional societies in a modern world*, London, Penguin African Library., 1972.

Le Vine VT., *The Cameroons from Mandate to Independence*, Los Angeles, University of California Press, 1964.

Lowe, R., *Education and the Second World War: studies in school and social change*, London, Falmer Press, 1992.

Lugard, F.D., *The Dual Mandate in British Tropical Africa*, London, Frank Cass and Co., 1965.

Madiba, E., Colonisation et évangélisation en Afrique: L'Héritage scolaire au Cameroun, Bern, Editions Peter Lang, 1980.

Mamadou D. and Mamood M., *(eds) Academic Freedom in Africa*, Dakar, Codesria Book Series, 1994.

Mamouni, A., *Education in Africa*, Translated by Phillis Nants, London, Maspero,1968.

Mangan J.A. (ed), *Benefits Bestowed: Education and British imperialism*, Manchester University Press, 1988.

Mannoni O, *Psychology of Colonisation.; Paris*, 1950.; translation by Prospero and Caliban, London, Mathuen, 1956,

Martin, J.Y., *L' Ecole et les sociétés traditionnelles au Cameroun septentrional*, ORSTOM, Yaounde, 1970.

Mayhew, A., *Education in the Colonial Empire*. London, Longmans and Green. 1938.

Mbala, O.R., *L' École coloniale au Cameroun: approche historico- sociologique*, Yaoundé, Imprimerie Nationale, 1986.

Mbiti, J.S., *Introduction to African Religion;* London, Heinemann Education, 1975.

Mbuagbaw, T.F., and Brain R., *A History of Cameroon*, London, Longmans., 1987.

Memmi A., *Portrait du Colonisateur et du Colonisé*, Paris, Souvenir Press.; 1974.

Migeod, F.W.H., *Through the British Cameroons*, London; Heath Cranton Limited., 1925.

Morgan, E. P., *The Administration of Change in Africa:* essays in the theory and practice of development administration in Africa, New York, Duriellen, 1974.

Morrison D.R., *Education and Politics in Africa, the case of Tanzania*, London, C. Hurst., 1976,

Murray, A.V., *The School in the Bush: A Critical Study of the Theory and Practice of Native Education in Africa*, London, Longmans and Green, 1929.

Mwereria, G K., *Re-Africanisation of Knowledge: The roots of the politics of African politics of education.*, Nairobi, Kenyatta University Press,1987.

Neil, S., *Colonialism and Christian Missions*, London, Lutterworth Press, 1966.

Ngoh, V.J., *Constitutional Developments in Southern Cameroons 1946-1961.*, Yaounde, CEPER., 1990.

Nicolson, I.F., *The Administration of Nigeria 1900-1960*, Oxford: 1969.

Njasse-Njoya, A., *De Njoya a Njimolu, Cent ans d'histoire des Bamouns*, Foumban, CEPER., 1984.

Njeuma M.Z, *Fulani Hegemony in Yola, (Old Adamawa)* 1809-1912, Yaounde, CEPER. 1978.

Njeuma M.Z., (ed) *Introduction to the History of Cameroon: Nineteenth and Twentieth Centuries*, New York, St. Martin's Press, 1989.

Njoroge R. J., and Bennards G.A., *Philosophy and Education in Africa: an introductory text for students of education*, Nairobi, Trans Africa., 1987.

Nuffield Foundation., *African Education: A study of Education Policy and Practice in British Tropical Africa*, London, Oxford University Press, 1953

Nyerere, J.K., *Education for Self-Reliance*, Dar es Salaam, Government Press. 1964.

Omenka, N.J., *The School in the Service of Evangelisation: The Catholic Education Impact in Eastern Nigeria, 1886-1950.*, Leiden, E.J. Brill., 1989.

Oldham, J.H., and Gibson B.D., *The Remaking of Man in Africa*, London, Humphy Milford., 1931.

Oliver, R., *The Missionary Factor in East Africa*, London, Longmans. 1965.

Perham, M., *Lugard; The Years of Authority, 1895- 1945*, London, Collins, 1960.

Perham, M., *Native Administration in Nigeria*, London, Oxford University Press., 1937.

Phillipson, Sir Sydney., *Financial, Economic and Administrative Consequences to the Southern Cameroons of separation from the Federation of Nigeria*, Lagos, Federal Government Press, 1959.

Porter, A.N., and Stockwell A.J., *British Imperial Policy and Decolonisation, 1938-1964*, Basingstoke, Macmillan., 1987.

Priollaud N., *La France colonisatrice*, Paris, Editions Levi-Messinger., 1983.

Read, M., *Education and Social Change in Tropical Africa*, London, University of London, Institute of Education., Thomas Nelson and Sons Limited, 1955.

Rodney, W., *How Europe underdeveloped Africa*, London, L' Ouverture Publications. 1971.

Roger-Louis, W. M., *Great Britain and Germany's lost Colonies 1914-1919, Oxford*, Clarendon Press,1980.

Rubin, N., *Cameroon: An African Federation*, London, Pall Mall, 1971.

Rudin H., *Germans in the Cameroons 1884 1914: a case study in Modern Imperialism*, Yale University Press, New Haven, 1938.

Scanlon, D.G., *(ed) Traditions of African Education*, New York, Columbia University Press., 1964.

Shu, S.N., *Landmarks in Cameroon Education*, Limbe, NOOREMAC Press. 1985.

Sieno, M., *Note on Cameroon History for Schools and Colleges.* Victoria, Presbook., 1968.

Smith, W.D., *The German Colonial Empire*, Chapel Hill, University of North Carolina Press, 1978.

Stoecker H, (ed), *German Imperialism in Africa: from the beginning until the Second*

World War; Translated by Bernd Miler, New jersey, Hurst and Company., 1986.
Tiberondowa, A.K., *Missionary teachers as agents of Colonisation,* Lusaka, National Educational Company of Zambia.1978.
Todd, L *Pidgins and Creoles,* Routledge and Kegan Paul., London, 1974.
Turner, V., (ed), *Colonialism in Africa 1870-1960,* Vol. III, Cambridge University Press, 1971.
Ukwu, I.U., Education for Self-Reliance and National Development in *Education for Self- Reliance,* Enugu, 1989.
Underhill, E. B., *Alfred Saker, Missionary to Africa,* London, The Carey Kingsgate Press, 1958.
Usman, Y. B., *The Transformation of Katsina (1400-1883): the emergence and overthrow of the Sarauta system and the establishment of the emirate,* Sokoto, Ahmadu Belo University Press, 1981.
Usman, Y. B., *For the Liberation of Nigeria: essays and lectures 1969-1978.* Sokoto, Ahmadu Belo University Press, 1980.
UNESCO Statistical Yearbook., UNESCO publication, Paris, 1991
Van Slageren, J., *Les Origines de l'Eglise Evangélique du Cameron: Mission Européennes et Christianisme Autochtone,* Leiden, E.J. Brill. 1972.
Vernon-Jackson H.O.H., *Language, Schools and Government in Cameroon,* New York, Teachers College Press., 1967.
Victoria Centenary Committee Victoria, *Southern Cameroons 1858-1958,* Victoria, Presbook., 1958.
Warnier J. P., *Echanges, développement et hiérarchies dans le Bamenda précolonial,* Stuttgart, Franz Steiner Verlag Wiesbaden GMBH., 1985.
Warmington, W.A., *A West African Trade Union: case study of the Cameroon Development Cooperation Workers Union and its relations with its employees,* London, Oxford University Press, 1960.
Watson, K., (ed) *Education in the Third World,* London, Croom Helen., 1982.
Weber C.W. *International Influences and Baptist Mission in West Cameroon: German-American Missionary endeavour under the International Mandate and British Colonialism,* Leiden. E.J. Brill., 1993.
Wight, M., *British Colonial Constitutions,* Oxford, Clarendon Press., 1947.
Williams, C., *The Rebirth of African Civilization,* Virginia, U.B. & U.S. Communications Systems, Inc. 1993.

Articles

Ardener E.W., 'The Nature of the Reunification of Cameroon" in Hazelwood, A., *African Integration and disintegration: case studies in economic and political union.,* Oxford university Press, 1967.
Ardener E.W., "Documentary and the linguistic Sources for the rise of the trading polities between Rio del Rey and Cameroon, 1500-1650" in I.M. Lewis., (ed) *History and Social Anthropology,* London, Tavistock Publication., 1963.
Adu Boahen, A., "African Perspectives on Colonialism" *in Journal of African History* 1987.
Afari-Gyan, "Nkrumah's Ideology" in Arhin, K., (ed.) *The Life and Works of Kwame Nkrumah,* African World Press, New Jersey, 1993. p.164
Akoulouze AR., «La Réforme de L' enseignement Primaire du Cameroun (1967-1984). Les causes de la non mise en application». Unpublished, Yaounde, 1984

Altbach P.G, "The distribution of knowledge in the third world: A case study in neocolonialism" in Altbach P.G, (ed) *Education and the colonial experience,* Transaction Books., New Brunswick., 1984. P 27

Altbach, P.G, '"Education and Neocolonialism: A note" in *Comparative Education Review,* 15.1., 1971.

Altbach P.G, "Education and Neocolonialism: A note." in *Comparative Education Review,* 15, 1. 1971.

Arnett, E.J., "Native Administration in West Africa: A Comparison of French and British Policy" *Journal of the African Society,* XXXII, 1923.

Austen, R, «Douala versus Germans in Cameroon: Economic Dimensions of a Political Conflict,» *Revue D'Histoire D'Outre Mer,* 64, 1977.

Bebe-Njoh., E. «La réforme éducative au Cameroun et le problème de l'intégration de deux systèmes scolaires», in *Education Comparée,* 22-27., 1981. pp. 47-54

Beck, A.,"Colonial Policy and Education in British East Africa" *in JOB,* May 1966.

Bederman, S.H., and DeLancey M.W. "The Cameroon Development Corporation: 1947-1977., Cameroonization and Growth. in Kofele-Kale N., (ed) *An African Experiment in Nation Building: The Bilingual Cameroon Republic since Reunification.,* Boulder-Colorado., Westerview Press., 1980. pp. 251-280.

Brown, Godfrey N., "British Education Policy in West and Central Africa.," *Journal of Modern African Studies,* III. 3., 1964.

Briggs, A., "The Study of the History of Education", *History of Education,* 1972(1).

Carter, F. Cooperation in Education In Uganda: Mission and Government in the inter war period", *Bulletin of the Society for African Church History, No.3,* 1967.

Chilver, E.M., "Native Administration in West Central Cameroon, 1902- 1954", in Robinson, K., and Malden, F., *Essays in Imperial Government presented to Magery Perham,* Oxford, Basil Blackwell., 1963. pp,89- 139.

Chilver, E.M., "The Bangwa and the Germans: A tail piece" in *Journal of the Historical Society of Nigeria,* Vol. IV No.I. 1967.

Clignet R.P. and Foster P.J., "French and British Colonial Education in Africa" in Com*parative Education Review,* 8.1., 1964.

Clignet R.P., "Damned if you do, damned if you don't; the dilemmas of colonizer-colonized relations" in *Comparative Education Review,* 15.1,1971. Also in (eds) Altbach P.G and Kelly GP., (eds), *Education and the colonial experience,* New Jersey, Transaction Books., 1984.

Cornevin, Robert., "Education in Black Africa; An Historical Account." *in Africa Quarterly,* January March 1968.

Cowan L.C., "British and French Education in Africa: A Critical Appraisal" in Piper D.C., and Cole T., (eds) *Post-primary Education and Political and Economic Development,* London, Cambridge University Press., 1964. pp.178-199.

Cowan L.G, "Education Policy in British Tropical Africa in *Education and National Building,* London, 1965, pp. 45-52.

Crouzet P., "Education in the French Colonies" in Kandel I.L. (ed) *The Education Yearbook of International Institute of Teachers College,* Columbia University Press, Columbia, 1931.

Crozier A.J. "The Establishment of the mandate system 1919-1925, some problems created by the Paris Peace Conference", in *Journal of Contemporary History,* 14,4. 1979. pp.483-515.

Elango L, "The Anglo-French Condominium in Cameroon, 1914-1916: The Myth and Reality" in *International Journal of African Studies*, 1987, p.82.

Fanso, V. U, "Background to the Annexation of Cameroon 1875-1885" *ABBIA*. No. 29 30, 1975.

Fohtung, M. U, edited by Chilver E.M., "Self- Portrait of a Cameroonian", in *Paideuma* 38, 1992.

Gardinier D.E., "The British in the Cameroons 1919-1939" in Gifford R and Louis W.R. (eds) *Britain and Germany in Africa: Imperial Rivals and colonial rule*, New Haven, Yale University Press., 1967.pp. 513-555.

Gardinier D.E., "Schooling in the states of Equatorial Africa", in *Canadian Journal of African Studies*, 8. 3., 1974.

Gensichen, H. W., "Evangelisation and Civilisation: The Germans", in *International Bulletin of Missionary Research*, No. 6, 1982, p. 52.

Gelzer, D., «Mission et Colonisation: Education au temps des Allemands» in *Flambeau* No. 19, 1966.

Henderson, W.O.," British Economic Activity in the German colonies, 1884-1914; Economic History Review, 15, 1945

Hussey, E.RJ., "The role of Education in assisting the people of West Africa to adjust to the changing conditions due to European contacts" in *Europe and West Africa: Some Problems and Adjustments*, (eds) Meek C.K. and Hussey E.R.J, London, Oxford University Press., 1940.

Hussey, E.R.J. "Education policy and Political Development in Africa in *Journal of African Affairs*, vol.44 of 1945.

Joseph, R., "Church, State and Society in Colonial Cameroun" in *International Journal of African Historical Studies*, No. 15, 1976.

Kala lobe., «Douala Manga Bell, Héros de la Résistance Douala» in *Grandes Figures Africaines de la Xxe siecle*, Tournai, 1977.

Kondo-Gete M.,» L'Enseignement Missionnaire dans le développement du. Congo Beige", in Ajayi J.F.A., (ed) *The Education Process and Historiography in Contemporary Africa,* UNESCO publication, Paris, 1985.

Lakowski "The Second World War" in Stoeker H., *German imperialism in Africa: From the beginning until the Second World War*, London., Hurst and Company, 1986. pp. 379-418.

Marchand, C., «Tentatives d'adaptation de l'enseignement au réalités Camerounais: enseignement agricole, 1921-1971» in *C.J.A.S.* vol.8, No.3 of 1974.

Mumford W.B., "Comparative study of native education in various dependencies" in *The Year Book of Education*, 1935. pp. 810-850.

Nwosu, S.N., "The British Idea of the Educability of the African: 1840-1939" *Etudes d'histoire africaine*, 8., 1976. pp.149-171.

Nyerere, J., "Education in Tanzania", in *Education in Africa: A comparative Survey.*, (ed) Fafunwa, A.B., and Aisiku J.0 Allen and Unwin., 1982.

Oldham J.H., "Education Policy of the British Government in Africa" in *International Review of Missions,1925*, p. 422.

Oshuntokun J., "Anglo-French Occupation and the Provisional partition of the Cameroons, 1914-1916" in *Journal of the Historical Society of Nigeria*, 7, 4. 1975.

Peshkin, A., "Education and National Integration in Nigeria" Journal *of Modern African Studies*, November 1967.

Quinn, F. "German and French Rule in the Cameroons" *Tarikh* London, 1974

Ranger, T. "African attempts to control Education in East and Central Africa, 1900-1939" *Pasp*, December 1965.

Sankie Maimo, A., "Early Education & Commerce in the Bamenda Grasslands *ABBIA.*, 3., 1963.

Shu, S., "Education in Cameroon" in Fanfunwa and Aisiku (eds) *Education in Africa: A Comparative Survey*, pp. 28-48, London, George Allen and Unwin., 1928.

Simon, J., "The History of Education in Past and Present", *Oxford Review of Education*, 3. 1., 1977.

Vernon Jackson, H.O.H., "A Chronology of the History of Academic Education in Cameroon 1844-1940", *ABBIA*, 3., 1963.

Webstel, C., "Changing perspectives in the History of Education", Oxford *Review of Education*, 2. 3., 1976.

Whitehead C., "Education Policy in British Tropical Africa: the 1925 White Paper in Retrospect", in *History of Education*, 1981 vol.10. No.3, pp. 195-203.

Whitehead C., "The impact of the Second World War on Education in British Colonial Empire" in Lowe R, (ed) *Education and the Second World War;* London, Falmer Press, 1992,

Wolfgang, H., "Education Policy" in Stoecker H., (ed), *German imperialism in Africa: from the beginning until the Second World War*, New Jersey, Hurst and Company., 1986

Theses

Abangma M.A., "A study of Primary teachers' attitudes towards the ruralization of school curriculum in English speaking Cameroon". PhD London, 1981.

Akoulouze A.R., "What education for what Society? The elite ideology of social change in Cameroon", Ph.D. Stanford, 1983.

Booth, B.F., "A Comparative Study of Mission and Government Involvement in Educational Development in West Cameroon, 1922 1969." PhD, UCLA, 1973.

Buchert, L., "Politics; Development and Education in Tanzania; 1q19-1986, An Historical Interpretation of Social Change", Ph.D., London, 1991.

Dah, J.N., "Missionary Motivations and Methods: A critical Examination of the Basel Mission in Cameroon 1886-1914" Ph.D., Basel, 1983.

Fajana, A., "The Evolution of Educational Policy in Nigeria", London, 1974.

Goodridge, R., "Society and Economy in the British Cameroons, 1916-1961" Ph.D. Ibadan, 1987.

Gwei, S.N., "Education in Cameroon: Western Pre-colonial and Colonial Antecedents and the Development of Higher Education" PhD Michigan University, 1975.

Lawrence, G, "An Evaluation of the Primary School Curriculum of West Cameroon in relation to its Social, Economic and Political import" PhD, Oregon, 1966,

Lekunze, E.F., "Chieftaincy and Christianity in Cameroon, 1886-1926; A Historical and Evangelical analysis of the evangelistic strategy of the Basel Mission" PhD, Chicago, 1987,

McLean, M., "A Comparative study of Assimilationist and Adaptationist, education policies in British Colonial Africa ,1925-1953, (With special reference to the

Gold Coast and Tanganyika)", PhD, London, 1978

Ndi, A.M., "Mill Hill Missionaries and the State in Southern Cameroons, 1922-1962", PhD, London, 1983.

Nfor-gwei S.N., "Education in Cameroon: Western Pre-colonial and colonial antecedents and the development of Higher education" Ph.D. Michigan, 1975.

Shu, S.N., "The Collaboration on policy in Cameroon Education 1910 to 1931: A study of the Policy of Collaboration between Government and Voluntary Agencies", PhD, London, 1971.

Snelson, P. D., "Educational Development in Northern Rhodesia 1883-1945", M.Phil., University of London 1971.

Stanley, W. R., "Educational Programs for West Cameroon, Africa: Suggestions for development." PhD., University of Northern Colorado, 1971.

Stonebreaker M.J., An analysis of the Teacher Role Expectations of Students and Teachers in selected secondary schools in the West Cameroon, PhD, UCLA., 1970.

Tembon, M., "The financing of Secondary Education in Mezam Division, North West Province, Cameroon. An uneasy partnership between family and state?", PhD, University of London, 1994.

Tosam, J. F., "Implementing Educational Change in Cameroon: Two Case Studies in Primary Education" PhD London, 1988.

Vernon Jackson, H.O.H., "Schools and School System, in Cameroon, 1844-1916," D.Ed., Columbia, 1968.

COLONIAL SYSTEMS OF EDUCATION

Type of school	THE GERMAN EDUCATIONAL SYSTEM Course
Mission vernacular school	Bush school in vernacular; 2 – 3 years
German school	Elementary school; 3 years
German school	Higher elementary; 2 years
Vocational and professional	Post-Primary Course; 2 - 3 years

The French School System During the Mandate

Type of school	Duration
Village or Rural school	3 years
Vocational schooling	1 - 3 years
Regional Schools	3 years
Higher Primary School	3 years

The British System During the Mandate

Type of school	Duration
Vernacular or Bush school	2 - 3 years
Infant Department	2 years
Elementary Department	4 years
Senior Primary Department	2 years
Middle School / Secondary School	6 Years
Teacher Training	Elementary teachers 2- 3 years

EDUCATIONALIONAL SYSTEMS SINCE REUNIFICATION

Age	Anglophone Before 1964		Francophone After 1964
4	Nursery 1	Nursery 1	Maternel 1
5	Nursery 2	Nursery 2	Maternel 2
6	Infant 1	Class 1	Cours d'initiation
7	Infant 2	Class 2	Cours Préparatoire
8	Standard 1	Class 3	Cours élémentaire 1
9	Standard 2	Class 4	Cours élémentaire 2
10	Standard 3	Class 5	Cours moyen 1
11	Standard 4	Class 6	Cours Moyen 2: CEPE
12	Standard 5	Class 7: FSLC	Sixiéme
13	Standard 6	Form 1	Cinquiéme
14	Form 1	Form 2	Quatriéme
15	Form 2	Form 3	Troisiéme **BEPC/ CAP**
16	Form 3	Form 4	Seconde
17	Form 4	Form 5: **GCE O/L**	Premiere **PROBATOIRE**
18	Form 5	Lower 6	Terminale **BACC**
19	Lower 6	Upper 6 **GCE A/L**	University/Professional
20	Upper 6	University/Professional schools	-
21	University	-	-

APPENDIX 3

CHRONOLOGY OF EDUCATIONAL DEVELOPMENT IN CAMEROON

1844	Opening of the first school by the British Baptist Missionary Society at Bimbia by Joseph Merrick.
1845	Opening of the second school by the same mission at Bethel by Alfred Saker.
1851	Opening of the first Teacher/Catechist training centre by the same mission.
1885	Arrival of the American Presbyterian Mission.
1886	Arrival of the Basel Mission.
1887	Appointment of the first Government teacher, Theodor Christaller.
1888	Opening of the first Government school in Douala.
1889	Basel Mission opens the first girls school.
1889	Establishment of Basel Mission Teacher/Catechists training centre.
1890	Arrival of the Roman Catholic Mission - the Pallotine Fathers.
1891	Opening of the first Catholic school.
1891	Arrival of the German Baptist Mission.
1892	The establishment of the first curriculum for government schools.
1903	The establishment of the first school in the Grassfield at Bali by the Basel Mission.
1906	Opening of the first government school in North Cameroon at Garoua.
1907	The first government conference on education at Douala by Governor Seitz.
1907	Opening of the first Catholic Mission seminary at Sasse for teacher/Catechist training.
1910	The first Government education policy on education establishing government control over all education provided in the territory.
1910	Government grants based on school performance in German language Examination.
1911	Compulsory government curriculum for all schools.

1911   The attachment of government subsidies to mission schools to success in Government designed German language

1912   Arrival of Sacred Heart Mission (Catholic).

1913   The establishment of the first Catholic school in the Grassfield at Shisong.

1914   The First World War and closure of schools.

1916   End of war in Cameroon. The Government and opening of mission schools in French Cameroon by Aymerich.

1916   Arrival of French Holy Ghost Mission in French Cameroon.

1917   Arrival of Paris Evangelical Mission in French Cameroon.

1917   Reopening of schools in the British sector.

1918   30 Government schools opened in nine administrative districts in French Cameroon.

1920   Reactivation of Native Baptist Church.

1920   Arrêté regulating private schools in French Cameroon.

1921   The High Primary School (Ecole Supérieure) opened in Yaoundé.

1921   Fees introduced in schools in British Cameroon. First inspection of schools with gloomy report.

1922   Arrival of Mill Hill Mission, (St. Joseph's Missionary Society). Creation of 10 Native Authority (N.A.) schools.

1922   Vocational education introduced in regional schools in French Cameroon.

1923   Mill Hill opened a higher elementary at Sasse.

1924   Arrêté revising policy for grants to mission schools in the French sector.

!925   Return of Basel Mission to British Cameroon and the reopening of their schools.

1925   The return of German plantation owners and business people.

1925   Opening of Government secondary school / Teachers Training Centre at Victoria.

1926   The Nigerian Education Ordinance of 1926 for implementation in British Cameroon.

1926   Return of the German Baptist Mission to British Cameroon.

1926   Transfer of Teachers Training Centre from Victoria to Buea.

1926   Arrival of Seventh Day Adventist Mission in French Cameroon.

1927   Revival of Baptist Mission education in British Cameroon.

1927   Opening of Catholic Girls' school at Bojongo.

1931   Implementation/adaptation of Nigerian Education Department Regulations in British Cameroon.

1931   Buea Teacher's Training Centre transferred to Kake, near Kumba.

1931	Basel Mission Girls elementary school started at Victoria.
1933	Special access to chiefs' children in schools in French Cameroon.
1934	Ayos Nursing School becomes more academic.
1936	Joint protestant teacher training school in Foulassi.
1937	Higher elementary school at Njinikom by the Catholic Mission.
1938	Higher elementary school at Soppo by the Baptist Mission.
1938	Five Year Plan for building new primary schools in British Cameroon.
1938	The publication of "Cameroons Chronicle".
1939	Opening of the first secondary school in British Cameroon at Sasse by the Catholic Mission.
1939	Village schools in French Cameroon became Rural schools.
1939	Beginning of the Second World War and the climax of jingoistic warfare between the Germans and the administering regimes in Cameroon
1940	Detention and eventual expulsion of all missionaries (teachers and school administrators inclusive) of German nationality.
1944	Teacher Training Centre transferred from Kake to Kumba.
1944	Visit of the Elliot commission to promote secondary and higher education.
1944	Opening of a Government secondary school in Yaoundé for Europeans.
1944	Brazzaville Conference.
1944	One year teachers training at Nyasoso by the Basel Mission.
1945	Fulani school opened at Jakiri.
1946	The Yaoundé Government Secondary School which eventually became Lycée Leclerc opened to Cameroonians and people of all races.
1946	Catholic teachers training centre opened at Makak.
1947	Opening of mission Teachers Training Centres at Bambui (Catholics), at Bali (Basel Mission, transferred in 1949 to Batibo).
1947	British post war colonial education policy in Nigerian Sessional Paper No.2. Free primary school of two cycles of four years each declared.
1947	Arrêté on education policy reform in French Cameroon.
1947	First lay private school opened at Nkol-Ossanaga.
1949	First Women Teachers Training Centre in British Cameroon at Fiango in Kumba by the Catholic Mission.
1949	The opening of the first secondary school in the Grassfield at Bali by the Basel Mission.
1951	G.C.E. replaces Matriculation Examinations in Britain, but the Cambridge Overseas Examinations Syndicate continues with school certificate
1952	Recommendations received on syllabus of secondary schools.

1952   Opening of the Government Technical College at Ombe.

1954   The achievement of regional status for Southern Cameroons and therefore attainment of autonomy for the first time over education and no more depending on Nigeria.

1954   Opening of Bambui rural education centre.

1954   Southern Cameroons Government disallowed departures to Nigerian secondary schools because of the political misunderstanding started in 1953.

1955   The Baptists established an elementary school at Great Soppo.

1956   The first Girls Secondary school was opened at Okoyong by the Catholic Mission.

1956   The Catholic Mission opened a Teacher's Training Centre at Bojongo.

1956   The Government ruled that teaching in vernacular should not be allowed except when more than 66.6 per cent of the pupils speak the local language.

1957   The West African School Certificate Examination replaced the Cambridge

1957   Teacher's Training Centre opened in Tatum by the Catholic Mission.

1957   Basel Mission hands over all activities (evangelical) except Education and Medical duties to an independent church, the Presbyterian Church in Cameroon.

1958   Bali and Douala languages demoted in favour of mother tongues.

1960   Independence for French Cameroon which became Republique du Cameroun

1960   Southern Cameroon Government abolishes vernacular teaching in primary schools.

1960   The National School of Agriculture (ENSA) opened in Nkolbissong in Yaounde.

1960   Opening of the Protestant Faculty of Theology in Yaoundé.

1961   Reunification of former French Cameroon with former British Southern Cameroon into a Federation where British Cameroon became West Cameroon while the former became East Cameroon.

1961   Reorganisation of education; the Ministry of National Education, Youth and Culture remains at Yaoundé, while the Secretariat of Education is established in Buea.

1961   A Presidential decree creates a National Institute of University Studies preparing for external examinations of French Universities.

1961   A Women Teacher's Training College is open in Bamenda by the Presbyterian Church in Cameroon/Basel Mission.

1961   Ecole Normale Supérieure (E.N.S.) opened in Yaoundé for the training of Secondary School Teachers.

1962   Opening of the first university, University of Yaoundé.

1962   Financial autonomy granted the university by Federal Law No. 62/DF/ 22 of 21 November 1962.

1962   A coeducational Teachers Training College opened at Mutengene by the Catholic Mission.

1962   The second Girl's Secondary School opened in Victoria by the Baptist Mission.

1963   The first national law aimed at unifying the two systems of education-Law No. 63/DF/13 of 19 June 1963.

1963   Opening of Cameroon College of Arts, Science and Technology at Kumba as the first Government institution in the Anglophone zone.

1963   The first Bilingual secondary school in the country opened temporary at Man O' War Bay in Victoria before being transferred to Molyko in Buea.

1963   A West Cameroon Education Policy Paper on the entire educational system.

1963   Opening of more secondary schools- Our Lady of Lourdes Secondary School, Mankon by the Catholic Mission. St. Bedes Secondary School, Njinikom, by the Catholic Mission. Presbyterian Secondary School, Kumba, by the Presbyterian Church/ Basel Mission, Joseph Merick Secondary School, Ndu.

1963   Opening of Teacher's Training College at Nyasoso by the Presbyterian Church/Basel Mission.

1963   Opening of Teachers Training Centre at Nchang by the Catholic Mission.

1964   Federal Law No. 6 4/DF/1 1 of 26 June 1964 regulating the provision of private lay secondary and technical colleges in Cameroon.

1964   East Cameroon Law No. 64/COR/3 of 9 June 1964 controlling the operation of private primary schools in East Cameroon.

1964   London G.C.E. replaces West African School Examination in Cameroon.

1964   Anglophone school year changed to agree with the Francophone school year.

1964   Opening of St. Augustine's Secondary School, Kumbo and Bishop Rogan Secondary School, Small Soppo, by the Catholic Mission.

1964   Opening of Presbyterian Secondary School, Besongabang by the Presbyterian Church in Cameroon/Basel Mission.

1964   Cameroon Development Corporation (C.D.C.) hands over their thirteen primary schools to the local Councils.

1964   Cameroon's College of Arts, Science and Technology transferred from Kumba to Bambili.

1964   The first nursery school opened in West Cameroon by Catholic Women Association.

1965   Introduction of West Cameroon education rating scheme aimed at making the first four years of schooling free.

1965   Anglophone school year brought down from eight years to seven years to eventually cut down to six years in response to harmonisation of the two systems as contained in Federal Law No. 63/DF/1 3 of 19 June 1963 mentioned above.

1965   Teacher Training Centre opened at Njinikom by the Catholic Mission.

1966   Meeting of the Higher Council of National Education presided by the Vice President of the Federal Republic proposed the name of C.G.E. (Certificate of General Education) for certificates marking the end of secondary school, course following the harmonisation.

1966   Basel Mission hands over all educational activities in Cameroon to the Presbyterian Church in Cameroon.

APPENDIX 4

LEAGUE OF NATIONS MANDATE

(THE BRITISH MANDATE FOR THE CAMEROONS)

The Council of the League of Nations:
Whereas by Article 119 of the Treaty of Peace with Germany signed at Versailles on June 28th, 1919,   Germany renounced in favour of the Principal Allied and Associated Powers all her rights over her overseas possessions, including therein the Cameroons; and

Whereas the Principal Allied and Associated Powers agreed that the Governments of France and Great Britain should make a joint recommendation to the League of Nations as to the future of the said territory; and; Whereas the Governments of France and Great Britain have made a joint recommendation to the Council of the League of Nations that a mandate to administer in accordance with Article 22 of the Covenant of the League of Nations that part of the Cameroons lying to the west of the line agreed upon in the Declaration of July 10th, 1919,   referred to in Article 1, should be conferred upon His Britannic Majesty; and; Whereas the Governments of France and Great Britain have proposed that the mandate should be formulated in the following terms; and; Whereas His Britannic Majesty has agreed to accept the mandate in respect of the said territory, and has undertaken to exercise it on behalf of the League of Nations in accordance with the following provisions;

Confirming the said mandate, defines its terms as follows:

Article 1
The territory for which a mandate is conferred upon His Britannic Majesty comprises that part of the Cameroons which lies to the west of the line laid down in the Declaration signed on July 10th, 1919, of which a copy is annexed hereto. This line may, therefore, be slightly modified by mutual agreement between His Britannic Majesty's Government and the Government of the French Republic

158

where an examination of the localities shows that it is undesirable, either in the interests of the inhabitants or by reason of any inaccuracies in the map, Moisel 1: 300,000, annexed to the Declaration, to adhere strictly to the line laid down therein. The delimitation on the spot of this line shall be carried out in accordance with the provisions of the said Declaration.

The final report of the Mixed Commission shall give the exact description of the boundary line as traced on the spot; maps signed by the Commissioners shall be annexed to the report. This report with its annexes shall be drawn up in triplicate: one of these shall be deposited in the archives of the League of Nations, one shall be kept by His Britannic Majesty's Government, and one by the Government of the French Republic.

Article 2

The Mandatory shall be responsible for the peace, order and good government of the territory, and for the promotion to the utmost of the material and moral well-being and the social progress of its inhabitants.

Article 3

The Mandatory shall not establish in the territory any military or naval bases, nor erect any fortifications, nor organise any native military force except for local police purposes and for the defence of the territory.

Article 4

The Mandatory:

1). shall provide for the eventual emancipation of all slaves, and for as speedy an elimination of domestic and other slavery as social conditions will allow;
2). shall suppress all forms of slave trade;
3). shall prohibit all forms of forced or compulsory labour, except for essential public works and services, and then only in return for adequate remuneration;
4). shall protect the natives from abuse and measures of fraud and force by the careful supervision of labour contracts and the recruiting of labour;
5). shall exercise a strict control over the traffic in arms and ammunition and the sale of spirituous liquors.

Article 5

In the framing of laws relating to the holding or transfer of land, the Mandatory shall take into consideration native laws and customs, and shall respect the rights and safeguard the interests of the native population.

No native land may be transferred, except between natives, without the previous consent of the public authorities, and no real rights over native land in favour of non-natives may be created except with the same consent.

The Mandatory shall promulgate strict regulations against usury.

Article 6

The Mandatory shall secure to all nationals of States Members of the League of Nations the same rights as are enjoyed in the territory by his own nationals in respect of entry into and residence in the territory, the protection afforded to their person and property, and acquisition of property, movable and immovable, and the exercise of their profession or trade, subject only to the requirements of public order, and on condition of compliance with the local law.

Further, the Mandatory shall ensure to all nationals of States Members of the League of Nations on the same footing as to his own nationals, freedom of transit and navigation, and complete economic, commercial and industrial equality; except that the Mandatory shall be free to organise essential public works and services on such terms and conditions as he thinks just.

Concessions for the development of the natural resources of the territory shall be granted by the Mandatory without distinction on grounds of nationality between the nationals of all States Members of the League of Nations, but on such conditions as will maintain intact the authority of the local Government.

Concessions having the character of a general monopoly shall not be granted. This provision does not affect the right of the Mandatory to create monopolies of a purely fiscal character in the interest of the territory under mandate and in order to provide the territory with fiscal resources which seem best suited to the local requirements; or, in certain cases, to carry out the development of natural resources, either directly by the State or by a controlled agency, provided that there shall result there from no monopoly of the natural resources for the benefit of the Mandatory or his nationals, directly or indirectly, nor any preferential advantage which shall be inconsistent with the economic, commercial and industrial equality hereinbefore guaranteed.

The rights conferred by this article extend equally to companies and associations organised in accordance with the law of any of the Members of the League of Nations, subject only to the requirements of public order, and on condition of compliance with the local law

Article 7

The Mandatory shall ensure in the territory complete freedom of conscience and the free exercise of all forms of worship which are consonant with public order and morality; missionaries who are nationals of States Members of the League of Nations shall be free to enter the territory and to travel and reside therein, to acquire and possess property, to erect religious buildings and to open schools throughout the territory; it being understood, however, that the Mandatory shall have the right to exercise such control as may be necessary for the maintenance of public order and good government, and to take all measures required for such control.

Article 8

The Mandatory shall apply to the territory any general international conventions applicable to his contiguous territory.

Article 9

The Mandatory shall have full powers of administration and legislation in the area subject to the mandate. This area shall be administered in accordance with the laws of the Mandatory as an integral part of his territory and subject to the above provisions.

The Mandatory shall therefore be at liberty to apply his laws to the territory under the mandate subject to the modifications required by local conditions, and to constitute the territory into a customs, fiscal or administrative union or federation with the adjacent territories under his sovereignty or control, provided always that the measures adopted to that end do not infringe the provisions of this mandate.

Article 10

The Mandatory shall make to the Council of the League of Nations an annual report to the satisfaction of the Council, containing full information concerning the measures taken to apply the provisions of this mandate.

Article 11

The consent of the Council of the League of Nations is required for any modification of the terms of this mandate.

Article 12

The Mandatory agrees that, if any dispute whatever should arise between the Mandatory and another Member of the League of Nations relating to the interpretation or the application of the provisions of the mandate, such dispute, if it cannot be settled by negotiation, shall be submitted to the Permanent Court of International Justice provided for by Article 14 of the Covenant of the League of Nations.

The present instrument shall be deposited in original in the archives of the League of Nations. Certified copies shall be forwarded by the Secretary-General of the League of Nations to all Members of the League.

Done at London, the twentieth day of July one thousand nine hundred and twenty-two.

The French Mandate For Cameroon

MANDATE for the administration of Part of the former German Territory of the Cameroons conferred upon the Government of the French Republic, confirmed and defined by the Council of the League of Nations; London, July 20, 1922.

The Council of the League of Nations:

Whereas by Article 119 of the Treaty of Peace with Germany, signed at Versailles on the 28th June, 1919, Germany renounced in favour of the Principal Allied and Associated Powers all her rights over her overseas possessions, including therein the Cameroons; and

Whereas the Principal Allied and Associated Powers agreed that the Governments of France and Great Britain should make a joint recommendation to the League of Nations as to the future of the said territory; and

Whereas the Governments of France and Great Britain have made a joint recommendation to the Council of the League of Nations that a mandate to administer, in accordance with Article 22 of the Covenant of the League of Nations, that part of the Cameroons lying to the east of the line agreed- upon in the Declaration of the 10th July, 1919, of which mention is made in Article 1 below, should be conferred upon the French Republic; and

Whereas the Governments of France and Great Britain have proposed that the mandate should be formulated in the following terms; and

Whereas the French Republic has agreed to accept the mandate in respect of the said territory, and has undertaken to exercise it on behalf of the League of Nations: Confirming the said mandate, defines its terms as follows:

Article 1.

The territory for which a mandate is conferred upon France comprises that part of the Cameroons which lies to the east of the line laid down in the Declaration signed on the 10th July, 1919, of which a copy is annexed hereto. This line may, however, be slightly modified by mutual agreement between His Britannic Majesty's Government and the Government of the French Republic where an examination of the localities shows that it is undesirable, either in the interests of the inhabitants or by reason of any inaccuracies in the map, Moisel 1: 300,000, annexed to the Declaration, to adhere strictly to the line laid down therein.

The delimitation on the spot of this line shall be carried out in accordance with the provisions of the said Declaration. The final report of the Mixed Commission shall give the exact description of the boundary line as traced on the spot; maps signed by the Commissioners shall be annexed to the report. This report, with its annexes, shall be drawn up in triplicate; one of these shall be deposited in the archives of the League of Nations, one shall be kept by the Government of the Republic and one by His Britannic Majesty's Government.

Article 2

The Mandatory shall be responsible for the peace, order and good government of the territory and for the promotion to the utmost of the material and moral well-being and the social progress of its inhabitants.

Article 3

The Mandatory shall not establish in the territory any military or naval bases, nor erect any fortifications, nor organise any native military force except for local police purposes and for the defence of the territory.

It is understood, however, that the troops thus raised may, in the event of general war, be utilised to repel an attack or for defence of the territory outside that subject to the mandate.

Article 4

The Mandatory:

(1) Shall provide for the eventual emancipation of all slaves, and for as speedy an elimination of domestic and other slavery as social conditions will allow;

(2) Shall suppress all forms of slave trade;

(3) Shall prohibit all forms of forced or compulsory labour, except for essential public works and services, and then only in return for adequate remuneration;

(4) Shall protect the natives from measures of fraud and force by the careful supervision of labour contracts and the recruiting of labour;

(5) Shall exercise a strict control over the trade in arms and ammunition and the sale of spirituous liquors.

Article 5

In the framing of laws relating to the holding or transference of land, the Mandatory shall take into consideration native laws and customs, and shall respect the rights and safeguard the interests of the native population.

No native land may be transferred, except between natives, without the previous consent of the public authorities, and no real rights over native land in favour of non-natives may be created except with the same consent.

The Mandatory shall promulgate strict regulations against usury.

Article 6

The Mandatory shall secure to all nationals of States members of the League of Nations the same rights as are enjoyed in the territory by his own nationals in respect of entry into and residence in the territory, the protection afforded to their person and property, movable and immovable, and the exercise of their profession or trade, subject only to the requirements of public order, and on condition of compliance with the local law.

Further, the Mandatory shall ensure to all nationals of States members of the League of Nations, on the same footing as his own nationals, freedom of transit and navigation, and complete economic, commercial and industrial equality; provided that the Mandatory shall be free to organise essential public works and services on such terms and condition as he thinks just.

Concessions for the development of the natural resources of the territory shall be granted by the Mandatory without distinction on grounds of nationality between the nationals of all States members of the League of Nations, but on such conditions as will maintain intact the authority of the local Government.

Concessions having the character of a general monopoly shall not be granted. This provision does not affect the right of the Mandatory to create monopolies of a purely fiscal character in the interest of the territory under mandate and in order to provide the territory with fiscal resources which seem best suited to the local requirements; or, in certain cases, to carry out the development of natural resources, either directly by the State or by a controlled agency, provided that there shall result there from no monopoly of the natural resources for— the benefit of the Mandatory or his nationals, directly or indirectly, nor any preferential advantage which shall be inconsistent with the economic, commercial and industrial equality hereinbefore guaranteed.

The rights conferred by this Article extend equally to companies and associations organised in accordance with the law of any of the members of the League of Nations, subject only to the requirements of public order, and on condition of compliance with the local law.

Article 7

The Mandatory shall ensure in the territory complete freedom of conscience and the free exercise of all forms of worship which are consonant with public order and morality; missionaries who are nationals of States members of the League of Nations shall be free to enter the territory and to travel and reside therein, to acquire and possess property, to erect religious buildings and to open schools throughout the territory; it being understood, however, that the Mandatory shall have the right to exercise such control as may be necessary for the maintenance of public order and good government, and to take all measures required for such control.

Article 8

The Mandatory shall apply to the territory any general international Conventions applicable to his contiguous territory.

Article 9

The Mandatory shall have full powers of administration and legislation in the area subject to the mandate. This area shall be administered in accordance with the laws of the Mandatory as an integral part of his territory and subject to the above provisions.

The Mandatory shall therefore be at liberty to apply his laws to the territory subject to the mandate, with such modifications as may be required by local conditions, and to constitute the territory into a customs, fiscal or administrative union or federation with the adjacent territories under his sovereignty or control; provided always that the measures adopted to that end do not infringe the provisions of this mandate.

Article 10

The Mandatory shall make to the Council of the League of Nations an annual report to the satisfaction of the Council. This report shall contain full information concerning the measures taken to apply the provisions of this mandate.

Article 11

The consent of the Council of the League of Nations is required for any modification of the terms of the present mandate,

Article 12

The Mandatory agrees that, if any dispute whatever should arise between the Mandatory and another member of the League of Nations relating to the interpretation or the application of the provisions of the mandate, such dispute, if it cannot be settled by negotiation, shall be submitted to the Permanent Court of International Justice provided for by Article 14 of the Covenant of the League of Nations.

The present instrument shall be deposited in original in the archives of the League of Nations. Certified copies shall be forwarded by the Secretary-General of the League of Nations to all members of the League.

Done at London, the 20th day of July, 1922.

UNITED NATIONS TRUSTEESHIPAGREEMENT

(THE TRUSTEESHIP AGREEMENT FOR THE BRITISH CAMEROONS)

Whereas the Territory known as Cameroons under British Mandate and hereinafter referred to as the Territory has been administered in accordance with Article 22 of the Covenant of the League of Nations under a Mandate conferred on His Britannic Majesty; and Whereas Article 75 of the United Nations Charter signed at San Francisco on 26th June, 1945, provides for the establishment of an international trusteeship system for the administration and supervision of such territories as may be placed thereunder by subsequent individual agreements; and Whereas under Article 77 of the said Charter the international trusteeship system may be applied to territories now held under Mandate; and

Whereas His Majesty has indicated his desire to place the Territory under the said international trusteeship system; and Whereas, in accordance with Articles 75 and 77 of the said Charter the placing of a territory under the international trusteeship system is to be effected by means of a Trusteeship Agreement; Now therefore the General Assembly of the United Nations hereby resolves to approve the following terms of trusteeship for the Territory.

Article I

The Territory to which this Agreement applies comprises that part of the Cameroons lying to the west of the boundary defined by the Franco-British Declaration of 10th July, 1919, and more exactly defined in the declaration made by the Governor of the Colony and Protectorate of Nigeria and the Governor of the Cameroons under French Mandate which was confirmed by the exchange of notes between His Majesty's Government in the United Kingdom and the French Government of 9th January, 1931. This line may, however, be slightly modified by mutual agreement between His Majesty's Government in the United Kingdom and the Government of the French Republic where an examination of the localities shows that it is desirable in the interests of the inhabitants.

Article 2

His Majesty is hereby designated as Administering Authority for the Territory, the responsibility for the administration of which will be undertaken by His Majesty's Government in the United Kingdom of Great Britain and Northern Ireland.

Article 3

The Administering Authority undertakes to administer the Territory in such a manner as to achieve the basic objectives of the international trusteeship system laid down in Article 76 of the United Nations Charter. The Administering Authority further undertakes to collaborate fully with the General Assembly of the United Nations and the Trusteeship Council in the discharge of all their functions as defined in Article 87 of the United Nations Charter, and to facilitate any periodic visits to the Territory which they may deem necessary, at times to be agreed upon with the Administering Authority.

Article 4

The Administering Authority shall be responsible (a) for the peace, order, good government and defence of the Territory, and (b) for ensuring that it shall play its part in the maintenance of international peace and security.

Article 5

For the above-mentioned purposes and for all purposes of this Agreement, as may be necessary, the Administering Authority:

a. shall have full powers of legislation, administration and jurisdiction in the Territory and shall administer it in accordance with his own laws as an integral part of his territory with such modification as may be required by local conditions and subject to the provisions of the United Nations Charter and of this Agreement;

b. shall be entitled to constitute the Territory into a custom, fiscal or administrative union or federation with adjacent territories under his sovereignty or control, and to establish common services between such territories and the Territory where such measures are not inconsistent with the basic objectives of the international trusteeship system and with the terms of this Agreement;

c. and shall be entitled to establish naval, military and air bases, to erect fortifications, to station and employ his own forces in the Territory and to take all such other measures as are in his opinion necessary for the defence of the Territory and for ensuring that it plays its part in the maintenance of international peace and security. To this end the Administering Authority may make use of volunteer forces, facilities and assistance from the Territory in carrying out the obligations towards the Security Council undertaken in this regard by the Administering Authority, as well as for local defence and the maintenance of law and order within the Territory.

Article 6

The Administering Authority shall promote the development of free political institutions suited to the Territory. To this end the Administering Authority shall assure to the inhabitants of the Territory a progressively increasing share in the administrative and other services of the Territory; shall develop the participation of the inhabitants of the Territory in advisory and legislative bodies and in the government of the Territory, both central and local, as may be appropriate to the particular circumstances of the Territory and its people; and shall take all other appropriate measures with a view to the political advancement of the inhabitants of the Territory in accordance with Article 76 (b) of the United Nations Charter. In considering the measures to be taken under this Article the Administering Authority shall, in the interests of the inhabitants, have special regard to the provisions of Article 5 (a) of this Agreement.

Article 7

The Administering Authority undertakes to apply in the Territory the provisions of any international conventions and recommendations already existing or hereafter drawn up by the United Nations or by the specialised agencies referred to in Article 57 of the Charter, which may be appropriate to the particular circumstances of the Territory, and which would conduce to the achievement of the basic objectives of the international trusteeship system.

Article 8

In framing laws relating to the holding or transfer of land and natural resources, the Administering Authority shall take into consideration native laws and customs, and shall respect the rights and safeguard the interests, both present and future, of the native population. No native land or natural resources may be transferred except between natives, save with the previous consent of the competent public Authority. No real rights over native land or natural resources in favour of non-natives may be created except with the same consent.

Article 9

Subject to the provisions of Article 10 of this Agreement, the Administering Authority shall take all necessary steps to ensure equal treatment in social, economic, industrial and commercial matters for all Members of the United Nations and their nationals and to this end:

a. shall ensure the same rights to all nationals of Members of the United Nations as to his own nationals in respect of entry into and residence in the Territory, freedom of transit and navigation, including freedom of transit and navigation by air, acquisition of property both movable and immovable, the protection of persons and property, and the exercise of professions and trades;

b. shall not discriminate on grounds of nationality against nationals of any Member of the United Nations in matters relating to the grant of concessions for the development of the natural resources of the Territory, and shall not grant concessions having the character of a general monopoly;

c. shall ensure equal treatment in the administration of justice to the nationals of all Members of the United Nations.

The rights conferred by this Article on nationals of Members of the United Nations apply equally to companies and associations controlled by such nationals and organised in accordance with the law of any Member of the United Nations.

Article 10

Measures taken to give effect to Article g of this Agreement shall be subject always to the over-riding duty of the Administering Authority in accordance with Article 76 of the United Nations Charter to promote the political, economic, social and educational advancement of the inhabitants of the Territory, to carry out the other basic objectives of the international trusteeship system, and to maintain peace, order and good government. The Administering Authority shall in particular be free:

a. to organise essential public services and works on such terms and conditions as he thinks just;

b. to create monopolies of a purely fiscal character in order to provide the Territory with the fiscal resources which seem best suited to local requirements, or otherwise to serve the interests of the inhabitants of the Territory;

c. where the interests of the economic advancement of the inhabitants of the Territory may require it, to establish or permit to be established, for specific purposes, other monopolies or undertakings having in them an element of monopoly, under conditions of proper public control; provided that, in the selection of agencies to carry out the purposes of this paragraph, other than agencies controlled by the Government or those in which the Government participates, the Administering Authority shall not discriminate on grounds of nationality against Members of the United Nations or their nationals.

Article 11

Nothing in this Agreement shall entitle any Member of the United Nations to claim for itself or for its nationals, companies and associations, the benefits of Article g of this Agreement in any respect in which it does not give to the inhabitants, companies and associations of the Territory equality of treatment with the nationals companies and associations of the State which it treats most favourably.

Article 12

The Administering Authority shall, as may be appropriate to the circumstances of the Territory, continue and extend a general system of elementary education designed to abolish illiteracy and to facilitate the vocational and cultural advancement of the population, child and adult, and shall similarly provide such facilities as may prove desirable and practicable in the interests of the inhabitants for qualified students to receive secondary and higher education, including professional training.

Article 13

The Administering Authority shall ensure in the Territory complete freedom of conscience, and, so far as is consistent with the requirements of public order and morality, freedom of religious teaching and the free exercise of all forms of worship. Subject to the provisions of Article 8 of this Agreement and the local law, missionaries who are nationals of Members of the United Nations shall be free to enter the Territory and to travel and reside therein, to acquire and possess property, to erect religious buildings and to open schools and hospitals in the Territory. The provisions of this Article shall not, however, affect the right and duty of the Administering Authority to exercise such control as he may consider necessary for the maintenance of peace, order and good government and for the educational advancement of the inhabitants of the Territory, and to take all measures required for such control.

Article 14

Subject only to the requirements of public order, the Administering Authority shall guarantee to the inhabitants of the Territory freedom of speech, of the press, of assembly, and of petition.

Article 15

The Administering Authority may arrange for the co-operation of the Territory in any regional advisory commission, regional technical organisation, or other voluntary association of States, any specialised international bodies, public or private, or other forms of international activity not inconsistent with the United Nations Charter.

Article 16

The Administering Authority shall make to the General Assembly of the United Nations an annual report on the basis of a questionnaire drawn up by the Trusteeship Council in accordance with Article 88 of the United Nations Charter. Such reports shall include information concerning the measures taken to give effect to suggestions and recommendations of the General Assembly and the Trusteeship Council. The Administering Authority shall designate an accredited representative to be present at the sessions of the Trusteeship Council at which the reports of the Administering Authority with regard to the Territory are considered.

Article 17

Nothing in this Agreement shall affect the right of the Administering Authority to propose, at any future date, the amendment of this Agreement for the purpose of designating the whole or part of the Territory as a strategic area or for any other purpose not inconsistent with the basic objectives of the international trusteeship system.

Article 18

The terms of this Agreement shall not be altered or amended except as provided in Article 79 and Articles 83 or 85, as the case may be, of the United Nations Charter.

Article 19

If any dispute whatever should arise between the Administering Authority and another Member of the United Nations relating to the interpretation or application of the provisions of this Agreement, such dispute, if it cannot be settled by negotiation or other means, shall be submitted to the International Court of Justice provided for in Chapter XIV of the United Nations Charter.

THE TRUSTEESHIP AGREEMENT FOR FRENCH CAMEROON

Whereas the territory known as the Cameroons Lying to the east of the line agreed upon in the Declaration signed on 10th July, 1919, has been under French administration in accordance with the mandate defined under the terms of the instrument of 20th July, 1922; and; Whereas, in accordance with Article g of that instrument, this part of the Cameroons has since then been "administered in accordance with the laws of the Mandatory as an integral part of his territory and subject to the provisions" of the mandate, and it is of importance, in the interests of the population the Cameroons, to pursue the administrative and political development of the territories in question, in such a way as to promote the political. economic and social advancement of the inhabitants in accordance with Article 76 of the Charter of the United Nations; and; Whereas France has indicated her desire to place under trusteeship in accordance with Articles 75 and 77 of the said Charter that part of the Cameroons which is at present administered by her; and; Whereas Article 85 of the said Charter provides that the terms of trusteeship are to be submitted for approval by the General Assembly; Now, therefore, the General Assembly of the United Nations approves the following terms of trusteeship for the said Territory.

Article I

The Territory to which the present Trusteeship Agreement applies comprises that part of the Cameroons Lying to the east of the boundary defined by the Franco-British Declaration of 10th July, 1919.

Article 2

The French Government in its capacity of Administering Authority for this Territory under the terms of Article 81 of the Charter of the United Nations, undertakes to exercise therein the duties of trusteeship as defined in the said Charter, to promote the basic objectives of the trusteeship system laid down in Article 76 and to collaborate fully with the General Assembly and the Trusteeship Council in the discharge of their functions as defined in Articles 87 and 88. Accordingly the French Government undertakes:

1. To make to the General Assembly of the United Nations the annual report provided for in Article 88 of the Charter, on the basis of the questionnaire drawn up by the Trusteeship Council in accordance with the said Article, and to attach to that report such memoranda as may be required by the General Assembly or the Trusteeship Council. To include in that report information relating to the measures taken to give effect to the suggestions and recommendations of the General Assembly or of the Trusteeship Council. To appoint a representative and, where necessary, qualified experts to attend the meetings of the Trusteeship Council or of the General Assembly at which the said reports and memoranda will be examined.

2. To appoint a representative and, where necessary, qualified experts to participate, in consultation with the General Assembly or the Trusteeship Council, in the examination of petitions received by those bodies.

3. To facilitate such periodic visits to the Territory as the General Assembly or the Trusteeship Council may decide to arrange, to decide jointly with these bodies the dates on which such visits shall take place, and also to agree jointly with them on all questions concerned with the organisation

and accomplishment of these visits.

4. To render general assistance to the General Assembly or the Trusteeship Council in the application of these arrangements, and of such other arrangements as these bodies may take in accordance with the terms of the present Agreement. The Administering Authority shall be responsible for the peace, order and good government of the Territory.

It shall also be responsible for the defence of the said Territory and ensure that it shall play its part in the maintenance of international peace and security.

Article 4

For the above-mentioned purposes and in order to fulfil its obligations under the Charter and the present Agreement, the Administering Authority:

Shall:

1. Have full powers of legislation, administration and jurisdiction in the Territory and shall administer it in accordance with French law as an integral part of the French territory, subject to the provisions of the Charter and of this Agreement.
2. Be entitled, in order to ensure better administration, with the consent of the territorial representative Assembly, to constitute this Territory into a customs, fiscal or administrative union or federation with adjacent territories under its sovereignty or control and to establish common services between such territories and the Trust Territory, provided that such measures should promote the objectives of the international trusteeship system.

May:

1. Establish on the Territory military, naval or air bases, station national forces and raise volunteer contingents therein.
2. Within the limits laid down in the Charter, take all measures of organisation and defence appropriate for ensuring:
    a). the participation of the Territory in the maintenance of international peace and security.
    b). the respect for obligations concerning the assistance and facilities to be given by the Administering Authority to the Security Council,
    c). the respect for internal law and order,
    d). the defence of the Territory within the framework of the special agreements for the maintenance of international peace and security.

Article 5

The Administering Authority shall take measures to ensure to the local inhabitants a share in the administration of the Territory by the development of representative democratic bodies, and, in due course, to arrange appropriate consultations to enable the inhabitants freely to express an opinion on their political regime and ensure the attainment of the objectives prescribed in Article 76 (b) of the Charter.

Article 6

The Administering Authority undertakes to maintain the application to the Territory of the international agreements and conventions which are at present in force there, and to apply therein any conventions and recommendations made by the United Nations or the specialised agencies referred to in Article 57 of the Charter, the application of which would be in the interests of the population and consistent with the basic objectives of the trusteeship system and the terms of the present Agreement.

Article 7

In framing laws relating to the holding or transfer of land, the Administering Authority shall, in order to promote the economic and social progress of the native population, take into consideration local laws and customs.

No land belonging to a native or to a group of natives may be transferred, except between natives, save with the previous consent of the competent public authority, who shall respect the rights and safeguard the interests, both present and future, of the natives. No real rights over native land in favour of non-natives may be created except with the same consent.

Article 8

Subject to the provisions of the following Article, the Administering Authority shall take all necessary steps to ensure equal treatment in social, economic, industrial and commercial matters for all States Members of the United Nations and their nationals and to this end:

1. Shall grant to all nationals of Members of the United Nations freedom of transit and navigation, including freedom of transit and navigation by air, and the protection of person and property, subject to the requirements of public order, and on condition of compliance with the local law.
2. Shall ensure the same rights to all nationals of Members of the United Nations as to his own nationals in respect of entry into and residence in the Territory, acquisition of property, both movable and immovable, and the exercise of professions and trades.
3. Shall not discriminate on grounds of nationality against nationals of any Member of the United Nations in matters relating to the grant of concessions for the development of the natural resources of the Territory, and shall not grant concessions having the character of a general monopoly.

4. Shall ensure equal treatment in the administration of justice to the nationals of all Members of the United Nations.

The rights conferred by this Article on the nationals of Members of the United Nations apply equally to companies and associations controlled by such nationals and formed in accordance with the law of any Member of the United Nations. Nevertheless, pursuant to Article 76 of the Charter, such equal treatment shall be without prejudice to the attainment of the trusteeship objectives as prescribed in the said Article 76 and particularly in paragraph (b) of that Article.

Should special advantages of any kind be granted by a Power enjoying the equality of treatment referred to above to another Power, or to a territory whether self-governing or not, the same advantages shall automatically apply reciprocally to the Trust Territory and to its inhabitants, especially in the economic and commercial field.

Article 9

Measures taken to give effect to the preceding article of this Agreement shall be subject to the overriding duty of the Administering Authority, in accordance with Article 76 of the Charter, to promote the political, economic, social and educational advancement of the inhabitants of the Territory, to carry out the other basic objectives of the international trusteeship system and to maintain peace, order' and good government. The Administering Authority shall in particular be free, with the consent of the territorial representative Assembly:

1. To organise essential public services and works on such terms and such conditions as it thinks just.
2. To create monopolies of a purely fiscal character in the interest of the Territory and in order to provide the Territory with the fiscal resources which seem best suited to local requirements.
3. To establish or to permit to be established under conditions of proper public control, in conformity with Article 76, paragraph (d), of the Charter, such public enterprises or joint undertakings as appear to the Administering Authority to be in the interest of the economic advancement of the inhabitants of the Territory.

Article 10

The Administering Authority shall ensure in the Territory complete freedom of thought and the free exercise of all forms of worship and of religious teaching which are consistent with public order and morality. Missionaries who are nationals of States Members of the United Nations shall be free to enter the Territory and to reside therein, to acquire and possess property, to erect religious buildings and to open schools and hospitals throughout the Territory.

The provisions of this Article shall not, however, affect the right and duty of the Administering Authority to exercise such control as may be necessary for the maintenance of public order and morality, and for the educational advancement of the inhabitants of the Territory.

The Administering Authority shall continue to develop elementary, secondary and technical education for the benefit of both children and adults. To the full extent compatible with the interests of the population it shall afford to qualified students the opportunity of receiving higher general or professional education. The Administering Authority shall guarantee to the inhabitants of the Territory freedom of speech, of the press, of assembly and of petition, subject only to the requirements of public order.

Article II
Nothing in this Agreement shall affect the right of the Administering Authority to propose at any future date the designation of the whole or part of the Territory thus placed under its trusteeship as a strategic area in accordance with Articles 82 and 83 of the Charter.

Article 12
The terms of the present Trusteeship Agreement shall not be altered or amended except as provided in Articles 79, 82, 83 and 85, as the case may be, of the Charter.

Article 13
If any dispute whatever should arise between the Administering Authority and another Member of the United Nations, relating to the interpretation or the application of the provisions of the present Trusteeship Agreement, such dispute, if it cannot be settled by negotiation or other means, shall be submitted to the International Court of Justice provided for by Chapter XIV of the Charter of the United Nations.

Article 14
The Administering Authority may enter, on behalf of the Territory, any consultative regional commission, technical organ or voluntary association of States which may be constituted. It may also collaborate, on behalf of the Territory, with international public or private institutions or participate in any form of international co-operation in accordance with the spirit of the Charter.

Article 15
The present Agreement shall enter into force as soon as it has received the approval of the General Assembly of the United Nations.

THE CONSTITUTION OF THE FEDERAL REPUBLIC OF CAMEROON

PART I The Federal Republic of Cameroon

1. (I) With effect from the 1st October 1961, the Federal Republic of Cameroon shall be constituted from the territory of the Republic of Cameroon, hereafter to be styled East Cameroon, and the territory of the Southern Cameroons, formerly under British trusteeship, hereafter to be styled West Cameroon.

2. The Federal Republic of Cameroon shall be democratic, secular and dedicated to social service;
   it shall ensure the equality before the law of all its citizens;
   and it proclaims its adherence to the fundamental freedoms written into the Universal Declaration of Human Rights and the Charter of the United Nations.

3. The official languages of the Federal Republic of Cameroon shall be French and English.

4. The motto shall be: "Peace, Work, Fatherland."

5. The flag shall be of three equal vertical stripes of green, red and yellow, charged with two gold stars on the green stripe.

6. The capital shall be Yaounde.

7. The national anthem of the Federation shall be: "O Cameroon, cradle of our forefathers."

8. The seal of the Federal Republic of Cameroon shall be a circular medallion in bas-relief, forty-six millimetres in diameter, bearing on the reverse and in the centre the head of a girl in profile turned to the dexter towards a coffee branch and flanked on the sinister by five cocoa pods, encircled beneath the upper edge by the words "Federal Republic of Cameroun" and above the lower edge by the national motto "Peace— Work—Fatherland."

9. The subjects of the Federated States shall be citizens of the Federal Republic with Cameroonian Nationality.

2. (I) National sovereignty shall be vested in the people of Cameroon who shall exercise it either through the members returned by it to the Federal

Assembly or by way of referendum;
nor may any section of the people or any individual arrogate to itself or to himself the exercise thereof.

(2) The vote shall be equal and secret, and every citizen aged twenty-one years or over shall be entitled to it.

(3) The authorities responsible for the direction of the State shall hold their powers of the people by way of election by universal suffrage, direct or indirect.

3. (I) Political parties and groups may take part in elections; and within the limits laid down by law and regulation their formation and their activities shall be free. (2) Such parties shall be bound to respect the principles of democracy and of the national sovereignty.

4. Federal authority shall be exercised by:

(a) the President of the Federal Republic, and

(b) The Federal National Assembly.

PART II Federal Jurisdiction

5. The following subjects shall be of federal jurisdiction:

(I) Nationality;

(2) Status of Aliens;

(3) Rules governing the conflict of Laws;

(4) National Defence;

(5) Foreign Affairs;

(6) Internal and External Security of the Federal State, and Immigration and Emigration;

(7) Planning, Guidance of the Economy, Statistical Services, Supervision and Regulation of Credit, Foreign Economic Relations, in particular Trade

Agreements;

(8) Currency, the Federal Budget, Taxation and other Revenue to meet federal expenditure;

(9) Higher Education and Scientific Research;

(10) Press and Broadcasting;

(11) Foreign Technical and Financial Assistance;

(I2) Postal Services and Telecommunications;

(I3) Aviation and Meteorology, Mines and Geological Research; Geographical Survey:

(14) Conditions of Service of Federal Civil Servants, Members of the Bench and Legal Officers;

(15) Regulation as to procedure and otherwise of the Federal Court of Justice;

(16) Border between the Federated States;

(I7) Regulation of Services dealing with the above subjects.

6. (1) The following subjects shall also be of federal jurisdiction:

(a) Human Rights;

(b) Law of Persons and of Property

(c) Law of Civil and Commercial Obligations and Contracts;

(d) Administration of Justice, including rules of Procedure in and Jurisdiction of all Courts (but not the Customary Courts of West Cameroon except for appeals from their decisions);

(e) Criminal Law:

(f) Means of Transport of federal concern (roads, railways, inland waterways, sea and air) and Ports;

(g) Prison Administration;

(h) Law of Public Property;

(i) Labour Law;

(1) Public Health;

(k) Secondary and Technical Education;

(I) Regulation of Territorial Administration;

(m) Weights and Measures.

(2) The Federated States may continue to legislate on the subjects listed in this article, and to run the corresponding administrative services until the Federal National Assembly or the President of the Federal Republic in its or his field shall have determined to exercise the jurisdiction by this Article conferred.

(3) The executive or legislative authorities as the case may be of the Federated States shall cease to have jurisdiction over any such subject of which the Federal authorities shall have taken charge.

7. (I) Wherever under the last preceding Article the authorities of the Federated States shall have been temporarily enabled to deal with a federal subject, they may legislate on such subject only after consultation with the Federal Co-ordination Committee.

(2) The chairman of the said Committee shall be a Federal Minister, and the members shall be nominated by the President of the Federal Republic in view of their special knowledge.

PART III The President of the Federal Republic

8. (I) The President of the Federal Republic of Cameroon, as head of the Federal State and head of the Federal Government, shall ensure respect for the Federal Constitution and the integrity of the Federation, and shall be responsible for the conduct of the affairs of the Federal Republic.

(2) He shall be assisted in his task by the Vice-President of the Federal Republic.

9. (I) The President and Vice-President of the Federal Republic
shall be elected together on the same list, both candidates on which may not
come from the same Federated State, by universal suffrage and direct
and secret ballot.

(2) Candidates for the offices of President and Vice-President of the Federal
Republic must be in possession of their civic and political rights, and
have attained the age of thirty-five years by the date of the election, the
nomination of candidates, the supervision of elections and the procla-
mation of the result being regulated by a federal law.

(3) The offices of President and Vice President of the Republic may not be
held together with any other office.

10. (1) The President of the Federal Republic shall be elected for five years
and may be re-elected.

(2) Election shall be by majority of votes cast, and shall be held not less
than twenty or more than fifty days before the expiry of the term of the
President in office.

(3) In the event of vacancy of the Presidency for whatever cause the powers
of the President of the Federal Republic shall without more devolve upon
the Vice-President until election of a new President.

(4) Voting to elect a new President shall take place not less than twenty or
more than fifty days after the vacancy.

(5) The President shall take oath in manner to be laid down by federal law. II.
(I) Ministers and Deputy Ministers shall be appointed by the President
of the Federal Republic from each Federated State at his choice, to be
responsible to him and liable to be dismissed by him.

(2) The office of Minister or Deputy Minister may not be held together with
elective office in either Federated State, office as member of a body representing nationally any occupation, or any public post or gainful activity.

12. The President of the Federal Republic shall—

(I) represent the Federal Republic in all public activity and be head of the
armed forces;

(2) accredit ambassadors and envoys extraordinary to foreign powers;

(3) receive letters of credence of ambassadors and envoys extraordinary
from foreign powers;

(4) negotiate agreements and treaties;

Provided that treaties dealing with the sphere reserved by Article 24 to the
federal legislature shall be submitted before ratification for approval in
the form of law by the Federal Assembly;

(5) exercise the prerogative of clemency after consultation with the Federal
Judicial Council;

(6) confer the decorations of the Federal Republic;

(7) promulgate federal laws as provided by Article 31

(8) be responsible for the enforcement of federal laws and also of such laws as may be passed by a Federated State under the last paragraph of Article 6;

(9) have the power to issue statutory rules and orders;

(I0) appoint to federal civil and military posts;

(11) ensure the internal and external security of the Federal Republic;

(12) set up, regulate and direct all administrative services necessary for the fulfilment of his task;

Provided that where he considers it advisable he may after consultation with the heads of the Governments of the Federated States assume authority over such of their services as exercise federal jurisdiction as defined by Article 5 or 6-and may by Decree delegate any part of his functions to the Vice-President of the Federal Republic.

13. The Governments of the Federated States shall be bound, before adopting any measure which may impinge upon the Federation as a whole, to consult the President of the Federal Republic who shall refer the matter to the Committee provided by Article 7 for its opinion.

14. The President of the Federal Republic shall refer to the Federal Court of Justice under Article 34 any federal law which he considers to be contrary to this Constitution, or any law passed by a Federated State which he considers to be in violation of the Constitution or of a federal law.

15. (I) The President of the Federal Republic may where circumstances require proclaim by Decree a State of Emergency, which will confer upon him such special powers as may be provided by federal law.

(2) In the event of grave peril threatening the nation's territorial integrity or its existence, independence or institutions, the President of the Federal Republic may after consultation with the Prime Ministers of the Federated States proclaim by Decree a State of Siege.

(3) He shall inform the nation by message of his decision.

(4) The Federal National Assembly shall without more be in session throughout the State of Siege.

PART IV The Federal Legislature

16. The Federal National Assembly shall be renewed every five years, and shall be composed of members elected by universal suffrage and direct and secret ballot in each Federated State in the proportion of one member to every eighty thousand of the population.

17. Federal laws shall be passed by simple majority of the members.

18. Before promulgating any bill the President of the Federal Republic may of his own accord or on request by the Prime Minister of either State request a second reading, at which the law may not be passed unless the majority required

by the last preceding Article shall include a majority of the votes of the members from each Federated State.

19. (1) The Federal National Assembly shall meet twice a year, the duration of each session being limited to thirty days, and the opening date of each session being fixed by the Assembly's steering committee after consultation with the President of the Federal Republic.

(2) In the course of one such session the Assembly shall approve the Federal Budget:

Provided that in the event of the Budget not being approved before the end of the current financial year the President of the Federal Republic shall have power to act according to the old Budget at the rate of one twelfth for each month until the new budget is approved.

(3) On request of the President of the Federal Republic or of two thirds of its membership the Assembly shall be recalled to an extraordinary session, limited to fifteen days, to consider a specific programme of business.

20. The Federal National Assembly shall adopt its own standing orders, and at the opening of the first session of each year shall elect its Speaker and steering committee.

The sittings of the Federal National Assembly shall be open to the public: Provided that in exceptional circumstances and on the request of the Federal Government or of a majority of its members strangers may be excluded.

21. Federal elections shall be regulated by a federal law.

22. Parliamentary immunity, disqualification of candidates or of sitting members, and the allowances and privileges of members shall be governed by a federal law.

PART V Relations Between the Federal Executive and Legislature

23. Bills may be introduced either by the President of the Federal Republic or by any member of the Federal Assembly.

24. Of the subjects of federal jurisdiction under Articles 5 and 6 the following shall be reserved to the legislature: (I) the fundamental rights and duties of the citizen, including: (a) protection of the liberty of the subject. (b) human rights. (c) labour and trade union law. (d) duties and obligations of the citizens in face of the necessities of national defence.

(2) the law of persons and property, including: (a) nationality and personal status. (b) law of moveable and immoveable property. (c) law of civil and commercial obligations.

(3) the political, administrative and judicial system in respect of: (a) elections to the Federal Assembly.

(b) general regulation of national defence.

(c) the definition of criminal offenses not triable summarily and the authorisation of penalties of any kind, criminal procedure, civil procedure, execution procedure, amnesty, the creation of new classes of Courts.

(4) the following matters of finance and public property: (a) currency. (b) federal budget. (c) imposition, assessment and rate of all federal dues and taxes. (d) legislation on public property.

(5) long-term commitments to economic and social policy, together with the general aims of such policy. (6) The Educational System.

25. Bills laid on the table of the Assembly shall be considered in the appropriate committee before debate on the floor of the House.

26. The text laid before the House shall be that proposed by the President of the Federal Republic when the proposal comes from him and otherwise the text as amended in committee; but in either case amendments may be moved in the course of the debate.

27. The President of the Federal Republic may at his request address the Assembly in person, and may send messages to it; but no such address or message may be debated in his presence.

28. Federal Ministers and Deputy Ministers shall have access to the Assembly and may take part in debates.

29. (1) The programme of business in the Assembly shall be appointed by the chairmen's conference, composed of party leaders, chairmen of committees and members of the steering committee of the Federal National Assembly, together with a Federal Minister or Deputy Minister.

(2) The programme of business may not include bills beyond the jurisdiction of the Assembly as defined by Articles 5, 6 and 24; nor may any bill introduced by a member or any amendment be included which if passed would result in a burden on public funds or an increase in public charges without a corresponding reduction in other expenditure or the grant of equivalent new supply.

(3) Any doubt or dispute on the admissibility of a bill or amendment shall be referred for decision by the Speaker or by the President of the Federal Republic to the Federal Court of Justice.

(4) The programme of business shall give priority, and in the order decided by the Government, to bills introduced or accepted by it.

(5) Any business shall on request by the Government be treated as urgent.

30. (1) The Government shall be bound to furnish to the Federal National Assembly any explanation and information on its activities in reply to written or oral questions by the Assembly or to any Committee of Inquiry set up by the Assembly to inquire into governmental activities.

(2) The procedure of all such inquiry and supervision shall be laid down by a federal law.

31. (1) The President of the Federal Republic shall promulgate laws passed

by the Federal National Assembly within fifteen days of their being forwarded to him, unless he receive a request for a second reading; and at the expiry of such period the Speaker may record his failure to promulgate and do so himself.

(2) Laws shall be published in both official languages of the Federal Republic.

PART VI: The Judiciary

32. (1) Justice shall be administered in the Federation in the name of the people of Cameroon by the competent Courts of each State.

(2) The President of the Federal Republic shall ensure the independence of the judiciary, and shall appoint to the bench and to the legal service of the Federated States.

(3) He shall be assisted in his task by the Federal Judicial Council, which shall give him its opinion on all proposed appointments to the bench and shall have over members of the bench the powers of a Disciplinary Council; and which shall be regulated as to procedure and otherwise by a federal law.

33. (I) The Federal Court of Justice shall have jurisdiction—

(a) to decide conflicts of jurisdiction between the highest Courts of the Federated States;

(b) to give final judgment on such appeals as may be granted by federal law from the judgments of the superior Courts of the Federated States wherever the application of federal law is in issue;

(c) to decide complaints against administrative acts of the federal authorities, whether claiming damages or on grounds of ultra vires;

(d) to decide disputes between the Federated States, or between either of them and the Federal Republic.

(2) The composition of, the taking of cognizance by, and the procedure of the Federal Court of Justice shall be laid down by a federal law.

34. Where the Federal Court of Justice is called upon to give an opinion in the case contemplated by articles 14 or 29, its numbers shall be doubled by the addition of personalities nominated for one year by the President of the Federal Republic in view of their special knowledge or experience.

35. Warrants. Orders and judgments of any Court of Justice in either Federated State shall be enforceable throughout the Federation

PART V II Impeachment

36. (I) There shall be a Federal Court of Impeachment which shall be regulated as to composition and taking of cognizance and in other respects by a federal law.

(2) The Federal Court of Impeachment shall have jurisdiction, in respect of

acts performed in the exercise of their offices, to try the President of the Federal Republic for high treason, and the Vice-President of the Republic and Federal Ministers, and Prime Ministers and Secretaries of State of the Federated States for conspiracy against the security of the State.

PART VIII Federal Economic and Social Council

37. There shall be a Federal Economic and Social Council which shall be regulated as to powers and in other respects by a federal law.

PART IX: The Federated States

38. (I) Any subject not listed in Articles 5 and 6, and whose regulation is not specifically entrusted by this Constitution to a federal law shall be of the exclusive jurisdiction of the Federated States, which within those limits, may adopt their own Constitutions.

(2) The House of Chiefs of the Southern Cameroons shall be preserved.

39. (I) The Prime Minister of each Federated State shall be nominated by the President of the Federal Republic and invested by a simple majority of the Legislature Assembly of that State.

(2) Secretaries of State shall be appointed to the Government by the President on the proposal of the Prime Minister after his investiture.

(3) The Secretaries of State may in like manner be dismissed.

40. (I) Legislative power shall be exercised in the Federated States by a Legislative Assembly, elected for five years by universal suffrage and direct and secret ballot in such manner as to ensure to each administrative unit representation in proportion to its population:

Provided that in West Cameroon the House of Chiefs may exercise specified legislative powers, to be defined, together with the manner of their exercise, by a law of the Federated State in conformity with this Constitution.

(2) There shall be one hundred representatives in the Legislative Assembly of East Cameroon, and thirty-seven representatives in the Legislative Assembly of West Cameroon.

(3) The electoral system, qualifications for candidates and disqualification of sitting members, parliamentary immunity and the allowances of representatives shall be regulated by federal law.

41. (I) Each Legislative Assembly shall adopt its own standing orders and shall annually elect its steering committee.

(2) It shall meet twice a year, the duration for each session being limited to thirty days, on dates to be fixed by the steering committee after consultation with the Prime Minister of the Federated State, and so that the opening date of the budgetary session shall be later than the approval of the federal budget.

(3) On request of the Prime Minister, of the President of the Federal Republic or of two thirds of its membership, it shall be recalled to an extraordinary session limited to fifteen days, to consider a specific programme of business.

42. The sittings of each Legislative Assembly shall be open to the public: Provided that in exceptional circumstances on the request of the Government or of a majority of its members strangers may be excluded.

43. Bills may be introduced either by the Government of each Federated State or by any representative in the Legislative Assembly, and shall be passed by a simple majority.

44. (I) A motion of no-confidence passed by a simple majority, or a vote of censure passed by an absolute majority shall oblige the Prime Minister to place his resignation in the hands of the President of the Federal Republic or be declared to have forfeited his office; and the President may then dissolve the Legislative Assembly.

(2) Persistent discord between the Government and the Legislative Assembly shall enable the President of the Federal Republic to dissolve. the latter of his own accord or on the proposal of the Prime Minister

(3) New elections shall be held within two months of dissolution.

(4) Until investiture of a new Prime Minister the outgoing Government be responsible for the despatch of current business.

45. (I) The Speaker of each Federated State shall within twenty-one days forward bills passed to the President of the Federal Republic, who shall within a further fifteen days promulgate them.

(2) Within the said period the President of the Federal Republic may either request a second reading by the Legislative Assembly or act under Article 14.

(3) At the expiry of such period the Speaker of the Legislative Assembly in question may record the President's failure to promulgate and do so himself.

46. In so far as they do not conflict with the provisions of this Constitution the existing laws of the Federated States shall remain in force.

PART X Amendment of the Constitution

47. (1) No bill to amend the Constitution may be introduced if it tend to impair the unity and integrity of the Federation.

(2) Bills to amend the Constitution may be introduced either by the President of the Federal Republic after consultation with the Prime Ministers of the Federated States, or by any member of the Federal Assembly:

Provided that any bill introduced by a member of the Assembly shall bear the signatures of at least one third of its membership.

(3) The amendment may be passed by a simple majority of the membership of the Federal Assembly:

Provided that such majority include a majority of the membership elected from each Federated State.

(4) The President of the Federal Republic may request a second reading of a bill to amend the Constitution as of any other federal bill, not in like manner.

PART XI: Transition and Special

48. The jurisdiction defined in Article 5 shall pass without more to the federal authorities as soon as they are set up.

49. The Government of each Federated State shall forward to the Federal Government all papers and records necessary for the performance of its task, and shall place at the disposal of the Federal Government the services destined to exercise federal jurisdiction under the authority of the latter.

50. Notwithstanding anything in this Constitution, the President of the Federal Republic shall have power, within the six months beginning from the 1st October 1961, to legislate by way of Ordinance having the force of law for the setting up of constitutional organs, and, pending their setting up, for governmental procedure and the carrying on of the federal government.

51. The President of the Republic of Cameroon shall be for the duration of his existing term the President of the Federal Republic.

52. For the duration of the term of the first President of the Federal Republic the Prime Minister of West Cameroon shall be Vice-President of the Federal Republic; and the disqualifications prescribed by Article g for the Vice-President of the Federal Republic shall during that period be inapplicable.

53. With effect from the 1st October, 1961 the National Assembly of the Republic of Cameroon and the House of Assembly of the Southern Cameroons shall become the first Legislative Assembly of East Cameroon and of West Cameroon respectively.

54. Until the 1st April, 1964 the Federal Assembly shall be composed of members elected from among themselves by the Legislative Assemblies of the Federated States according to the population of each State in the proportion of one member to every eighty thousand of the population.

55. Notwithstanding the provisions of Article 11, and until the election of a Federal Assembly under Article 16, the offices of Federal Minister and Deputy Minister may be held together with parliamentary office in either Federated States.

56. The Government of the Republic of Cameroon and the Government of the Southern Cameroons under British trusteeship respectively shall become on the 1st October, 1961 the Governments of the two Federated States.

57. Pending the setting up of the Federal Economic and Social Council, the Economic and Social Council of the Republic of Cameroon shall be preserved.

58. Pending approval of a definitive federal budget a provisional federal budget shall be drawn up and shall be financed by contributions from each Federated State to be settled after agreement with the Government of each such State.

59. This Constitution shall replace the Constitution of the Republic approved on the 21st February, 1960 by the people of Cameroon; shall come into force on the 1st October, 1961; and shall be published in its new form in French and in English, the French text being authentic.

60. (I) For the purposes of this Constitution the population of each Federated State shall on the faith of the statistics of the United Nations Organisation, be taken to be as follows:

East Cameroon 3,200,000, West Cameroon 800,000

(2) Such figures may be amended by a federal law in the light of significant variation established by census.

Yaoundé, the 1st September, 1961, Ahmadou Ahidjo

INDEX

Printed in the United States
By Bookmasters